CONTENTS

TABLES AND FIGURES

EXECUTIVE SUMMARY

I. INTRODUCTION

The Commission on the National Guard and Reserves was established by the Ronald Reagan National Defense Authorization Act of 2005. Congress chartered the 13-member body to conduct a comprehensive, independent assessment of the reserve components of the United States. The purpose of the assessment is expressed in the following mission statement:

To identify and recommend changes in policy, law, regulation, and practice to ensure that the National Guard and Reserves are organized, trained, equipped, compensated, and supported to best meet the national security requirements of the United States.

The United States Congress has directed the panel to deliver three separate reports to the House and Senate Armed Services Committees:

- An initial organizational report due within 90 days of the Commission's first official meeting.

- A second report providing our recommendations and supporting analyses on a set of specific legislative proposals bearing predominantly on matters related to the National Guard, no later than March 1, 2007.

- A concluding report providing our final assessments, findings, and recommendations, no later than January 31, 2008.

The first of these reports, detailing the status of the Commission's organization and the progress of our work, was submitted to the Senate Armed Services Committee, the House Armed Services Committee, and Secretary of Defense Donald Rumsfeld on June 5, 2006. The report is available on the Commission's Web site, www.cngr.gov.

The report we submit herewith is the second of our three products, and responds to the instructions set forth in the National Defense Authorization Act for Fiscal Year 2007 (P.L. 109-364). The law directed the Commission to report to Congress, no later than March 1, 2007, on the advisability and feasibility of 17 proposals bearing mainly on the status and activities of the National Guard Bureau, its Chief, and related matters.

March 1, 2007, Report: Approach and Structure

The issues that Congress instructed the Commission to address in this report are, for the most part, provisions of freestanding legislation titled the National Defense Enhancement and National Guard Empowerment Act of 2006 (S. 2658/H.R. 5200), introduced in both the U.S. Senate and House of Representatives in the 109th Congress. The legislation was reintroduced in the 110th Congress as the National Guard Empowerment Act of 2007 (S. 430/H.R. 718). The legislation, in general, seeks to enhance the stature, authority, and resources of the National Guard and the National Guard Bureau, the Department of Defense organization charged with managing joint aspects of the Air and Army Guard and other responsibilities, and particularly to improve the National Guard's capabilities to provide military assistance to civilian authorities in times of man-made or natural disaster here at home.

The recommendations in this report are not the full sum of our conclusions and recommendations on topics related to the National Guard. Rather, they are the ones we believe are directly related to the mandate we received from Congress in the 2007 NDAA. In the final section of this Executive Summary, we identify some of the related topics still under review by the Commission as we address the extensive requirements of our charter.

The National Guard Empowerment Act and Its Implications

The sponsors of the legislation have stated that at a time when we are asking more of the National Guard both at home and abroad, its effectiveness is hampered by Cold War structures and a lack of institutional power within the Pentagon commensurate with its increasingly important role. In summary, the proponents conclude that

- The Department of Defense and the parent services of the National Guard have not adapted to the significant role of the National Guard in the post-9/11 security environment.

- Decision-making processes within the Department of Defense do not adequately consider the interests of the National Guard and do not always include National Guard participation and input at the appropriate level.

- DOD's failure to appropriately consider National Guard needs and funding requirements has produced a National Guard that is not fully ready to meet current and emerging missions.

We believe that addressing the fundamental problems facing the National Guard requires a broader approach than the legislation envisions. It requires a strategic framework that focuses not only on the National Guard Bureau but also on the parent services of the National Guard, the organizational structure of DOD as a whole, the role of United States Northern Command (NORTHCOM), the role of the states and their governors, and the role of other government agencies involved in homeland security missions. In that regard, the Commission believes it necessary to consider how best to empower not exclusively the National Guard Bureau but rather overall national security capabilities—including those of the National Guard, as part of a much broader, integrated team.

As described in its organic statute, the National Guard Bureau is neither a reserve component nor an operational command. Its chief missions are to participate in the formulation, development, coordination, and administration of programs, policies, and plans pertaining to the Army and Air National Guard based on guidance from the Army and Air Force; and to participate with and assist the states in the organization, maintenance, and operation of their National Guard units so as to provide trained and equipped units available for service in time of war or emergency to augment the active Army and Air Force.

The bulk of the National Guard Bureau's statutory responsibilities are reflected in its charter, including the responsibility to allocate unit structure, strength authorizations, and resources to the Army and Air National Guard; to prescribe training discipline and requirements; to monitor and assist the states in the organization, maintenance, and operation of National Guard units; to plan and administer the National Guard budget; and to supervise the acquisition, supply, and accounting of federal property issued to the National Guard.

The statute and charter do not tell the full story of the Bureau's functions, as they do not yet include all the duties currently required to be performed by the Chief of the National Guard Bureau based on today's challenging security environment. The CNGB today oversees a joint force of more than 450,000 Army and Air Guard members (larger than the strength of all the other reserves combined), more than 200 general officers, and more than 3,000 facilities nationwide. He administers 54 Joint Force Headquarters; provides liaison with every governor—each a state or territorial commander in chief; coordinates National Guard domestic emergency response, homeland defense, and support to homeland security operations nationwide; supports combatant commanders, including the five regional combatant commanders, through 54 state partnership programs; and manages the readiness and resourcing of the Army and Air National Guard for the federal Title 10 warfighting mission.

The nation's response to the terrorist attacks of 9/11 emphasized the role of the Chief of the National Guard Bureau as the nationwide coordinator of the Guard. The National Guard Bureau became a crucial link between state and federal emergency response capabilities. The Bureau coordinated the deployment of 11,000 members of the Army and Air National Guard to assist law enforcement and other federal agencies in securing more than 440 of America's commercial airports. Similarly, it identified National Guard volunteers to defend critical infrastructure and it oversaw the establishment of a weapons of mass destruction civil support team in each state and territory in the United States. All the while, it was continuing to source the Army and Air Force's expanding requirements to sustain the deployment of National Guard units for the global war on terrorism.

Executive and legislative branch investigations into the response to Hurricane Katrina indicate that the Chief of the National Guard Bureau acted appropriately and efficiently, but beyond the authorities set forth in the National Guard Bureau's charter, in ways that must be more formally established. The National Guard Empowerment Act, in part, is one approach to formalize those responsibilities.

The Commission believes that the goal of reform should be to ensure better national security outcomes by modernizing the authorities given to the National Guard and providing it with influence, stature, and participation commensurate with its current expanded and critical role. Reform efforts should ensure that the Guard is integrated with other military entities—not set it apart. To be successful, reforms should systemically enhance the National Guard within a set of organizations and processes redesigned to

- Reflect the higher priority placed on domestic missions.

- Improve the advice the Secretary of Defense receives about reserve matters.

- Increase cooperation among DOD—including the National Guard Bureau and U.S. Northern Command— the Department of Homeland Security, and governors on homeland matters.

- Harmonize the NGB with the goals and principles of the Goldwater-Nichols Department of Defense Reorganization Act of 1986.

- Strengthen the National Guard's ability to perform both its overseas (Title 10) and homeland missions.

- Increase the influence of states and their governors, thereby enhancing national security at home.

Accordingly, the Commission concludes that the scope of reforms necessary to achieve better national security outcomes related to the National Guard is broader than those in the proposed legislation.

Structure of the Report

In this report, the Commission first assesses the current and emerging security environment, the military capabilities necessary to keep America secure in this environment, and the current state of the National Guard, which is the major focus of the legislation. We do so to provide the proper context for possible reforms.

Second, with this context firmly in mind, we identify those changes to law and policy that we believe are necessary, in the areas raised by the legislation, to meet U.S. national security objectives now and in the years ahead. We identify the key problems that impede DOD's ability to create the kind of National Guard force necessary to carry out the nation's security, defense, and military strategies, and we make recommendations we believe must be adopted to solve those problems.

In evaluating and recommending proposed reforms, including the proposals referred to us by the National Defense Authorization Act, we asked the following questions: do the reforms

- Improve the ability of the National Guard to meet both its overseas (Title 10) and homeland responsibilities as required by U.S. military, defense, and homeland security strategies?

- Enhance the ability of the National Guard to be a reserve force overseas, backing up the active force, and an operational force in the homeland, backed up by the active force?

- Build jointness among the military services as envisioned by the Goldwater-Nichols Act?

- Further integrate the active and reserve components to promote military effectiveness while respecting the necessary and fundamental differences between these two elements of the total force?

- Promote cooperation and proper interrelationships among the chief institutions responsible for homeland defense and homeland security?

- Clarify lines of authority and align responsibility and accountability?

- Build organizational structures with clear roles and missions?

- Establish resource allocation and policymaking processes and procedures that are equitable, are inclusive, and take into account the full range of inputs, including those of governors?

- Ensure that military command structures and manning decisions are based on national security requirements, merit, and capability rather than on a desire to preserve historic service or component turf?

Applying these criteria, we make findings, conclusions, and recommendations on six topic areas that address the problems and proposals raised by the National Guard Empowerment Act:

A. The Defense Department's Role in the Homeland

B. The Role of States and Their Governors

C. The National Guard Bureau

D. U.S. Northern Command

E. Reserve Policy Advice

F. Reserve Component Officer Promotion

Our conclusions dealing only with the specific proposals of the 2007 National Defense Authorization Act and National Defense Enhancement and Guard Empowerment Act can be found in Appendix 1 of this report.

Our analysis has been informed by 12 days of public hearings, more than 300 interviews with officials and other subject matter experts, and the analysis of documents and other data supplied at the Commission's request.

While this report recommends major changes to some government institutions, the recommendations are not intended to provide an evaluation of how the leaders of those institutions have performed. The leaders of DOD and the other government elements whose reorganization we advocate are serving with distinction. However, some are working within the strictures and constraints of policies and institutions that, in many instances, have not been updated since shortly after World War II and are in urgent need of reform. Other institutions, such as NORTHCOM and the Department of Homeland Security (DHS), are relatively new and still building their capacities. Moreover, efficient unity of effort among departments and agencies is impeded by a lack of clarity and mutual understanding of roles, missions, and spheres of authority in the homeland mission set, as well as the conflicts over turf common to all governments and any administration.

II. THE CONTEXT FOR OUR REPORT

A. The National Guard and Reserves in Today's Security Environment

The first step in ensuring that the National Guard and Reserves are properly organized, equipped, trained, compensated, and supported is to understand the strategic environment in which they must operate and the capabilities necessary to meet national security objectives.

America faces the most diverse, complex, uncertain, and unpredictable security environment in our history, consisting of many different threats, each of which may require a U.S. military response, alone or in coordination with an interagency and inter-governmental response. Such threats include

- The proliferation of weapons of mass destruction that constitute a growing threat across the globe, including to the U.S. homeland, and the potential access to such weapons by individuals or terrorist groups who wish to use them indiscriminately on civilian populations.

- The "long war"—enduring threat of violent Islamic extremists who want to control populations and geographic areas, attack U.S. soil, and harm U.S. interests and values throughout the world.

- Pandemic disease, whether natural or man-made, and natural dis-asters, such as hurricanes, earthquakes, and floods, that can threaten and harm populations in magnitudes that can equal or exceed the losses incurred by war.

- Failed states and numerous ethnic, tribal, and regional conflicts throughout the world that can endanger global stability.

- The potential for an emerging world power to engage the United States and our allies in traditional peer-to-peer conflict.

The modern threat environment requires that the United States bring to bear all instruments of national power to achieve national security objectives. Among these instruments is the U.S. military, including the National Guard and Reserves, which must possess the multitude of capabilities necessary to meet the array of traditional, irregular, catastrophic, and disruptive threats to America both at home and abroad. These capabilities are

- The ability to engage any adversary, sustain the fight, and win on the battlefield in many different kinds of environments and circumstances.

- The ability to prevent and recover from warfare through peace-keeping, stability operations, capacity building, and civil support activities.

- The ability to respond to the national security requirements arising from an adversary's use of a weapon of mass destruction.

- The ability to support civil authorities at all levels of government in responding to domestic emergencies, where military manpower, assets, and capabilities must be used to save lives or property, secure communities, or mitigate consequences or recover from major disaster.

B. The Current State of the National Guard

The proposals we have been asked to consider focus mainly on the status of the National Guard. However, the Army and Air National Guard are only two of seven reserve components. In this section, we evaluate the status of the Guard as part of the reserves in their totality, in order to place in context our subsequent recommendations, which focus on the National Guard, but which are broader in scope than the National Guard Empowerment Act provisions. The Commission makes the following observations with regard to the status of the Guard and Reserves:

- The National Guard and Reserves are at a high operational tempo, playing a key role, and performing well, across an array of missions: warfighting, peacekeeping and stability operations, and civil support.

- The practice known as *cross-leveling*, which primarily involves ground combat forces, has degraded unit cohesion and, therefore, overall military effectiveness.

- The failure to utilize the Army's Individual Ready Reserve in any meaningful way has contributed to the degree of cross-leveling that has occurred to date.

- Over the past decade, from fiscal year 1997 to fiscal year 2006, the number of prior active duty personnel enlisting in the reserves has steadily decreased in all the reserve components.

- The long-term viability for both recruiting and retention remains highly problematic. Despite an upturn in reserve component recruiting for fiscal year 2006 (reversing a falling trend that had lasted several years), polling data from young people, their parents, and other youth influencers show that favorable attitudes toward military service continue to decline. On the retention side, surveys of spouses in all pay grades and all reserve components show a significant drop in support for reserve service.

- Increasing levels of financial inducements have been necessary to meet recruiting and retention goals for both active and reserve components.

- While the operational tempo of all the reserve components has increased substantially, resourcing has not kept pace.

- The lack of sufficient and ready equipment is a problem common to active and reserve components. In particular, the equipment readiness of the Army National Guard is unacceptable and has reduced the capability of the United States to respond to current and additional major contingencies, foreign and domestic.

- The administration's FY 2008 budget seeks large increases for National Guard equipment. However, DOD historic budget data show that Army plans for projected funding increases for the Army National Guard are not reliably carried through.

- Despite the extraordinarily high operational tempo for the reserve component, many of the underlying laws, regulations, policies, funding mechanisms, pay categories, mobilization processes, and personnel laws have not been modified to support its evolution into an operational force.

In conclusion, DOD has declared that we have an operational reserve without also making the changes necessary to ensure that such a change is sustainable. We believe that the current posture and utilization of the National Guard and Reserve as an "operational reserve" is not sustainable over time, and if not corrected with significant changes to law and policy, the reserve component's ability to serve our nation will diminish.

III. COMMISSION FINDINGS, CONCLUSIONS, AND RECOMMENDATIONS

A. The Defense Department's Role in the Homeland

> **Conclusion:** Although the current Department of Defense *Strategy for Homeland Defense and Civil Support* states that securing the U.S. homeland is "the first among many priorities," the Defense Department in fact has not accepted that this responsibility requires planning, programming, and budgeting for civil support missions.

Finding: The Department of Defense does not explicitly budget and program for civil support missions because the Department views them as derivative of its wartime missions. This is a flawed assumption.

Finding: The Department of Homeland Security does not have a National Guard presence sufficient to promote necessary levels of cooperation.

Finding: The commander of U.S. Northern Command does not sufficiently advocate for the full range of civil support requirements affecting the National Guard and Reserves. Neither do the Chiefs or Vice Chiefs of the Army and Air Force.

Finding: The National Response Plan and related preparedness efforts have not been translated adequately into Department of Defense programming and budgeting requirements.

Finding: The Department of Homeland Security has not identified the requirements that the Department of Defense must meet to adequately perform domestic civil support missions.

Finding: The system for funding and equipping the National Guard under both state and federal status, including for homeland-related missions, is inadequate in that requirements for civil support are rarely considered when Department of Defense funding is prioritized.

Finding: The Department of Defense is not adequately equipping the National Guard for its domestic missions.

Recommendations:

1. The Secretary of Homeland Security, with the assistance of the Secretary of Defense, should generate civil support requirements, which the Department of Defense will be responsible for validating as appropriate. The Department of Defense should include civil support requirements in its programming and budgeting. In a new advisory role, the Chief of the National Guard Bureau should advise the U.S. Northern Command commander, the Secretaries of the Air Force and Army, and, through the Chairman of the Joint Chiefs of Staff, the Secretary of Defense regarding gaps between federal and state emergency response capabilities.

2. The Department of Defense (including combatant commands and the National Guard Bureau) and Department of Homeland Security Headquarters should exchange representatives to improve the knowledge of National Guard and Reserve capabilities; to improve planning, training, and exercising; and to assist the Secretary of Homeland Security with generating requirements for military civil support missions. The Commission recommends that a plan to exchange personnel be developed and implemented by the Secretary of Defense and the Secretary of Homeland Security within 180 days. The Commission notes the urgency of this recommendation.

3. The Secretary of Defense and Secretary of Homeland Security should jointly submit an annual report to Congress on those civil support requirements generated by the Secretary of Homeland Security and those validated as well as funded by the Secretary of Defense, and the Chief of the National Guard Bureau should play a role in the preparation of that report as directed by the Secretary of Defense.

4. The commander of U.S. Northern Command should advocate for civil support requirements in the Department of Defense's capabilities development, requirements generation and validation, and programming systems. The military services should ensure that civil support requirements are included in their respective budget processes.

5. The budget information for National Guard training and equipment for military assistance to civil authorities and other domestic operations should be included in appropriate sections of the Department of the Army and Department of the Air Force budget documents, respectively. There should not be separate budget documents for National Guard training and equipment for military assistance to civil authorities and other domestic operations.

B. The Role of States and Their Governors

> **Conclusion: The priorities of the states and their governors are not adequately considered in the Department of Defense's policy and resourcing decisions related to the National Guard, even though governors are, and likely will continue to be, the leaders of most domestic emergency response efforts involving the National Guard.**

Finding: Governors do not have a formal mechanism to consult with the Department of Defense on decisions affecting the National Guard of their state, including how the National Guard is organized, manned, trained, equipped, and utilized.

Finding: There is no established process whereby governors can have operational control over federal military assets within a state to respond to emergencies.

Recommendations:

6. Congress should establish a bipartisan Council of Governors composed of 10 governors, with bipartisan co-chairs, appointed by the President in consultation with the National Governors Association, to meet and advise the Secretary of Defense, the Secretary of Homeland Security, and the White House Homeland Security Council on matters related to the National Guard and civil support missions. The Council should meet at least semiannually or as otherwise requested by the Secretary of Defense and the Secretary of Homeland Security or the co-chairs.

7. Laws and procedures should be put into place to enable the President of the United States and a governor to consent in advance that National Guard officers called to federal duty are not relieved of their National Guard state commission, can continue to command National Guard troops, and are exempt from the provisions of the Posse Comitatus Act.

8. As part of Department of Defense efforts to develop plans for consequence management and support to civil authorities that account for state-level activities and incorporate the use of National Guard and Reserve forces as first military responders (see Recommendation 19), the Department of Defense should develop protocols that allow governors to direct the efforts of federal military assets responding to an emergency such as a natural disaster.

C. The National Guard Bureau

> **Conclusion: The National Guard Bureau and other elements of the Department of Defense are not properly structured to fully integrate the National Guard into domestic contingency planning, training, exercising, and operations.**

Finding: Since September 11, 2001, the National Guard Bureau has assumed increased responsibilities for homeland-related missions. This trend will continue in the future.

Finding: The global war on terrorism has placed increased demands on and created new missions for the National Guard to provide forces for both overseas and domestic missions.

Finding: Under its current structure, the National Guard Bureau is not optimized to communicate, collaborate, and coordinate with U.S. Northern Command, the Joint Directorate of Military Support, Joint Forces Command, and the Department of Homeland Security with regard to domestic civil support missions.

Finding: National Guard forces are no longer the Cold War strategic reserve they were when the National Guard Bureau was established. The joint bureau structure of the National Guard Bureau is not sufficiently flexible to adjust to their increased use for domestic and overseas missions.

Finding: The Chief of the National Guard Bureau's detailed understanding of the status and capabilities of National Guard forces would best be utilized by better integrating the Chief and the National Guard Bureau into the workings of U.S. Northern Command, the joint command in charge of most Title 10 homeland defense and civil support activities.

Recommendations:

9. The National Guard Bureau should be made a joint activity of the Department of Defense, rather than a joint bureau of the Army and Air Force. This designation should not change the National Guard Bureau's relationship with the Army and Air Force related to Title 10 matters and planning and budgeting for Title 32 mission requirements.

10. The statute authorizing the National Guard Bureau Charter should be amended to make the Chief of the National Guard Bureau a senior advisor to the Chairman of the Joint Chiefs of Staff and, through the Chairman, to the Secretary of Defense, for matters pertaining to the

National Guard in its nonfederal role. The charter also should be revised to create an advisory relationship between the Chief of the National Guard Bureau and the commanders of the combatant commands for the United States, and between the Chief of the National Guard Bureau and the Department of Homeland Security.

11. The statute authorizing the National Guard Bureau Charter should be amended to include the Bureau's responsibility for "Facilitating and coordinating with other Federal agencies, with Combatant Commands, and with the several States on the use of the National Guard not in active Federal service," and other such changes as necessary to implement the spirit and letter of the Commission's recommendations. The National Guard Bureau should not become an operational command.

12. Immediately after enactment of the statutory changes suggested above, the Secretary of Defense should draft a new charter for the National Guard Bureau, in consultation with the Secretaries of the Army and Air Force and the Chairman of the Joint Chiefs of Staff, reflecting the statutory changes suggested in Recommendations 10 and 11; the charter should be reviewed periodically to ensure that it is updated appropriately.

13. The grade of the Chief of the National Guard Bureau should be increased to general, O-10, and the position should be reevaluated periodically to ensure that the duties required to be performed by the CNGB remain commensurate with grade O-10.

14. The Chief of the National Guard Bureau should not be a member of the Joint Chiefs of Staff.

15. The current position of Assistant to the Chairman of the Joint Chiefs of Staff for National Guard Matters should not be eliminated.

D. U.S. Northern Command

Conclusion: U.S. Northern Command does not adequately consider and utilize all military components—active and reserve, including the National Guard—in planning, training, and exercising and in the conduct of military operations while in support of a governor, in support of another lead federal agency, or in the defense of America.

Finding: The commander of U.S. Northern Command is responsible for the planning, exercising, and command and control of assigned and apportioned Title 10 forces in response to a domestic emergency. The National Guard Bureau coordinates the movement of nonfederalized National Guard forces. This arrangement can impair the coordination of the military response to disaster.

Finding: In accordance with Department of Defense policy, U.S. Northern Command's primary mission has been homeland defense, while civil support has been treated as a lesser included mission.

Finding: U.S. Northern Command is staffed predominantly by active duty personnel who are not fully aware of the capabilities that the reserve component can bring to civil support missions.

Recommendations:

16. Because U.S. Northern Command is a command with significant responsibility for domestic emergency response and civil support, a majority of U.S. Northern Command's billets, including those for its service components, should be filled by leaders and staff with reserve qualifications and credentials. Job descriptions for senior leaders and other key positions at U.S. Northern Command should contain the requirement of significant Reserve or National Guard experience or service.

17. Either the officer serving in the position of the commander or the officer serving in the position of deputy commander of U.S. Northern Command should be a National Guard or Reserve officer at all times.

18. There should be only one U.S. deputy commander at U.S. Northern Command.

19. U.S. Northern Command should develop plans for consequence management and support to civil authorities that account for state-level activities and incorporate the use of National Guard and Reserve forces as first military responders.

E. Reserve Policy Advice

Conclusion: The Secretary of Defense does not have mechanisms to generate and receive the best possible advice on reserve policy matters. The Reserve Forces Policy Board is not structured to obtain and provide to the Secretary of Defense a wide range of independent advice on National Guard and Reserve matters because of the nature of its membership, and because it is subordinated to other offices within the Office of the Secretary of Defense.

Finding: Statutes establishing the Reserve Forces Policy Board and the Office of the Assistant Secretary of Defense for Reserve Affairs conflict about which organization has the primary responsibility to provide advice to the Department of

Defense leadership on National Guard and Reserve matters.

Finding: Uncertainty about which entity has the primary responsibility for making recommendations to the Secretary of Defense involving National Guard and Reserve matters creates conflicting lines of communication and hinders integrated decision making.

Finding: The organization and membership of the Reserve Forces Policy Board and the limits on the topics it may consider prevent decision makers from obtaining the wide range of inputs necessary for them to formulate appropriate and sustainable policies.

Recommendation:

20. To improve the quality and timeliness of independent policy advice to the Secretary of Defense, the Reserve Forces Policy Board statute should be amended to create instead a Reserve Policy Board, composed of 20 members appointed by the Secretary of Defense from outside the Department of Defense. The chairman of the Reserve Policy Board should have extensive knowledge of and experience with the National Guard and Reserves.

F. Reserve Component Officer Promotion

Conclusion: National Guard and Reserve general and flag officers do not have the opportunities to achieve the joint experience and education necessary to be seriously considered for O-9 and O-10 positions. This disparity in opportunity must change. Policies must be put into place that recognize the constraints of a reserve component and provide reserve component personnel adequate opportunities to obtain joint education and joint experience.

Finding: Reserve component officers often serve in a joint environment in positions for which they currently do not receive joint duty credit.

Finding: There are general and flag officers in the National Guard and Reserves who are qualified to hold the rank of O-10.

Finding: Joint Professional Military Education (JPME I & II), required for full joint qualification, is difficult for reservists and national guardsmen to obtain.

Finding: Reserve component members do not have adequate opportunity to gain qualifying joint experience.

Finding: Those reserve component general and flag officers who do not have the opportunity to meet the joint standards imposed by Goldwater-Nichols are often considered less well qualified for senior positions than their active duty counterparts. These reserve component general and flag officers often have valuable civilian experience that is not counted.

Finding: Any attempt to increase the number of reserve component officers serving in joint billets of importance and responsibility must be predicated on increased opportunity, at mid-grade, to gain Joint Professional Military Education and joint experience qualifications. Gradually, all officers should be held to the same standards, although the path to qualifications may vary for reservists.

Recommendations:

21. The Department of Defense should modify joint experience qualifications and Joint Professional Military Education delivery methods in ways that significantly enhance the opportunities for reserve component officers. This should include consideration of credit for the quality of reserve component experience, not simply the quantity.

22. The Department of Defense should strive to ensure that Reserve and National Guard flag and general officers have the opportunity to serve in joint assignments, obtain joint experience, and acquire joint qualifications to compete for promotion to O-9 and O-10 positions, including combatant commanders and senior joint and service positions. Reserve and National Guard flag and general officers should be routinely considered for these positions, a practice that is not now the case.

23. The President of the United States should not be required to certify that all eligible reserve component officers were considered for promotions to the grade of O-9.

IV. THE PATH FORWARD

The conclusions and recommendations in this report address primarily those issues associated with the National Guard Empowerment Act. The Commission's final report will be more comprehensive with respect to the National Guard and the other reserve components as we address the full spectrum of the Commission's charter, including the reserve components' roles and mission, purposes, capabilities, organization and structure, command and control, training, readiness, equipment, mobilization, compensation and benefits, career paths, and funding.

Our effort will include building on the organizational reforms here—such as undertaking an examination of the reserve structures within the Office of the Secretary of Defense, the military departments, and the services to ensure that they are optimal for achieving national security objectives—and reviewing personnel and mobilization policies. The Commission also intends to examine the grade structure of reserve component senior officers to ensure that their duties and responsibilities are described accurately and are current with regard to the requirements necessary to support the global war on terrorism, both overseas and domestically, and to examine whether the National Guard and the other reserve components are adequately funded to properly support mission requirements for both overseas and domestic missions.

As the Commission continues with our work, information may come to light that causes us to modify some of our findings, conclusions, or recommendations in this document; we will highlight any such modifications in our final report.

I. INTRODUCTION

The Commission on the National Guard and Reserves was established by the Ronald Reagan National Defense Authorization Act of 2005. Congress chartered the 13-member body to conduct a comprehensive, independent assessment of the reserve components of the United States. The purpose of the assessment is expressed in the following mission statement:

To identify and recommend changes in policy, law, regulation, and practice to ensure that the National Guard and Reserves are organized, trained, equipped, compensated, and supported to best meet the national security requirements of the United States.

The United States Congress, through the Commission's founding statute and subsequent legislative modifications, has directed the panel to deliver three separate reports to the House and Senate Armed Services Committees:

- An initial organizational report due within 90 days of the Commission's first official meeting.

- A second report providing our recommendations and supporting analyses on a set of legislative proposals bearing predominantly on matters related to the National Guard, no later than March 1, 2007.

- A concluding report providing our final assessments, findings, and recommendations, no later than January 31, 2008.

The first of these reports, detailing our organizational structure, the scope of our activities, and the progress of our work, was submitted to the Senate Armed Services Committee, the House Armed Services Committee, and Secretary of Defense Donald Rumsfeld on June 5, 2006. The report is available on the Commission's Web site, www.cngr.gov.

The report we submit herewith is the second of our three products, and responds to the instructions set forth in the National Defense Authorization Act for Fiscal Year 2007 (P.L. 109-364). The law directed the Commission to report, no later than March 1, 2007, on the advisability and feasibility of 17 proposals bearing mainly on the status and activities of the National Guard Bureau, its Chief, and related matters.

The issues Congress asked the Commission to address in Public Law 109-364 are, for the most part, provisions that appeared in freestanding legislation titled the National Defense Enhancement and National Guard Empowerment Act of 2006 (S. 2658/H.R. 5200), introduced in both the U.S. Senate and House of Representatives in the 109th Congress. Recently the bills were reintroduced in the 110th Congress as the National Guard Empowerment Act of 2007 (S. 430/H.R. 718).

IMPETUS FOR THE PROPOSED LEGISLATION

When they introduced S. 2658 and H.R. 5200, the sponsors of the legislation, Senators Kit Bond and Patrick Leahy in the Senate and Representatives Tom Davis and Gene Taylor in the House, identified a set of specific problems that they argued the National Defense Enhancement and National Guard Empowerment Act would remedy. These significant problems fall into three broad groups:

- The Department of Defense (DOD) and the parent services of the National Guard have not adapted to the significant role of the National Guard in the post-9/11 security environment.

- Decision-making processes within DOD do not adequately consider the interests of the National Guard and do not always include National Guard participation and input at the appropriate level.

- DOD's failure to appropriately consider National Guard interests and funding requirements has produced a National Guard that is not ready to meet current and emerging missions.

The authors of the legislation cite the enormous contribution that National Guard units have made not only in responding to day-to-day emergencies under their state authorities but also in providing military manpower and capabilities to support major national contingencies, including post-9/11 homeland security initiatives, the wars in Afghanistan and Iraq, the response to major natural disasters such as Hurricanes Rita and Katrina, and many other security operations. The proponents point out that in this era of a "long war" against terrorism and of enhanced threats to the homeland—including the potential use of weapons of mass destruction, as well as the possibility of a pandemic—the National Guard will be an increasingly vital part of our overall national security, homeland security, and emergency response tool kit.[1]

Witnesses before the Commission also spoke of this changing role for the National Guard both at home and in its participation in overseas missions. Major General Raymond F. Rees testified that "[f]or decades, the readiness of National Guard units to perform that domestic role has been a by-product—a second order effect—of resources invested in its role as a reserve force. The post 9/11 world, however, has added a new level of expectations for its operational use here in the homeland."[2]

However, the proponents of the act believe that the National Guard is hampered in its ability to perform its missions by Cold War structures and that it lacks institutional power within the Pentagon to match its increasingly important role. They assert that planning for the reserve components often takes place in a joint decision-making environment, such as the Quadrennial Defense Review or the Base Realignment and Closure (BRAC) process, or

---

[1] Statement of Senator Patrick Leahy, 109th Cong., 2nd sess., *Congressional Record* 152, no. 47 (April 26, 2006): S3593–S3597.

[2] Major General Raymond F. Rees, Adjutant General, State of Oregon, prepared testimony before the CNGR, Hearing on Proposed Changes to the National Guard, December 14, 2006 (www.cngr.gov/hearing121314/ReesTestimony1206.pdf), p. 3.

in decision-making forums, such as the Joint Chiefs of Staff, where the interests of the reserve components are represented by their respective services. A consistent theme of the proponents is that the reserve components are not adequately funded because the Guard is not allowed to contribute adequately to discussions about force structure, personnel, equipment, and readiness, and that Guard interests are given short shrift in these processes.[3] The result was that "[w]ith respect to the domestic civil support mission of the Guard, decision makers who do not fully understand these paramount state missions are making the decisions that affect the governors' abilities to respond appropriately to natural and man-made disasters."[4]

Perhaps the most glaring symptom of the need for reform is the state of National Guard readiness and equipping. The Commission has collected information from a wide variety of sources indicating that National Guard readiness has been reduced by chronic equipment shortages. In testimony before the Commission, Janet St. Laurent, Government Accountability Office Director, Capabilities and Management, stated, "The Army National Guard and Army Reserve currently have shortages in the equipment they need to train and deploy and, in the case of the Army National Guard, to respond to domestic emergencies."[5] Army Chief of Staff General Peter J. Schoomaker also acknowledged the situation; as he explained, "To make reserve component units combat ready, we had to pool personnel and equipment from across the force. We also cascaded older equipment to the reserve components."[6] The Army's decision to quadruple funding for the Army National Guard by 2011, with more than $21 billion for ground systems procurement and $1.9 billion in aviation equipment, is in part validation that the concerns raised by the proponents of the National Defense Enhancement and National Guard Empowerment Act have merit.[7]

---

[3] Timothy J. Lowenberg, Adjutant General, State of Washington, pointed to "(1) the BRAC 2005 withdrawal of state National Guard aircraft responsible for moving 1 out of every 2 soldiers and airmen and 1 out of every 3 short tons of equipment that were airlifted into the Gulf Coast states after Hurricane Katrina hit land fall in August 2005, (2) the January 2006 elimination of force structure authorizations and budget authority for 34,000 Army and Air National Guard positions, (3) the removal of $1.2 Billion in military equipment and supplies from Army National Guard units [leaving the Army National Guard with less than 34 percent of its authorized and required equipment], (4) the July 2006 removal of two years' worth of Governor and Adjutant General–validated military construction projects from the Future Years Defense Plan, and (5) the Defense Department's request for legislation giving the President authority to take control of a State's National Guard away from the Governor in the event of any 'serious natural or manmade disaster, accident or catastrophe'" (statement before the House Homeland Security Subcommittee on Economic Security, Infrastructure Protection, and Cybersecurity Subcommittee on Emergency Preparedness, Science and Technology, August 8, 2006). See also Senator Patrick Leahy on the National Defense Authorization Act for 2007, 109th Cong., 2nd sess., *Congressional Record* 152, no. 125 (September 29, 2006): S10808–S10809; General Richard Cody, USA, Vice Chief of Staff, testimony before the House Armed Services Committee, June 13, 2006.
[4] Senators Kit Bond and Patrick Leahy, prepared remarks before the CNGR, Hearing on Roles and Missions, March 8, 2006 (www.cngr.gov/hearing308-9/Bond-Leahy.pdf), p. 1.
[5] Janet St. Laurent, GAO Director of Defense Capabilities and Management, prepared statement before the CNGR, Hearing on National Guard and Reserve Issues, September 21, 2006 (www.cngr.gov/hearing918-21/ReserveCommissiontestimonyGAO.pdf), p. 6.
[6] General Schoomaker, prepared testimony before the CNGR, Hearing on Proposed Changes to the National Guard, December 14, 2006 (www.cngr.gov/hearing121314/General%20Schoomaker%2014%20DEC%20Record%20Version.pdf), p. 4.
[7] Francis J. Harvey, Secretary of the Army, prepared statement before the CNGR, Hearing on Proposed Changes to the National Guard, January 31, 2007 (www.cngr.gov/hearing13107/SecArmy%27s%20Testimony%20--%20Commission%20on%20the%20National%20Guard%20and%20Reserve%20--%20Record%20Version.pdf), p. 3.

The Commission's own investigation of the specific events identified by the proponents of the legislation as examples of National Guard exclusion from deliberation and decisional processes leads us to believe that National Guard leaders did participate in many of the discussions contributing to these decisions. Nevertheless, the divisive outcomes, poor state of National Guard readiness, and discord generated clearly warrant an examination of whether DOD has mechanisms in place to properly consider and incorporate National Guard priorities, especially those unique to the Guard's dual status. Together, these problems bring into question the adequacy of the posture of the National Guard to meet current and emerging requirements. They provide a convincing case for changing the present organization of the National Guard within the overall structure of the Department of Defense and for improving coordination and planning for homeland defense and civil support missions. The question then becomes, how best to effect the desired changes?

As one of the sponsors declared: "The men and women of the National Guard have earned the right to be represented at the highest levels of the Department of Defense" and "to ensure the appropriate representation, manpower, training and equipment are provided to the National Guard for their future missions at home and abroad."[8] Another of the bill's architects described it as designed to give the National Guard the "institutional muscle commensurate with [its] missions."[9] We agree that improvement in this area is critically needed, and ask, what is the right kind of institutional muscle to achieve this objective and the overarching goal of improving national security by enhancing overall military effectiveness?

APPROACH

To inform its work, the Commission held a series of public hearings and received compelling testimony from experts and officials who offered the full range of viewpoints on the proposals of the National Guard Empowerment Act and related issues. We conducted interviews and received briefings on the many aspects of the issues, and we studied relevant documents, data, and other inputs requested of the Department of Defense, think tanks, academia, and other relevant stakeholders, experts, and authorities. Transcripts of the public hearings are available on the Commission's Web site.

This information-gathering process produced a useful set of criteria by which to evaluate the proposed changes bearing on the National Guard. We asked, do the reforms

1. Improve the ability of the National Guard to meet both its overseas and homeland responsibilities as required by U.S. military, defense, and homeland security strategies?[10]

---

[8] Statement of Representative Thomas Davis, 109th Cong., 2nd sess., *Congressional Record* 152, no. 47 (April 26, 2006): E613–E615.

[9] Senator Leahy, *Congressional Record* (April 26, 2006), p. S3597.

[10] See the prepared witness statements before the CNGR, Hearing on Roles and Missions, March 8–9, 2006, of David S. C. Chu, Under Secretary of Defense for Personnel and Readiness (www.cngr.gov/hearing308-9/Chu.pdf), p. 8; Andrew F. Krepinevich, Center for Strategic and Budgetary Assessments (www.cngr.gov/hearing308-9/Krepinevich.pdf), p. 4; and General Robert Magnus, Assistant Commandant of the Marine Corps (www.cngr.gov/hearing308-9/Magnus.pdf), p. 11.

2. Enhance the ability of the National Guard to be a reserve force overseas, backing up the active force, and an operational force in the homeland, backed up by the active force?[11]

3. Build jointness among the military services as envisioned by the Goldwater-Nichols Act?[12]

4. Further integrate the active and reserve components to promote military effectiveness while respecting the necessary and fundamental differences between these two elements of the total force?[13]

5. Promote cooperation and proper interrelationships among the chief institutions responsible for homeland defense and homeland security?[14]

6. Build organizational structures with clear roles and missions?[15]

7. Establish resource allocation and policymaking processes and procedures that are fair, inclusive, and take into account the full range of inputs, including those of governors?[16]

Using these criteria, the Commission envisions a National Guard that is properly organized and structured to operate in the joint-warfighting environment; brings unity of effort to federal and state emergency response capabilities; participates in an integrated, more systemic and interagency approach to solving problems; and benefits from a greater role in national security decision-making for our nation's governors.

---

[11] See the prepared witness statements before the CNGR, Hearing on Roles and Missions, March 8, 2006, of Congressman Ike Skelton (www.cngr.gov/hearing308-9/Skelton.pdf), p. 3, and Senator Ben Nelson (www.cngr.gov/hearing308-9/Nelsontestimony.doc), p. 4.

[12] See the prepared witness statements of General Lance Smith, USAF, Commander U.S. Joint Forces Command, before the CNGR, Hearing with Combatant Commanders, October 5, 2006 (www.cngr.gov/hearing1005/General%20Smith%20testimony.doc), p. 4; Major General Roger P. Lempke, President, Adjutants General Association of the United States and Adjutant General, Nebraska, before the CNGR, Hearing on Changes to the National Guard, December 14, 2006 (www.cngr.gov/hearing121314/Lempke%20Testimony%2014%20Dec%2006.pdf), p. 4.

[13] See the prepared witness statements before the CNGR, Hearing on Roles and Missions, March 8–9, 2006, of Admiral Robert F. Willard, USN, Vice Chief of Naval Operations (www.cngr.gov/hearing308-9/Willard.doc), p. 4; General Richard A. Cody, USA, Vice Chief of Staff (www.cngr.gov/hearing308-9/Cody.pdf), p. 2; Senator John Warner (www.cngr.gov/hearing308-9/Witness%20Statement%20Sen.%20Warner%20Comm%20on%20NG%20and%20Reserve%208%20Mar%2006%20V4.doc), p. 2; and Congressman Skelton, p. 2.

[14] See the prepared witness statement of Admiral Willard, p. 7, and the prepared witness statements before the CNGR, Hearing on Proposed Changes to the National Guard, December 13–14, 2006, of David S. C. Chu, Under Secretary of Defense for Personnel and Readiness, and Thomas F. Hall, Assistant Secretary of Defense for Reserve Affairs (www.cngr.gov/hearing121314/Chu-Hall%20Statement.pdf),p. 11, and General Peter J. Schoomaker, USA, Chief of Staff (www.cngr.gov/hearing121314/ General%20Schoomaker%2014%20DEC%20Record%20Version.pdf), p. 7.

[15] See the prepared witness statements before the CNGR, Hearing on Roles and Missions, March 8, 2006, of Senator Nelson, p. 5, and Lieutenant General Raymond T. Odierno, USA, Assistant to the Chairman, Joint Chiefs of Staff (www.cngr.gov/hearing308-9/Odierno.pdf), p. 4.

[16] See National Governors Association, letter to Major General Arnold L. Punaro, USMC (ret.), Chairman of the CNGR, January 26, 2007.

In evaluating proposed reforms, the Commission also believes that the Goldwater-Nichols Department of Defense Reorganization Act of 1986 is instructive for our work. Goldwater-Nichols sought to improve military effectiveness by modernizing organizational structures and relationships within the Department of Defense, improving the quality of military advice, increasing the power of combatant commanders, reaffirming civilian control of the military, and increasing jointness among the military services. This legislation helped transform and modernize the military services.

The organizational structures within the Department relating to the reserve components, including particularly the National Guard Bureau, were not altered by Goldwater-Nichols. Many of the proposals in the legislation we have been asked to consider reflect the strain caused by outdated structures and policies. Thus, an important objective of the Commission is to ensure that reforms to the reserve components further and are consistent with the Goldwater-Nichols reforms.

Although we believe that reforms are needed to increase the influence of the National Guard in DOD's decisions on policy and resourcing, we think that this reform effort will necessarily have implications beyond the proposals in the legislation; we therefore recognize the significant role played by governors of states, as well as the role of other Defense Department commands such as U.S. Northern Command and of other federal agencies, most notably the Department of Homeland Security. This wider purview is critical, because military power is only one aspect of U.S. capabilities at the federal, state, and local levels. In reporting to Congress on the National Defense Enhancement and National Guard Empowerment Act, the Commission delivers its findings, conclusions, and recommendations in this broader context, including needed reforms affecting the National Guard as a critical member of the entire national security team.

II. THE CONTEXT FOR OUR REPORT

A. THE SECURITY ENVIRONMENT AND ITS IMPLICATIONS FOR THE RESERVE COMPONENT

The Commission believes that the first step in ensuring that the National Guard and Reserves are properly organized, equipped, trained, compensated, and supported is to understand the strategic environment in which they must operate.

THE THREAT IN THE POST-9/11 ERA

The United States today faces strategic national security challenges that are far different than those of a generation ago. The terrorist attacks of September 11, 2001, crystallized the sea change in the nature of the threats we face, changes that began to become more evident following the end of the Cold War.

U.S. strategy and military resources must be ready to address a broad range of scenarios and contingencies posed by existing and aspiring regional powers; violent Islamic extremists; growing weapons proliferation; local conflicts and humanitarian crises that threaten to spark wider instability; transnational threats, including organized crime, drug trafficking, pandemic flu, and natural disasters; and domestic homeland security threats, including terrorist acts and natural disasters.

National security and strategy documents focus on the need to protect the homeland, and they underscore that the nation is engaged in a "long war" against terrorism that will make it increasingly important that our armed forces possess diverse, complex, and specialized skills.[1] Owing to the varied civilian backgrounds of service members, many of these capabilities may uniquely reside in the reserve component; and because the National Guard, in particular, is forward deployed throughout the United States, that force is especially critical to the homeland mission set.

Even before 9/11, the use of the National Guard and Reserves was on the rise, and reliance on these forces to achieve national security objectives is likely to increase. Missions in which National Guard units have been heavily involved include wars in Iraq and Afghanistan, stability operations, counterterrorism, natural disasters, homeland security, domestic disaster relief, border protection, and narcotics interdiction.

The Commission does not presume to know if or when the historically high demand on the Guard and Reserves will abate. Nor do we know how future threats might evolve, requiring

---

[1] *Quadrennial Defense Review Report* ([Washington, DC: Department of Defense,] 2006), pp. v–ix. See also *National Security Strategy of the United States of America* ([Washington, DC: The White House,] 2006), *National Defense Strategy of the United States of America* ([Washington, DC: Department of Defense], 2005), and *Strategy for Homeland Security and Civil Support* ([Washington, DC: Department of Defense], 2005).

the reserve components to take on new roles and missions. The testimony we have received from a wide variety of experts on the evolving security environment and its implications for the National Guard and Reserves was best summarized by Senator John Warner:

> The continuing operational demands placed on Guardsmen, Reservists and their families, at home and abroad, during a time of transformational change for the Armed Forces have raised critically important questions about the appropriate roles for the state National Guards and our Reserve Forces. Careful consideration needs to be given to the missions assigned to the Guard and Reserves, to the level of resources and equipment that must be provided for their use, and other career paths and benefits that should be available to Guardsmen and Reservists.[2]

TRANSFORMATION AND BUDGET

The Commission recognizes that our recommendations are not being formulated in a vacuum. Several factors of national importance are influencing the scope and pace of change, including the ongoing effort to transform the Department of Defense and the realities of the national budgeting process.

Right now, the Defense Department is seeking to make U.S. forces more agile and expeditionary by leveraging technological advances, "adjusting the U.S. global military force posture," and emphasizing "the ability to surge quickly to trouble spots across the globe."[3] Together with all other components, the National Guard and Reserves are undergoing transformation, and further reforms affecting them must take account of this reality.

Like all participants in the federal budget process, the reserve components must compete for scarce resources. Reserve funding requirements are planned, programmed, and budgeted for in each service's budget process and are considered as part of total force requirements.[4] Finding sufficient funding for these requirements will remain an ongoing challenge, given the tight fiscal environment, competing budget priorities, and the demands on DOD in allocating its resources. We realize that policymaking is often driven by resource constraints and that trade-offs are necessary. Our recommendations will reflect what courses we believe are optimal for achieving national security objectives.

The world is and will remain a dangerous place. The courage and skill of America's brave men and women in uniform will be needed on many missions across the globe. Given the national security environment, the role played by the National Guard and the Reserves will become increasingly vital. In the best tradition of the citizen-soldier, national guardsmen and reservists will confront enemies, whether they are nation-states or terrorists; defuse regional conflicts; stop the spread of weapons of mass destruction; confront such

---

[2] Senator John Warner, statement provided to the CNGR, March 2006.
[3] *Quadrennial Defense Review Report* (2006), p. v.
[4] Derived from information provided by Air National Guard Directorate and Army Program Analysis and Evaluation Directorate, November 2006.

transnational threats as crime, drugs, and pandemics; provide humanitarian comfort to the victims of natural disasters; help stabilize and build countries in transition; and provide homeland defense and civil support here at home.

As it always has, the United States will continue to promote human freedom, dignity, and greater economic opportunity. To pursue those ends, the nation must be able to identify precisely what is expected of our National Guard and Reserves in meeting the demands of the 21st century. The Commission on the National Guard and Reserves is committed to helping Congress and the administration gain essential perspectives on these vital issues.

B. The Current State of the National Guard

The Commission believes that to properly assess the need for and desirability of reforms to the National Guard and its institutions, it is vital to establish a baseline and to clearly comprehend the status of the National Guard with respect both to the other reserve components and to the active component. Key indicators such as manpower levels, mission, utilization, recruitment, retention, incentive levels, equipment, and funding contribute to an overall understanding of the posture and health of the force.

There is no doubt that the reserve components are today being employed as an operational force. The Center for Strategic and International Studies, in its report *The Future of the National Guard and Reserves*, finds: "Employing the Reserve Component as part of the operational force is mandatory, not a choice. DoD cannot meet today's operational requirements without drawing significantly on the Reserve Component."[1] There also seems little question about the Department of Defense's intent to continue to employ them operationally. Dr. David S. C. Chu, Under Secretary of Defense for Personnel and Readiness, described how the shift from a strategic reserve to an operational reserve has gradually taken place since the 1990 involuntary mobilizations for Operations Desert Shield and Desert Storm. He also described how the reserve components, as envisioned in the most recent Quadrennial Defense Review, will become even more operational—specifically, "more accessible and more readily deployable" in the future.[2]

Lieutenant General Raymond T. Odierno, then Assistant to the Chairman of the Joint Chiefs of Staff, defined an operational reserve for the Commission: "Current terminology defines an operational Reserve as a trained, predominantly part-time force, a portion of which is mission-tasked and engaged at all times. This force, a part of which is designed, structured, missioned and resourced to conduct operational missions on a continuous basis, assumes full-time roles and functions. The remainder of the force, then, is readily available to be placed on Active duties to conduct operational missions as needed."[3]

De facto use of the reserve components as an operational force and the declarations that it is so do not ensure that such use is feasible or sustainable. A crucial question that must be answered before determining the need for reform and the scope of any change required is whether the current posture of the National Guard is sustainable.

The Commission recognizes that we are reviewing the National Guard during a time of increased operational tempo. Whether such a tempo remains high for the indefinite future depends on events we cannot anticipate. We must be careful about drawing conclusions based on a status that, along with current contingencies, may change. However, as we have pointed out, U.S. national security plans anticipate that the fight against violent Islamic

---

[1] Christine E. Wormuth, Michèle A. Flournoy, Patrick T. Henry, and Clark A. Murdock, *The Future of the National Guard and Reserves: The Beyond Goldwater-Nichols Phase III Report* (Washington, DC: Center for Strategic and International Studies, 2006), p. ix.

[2] Dr. David S. C. Chu, prepared witness statement before the CNGR, Hearing on Roles and Missions, March 8, 2006 (www.cngr.gov/hearing308-9/Chu.pdf), pp. 5–6.

[3] Lieutenant General Odierno, testimony before the CNGR, Hearing on Roles and Missions, transcript of March 8, 2006, hearing (www.cngr.gov/pdf/0308cngr.pdf), p. 95.

extremism will be a "long war"—and as our analysis of the security environment demonstrates, it would be imprudent for us to assume that the operational tempo of current forces will necessarily diminish and remain lower in the long run. Certainly the trends since the first Iraq war are the ever-increasing reliance on and utilization of the reserve component.

MANPOWER/FORCE STRUCTURE

The reserve component consists of the Army National Guard, Army Reserve, Air National Guard, Air Force Reserve, Navy Reserve, Marine Corps Reserve, and Coast Guard Reserve. Since the end of the Cold War, the size of both the active and reserve components has decreased significantly, with a concomitant reduction in reserve force structure as well, as illustrated in Figures 1 and 2. The totals have gone from 2.2 million to 1.4 million active duty personnel and from 1.2 million to 800,000 Selected Reservists.

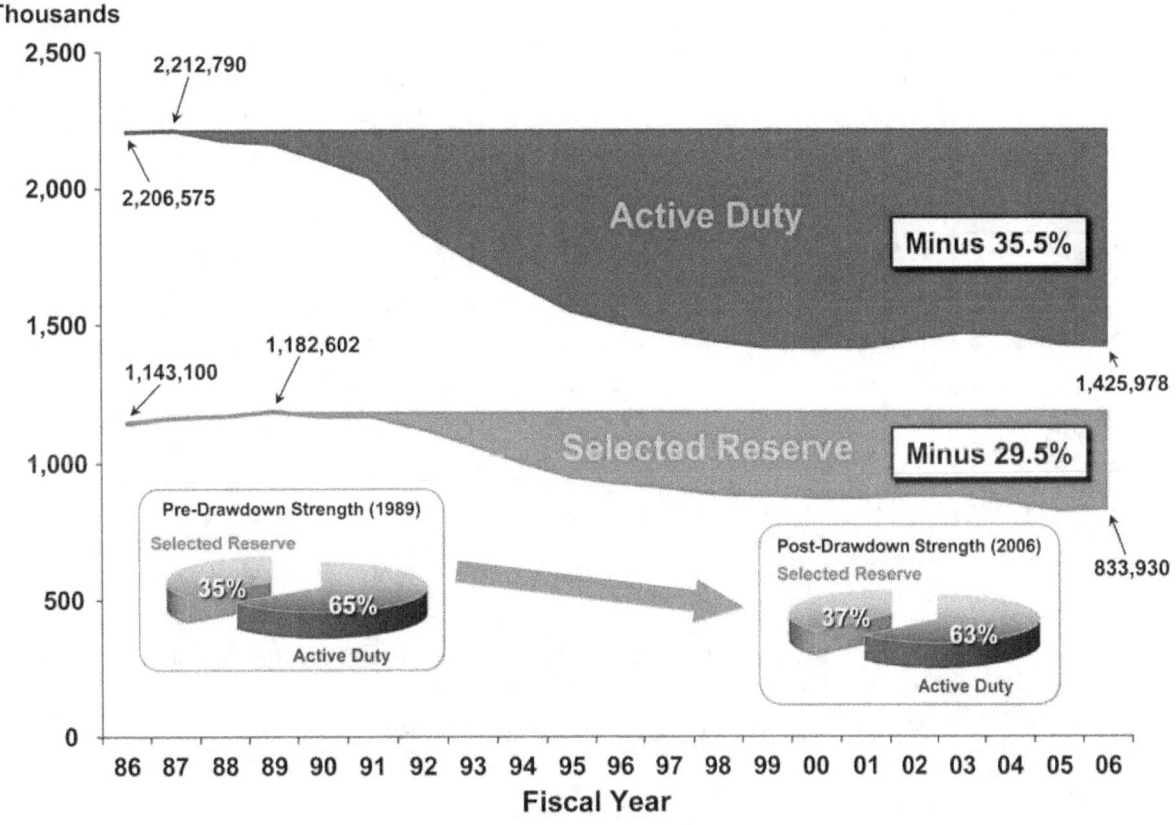

Source: Briefings prepared by the Office of the Assistant Secretary of Defense for Reserve Affairs (OASD-RA), March 13, 2006; January 2007, slide 8.

Figure 1. End-Strength Trend (Actual Strengths, FY 1986 – FY 2006)

Overall, the reserve component constitutes a major portion of the nation's military force capability for current and future contingencies. As shown in Figure 3, the Ready Reserve—which includes both the Selected Reserve, whose members train regularly, and the Individual Ready Reserve, a prior-service manpower pool with no training requirements—provides 44 percent of the total force.

	Cold War	Post–Cold War/GWOT
Army Guard 475K to 350K (+ 8.2K by FY 13)	10 Divisions, 24 Separate Brigades, & Combat Support (CS)/Combat Service Support (CSS)	8 Divisions, 15 "Enhanced" Separate Brigades…to Division HQs with 28 Modular Brigade Combat Teams
Army Reserve 319K to 205K (+1K by FY 13)	Combat, CS & CSS	CS & CSS… Developing Expeditionary Force Packages
Naval Reserve 152K to 70K	Combat & Combat Support plus Active Unit Augmentation	Surge Ready Maritime Total Force, Stand-alone Combat Support, and Augmentation to Combat Units
USMCR 43.6K to 39.6	Mirror image active component, 1 Division, 1 Marine Logistics Group, and 1 Marine Air Wing	Continues to augment and reinforce USMC
Air Guard 116K to 107K	12.5 Fighter Wing Equivalent (FWE), Tactical Lift	7 FWE, Bombers, Continental Air Defense, Future Total Force, Unmanned Aerial Vehicles, Information Operations, More Associate Units
Air Reserve 83K to 74K	Strategic (STRAT) Lift, & Tankers CSS	STRAT Lift, Tankers & CSS More Associate Units, future Total Force
Coast Guard Reserve 12K to 10K	Port Security Units; Marine Safety Units; Command, Control, and Communications; Ops Shore Facilities; Vessel & Air Station Augmentation	Active Coast Guard Unit Augmentation (by individual), Port Security Units (CS)

Source: Office of the Assistant Secretary of Defense for Reserve Affairs (OASD/RA) Briefing, slide 16, dated January 24, 2007 (www.dod.mil/ra/documents/RA%20101%20FY%2006.ppt).

Figure 2. Reserve Component Force Structure

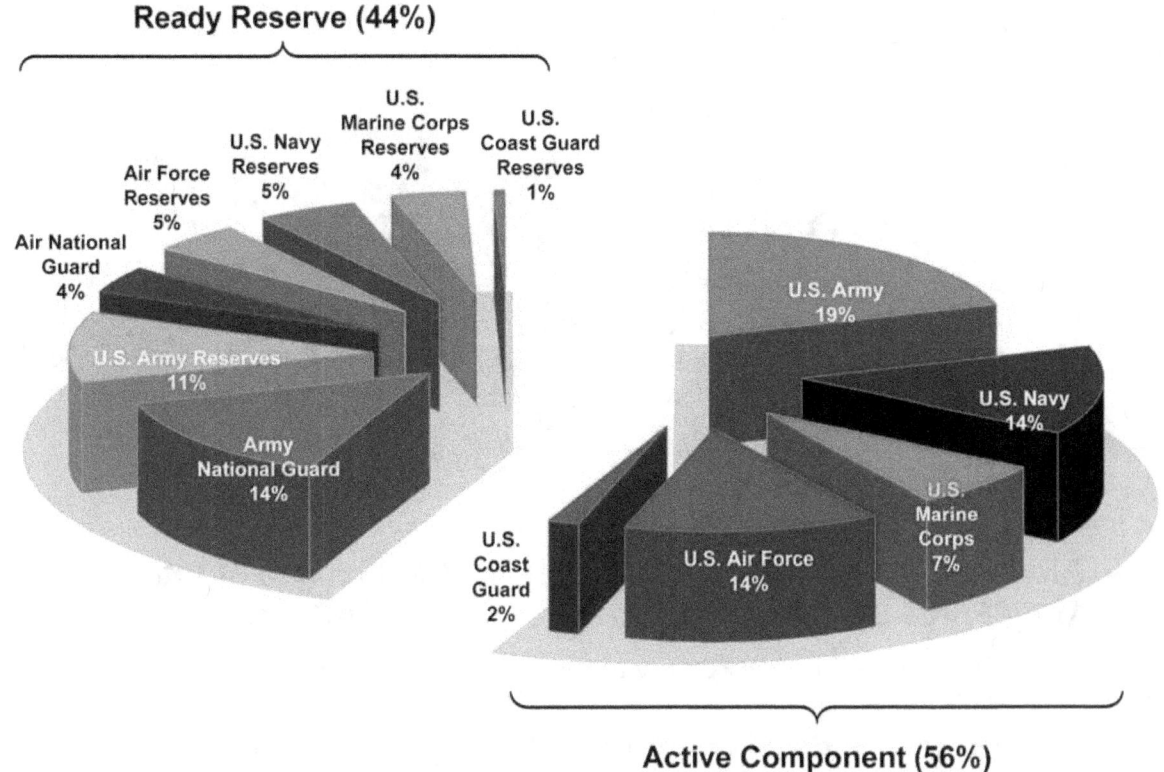

Source: The OASD-RA, December 2006.

Figure 3. Total Force — 2.4 Million

MISSION

The core mission of "each reserve component is to provide trained units and qualified persons available for active duty in the armed forces in time of war or national emergency[.]"[4] Although they regularly perform missions in support of the active component, the Army and Air National Guard, under their state and other authorities, also have a unique responsibility—providing military assistance during state and national emergencies and maintaining the defense and security of the homeland.

The Army National Guard participates in both missions through the utilization of its brigade combat teams, supporting brigades, and smaller or specialized units. At this time, Army National Guard soldiers are participating in the global war on terror in Iraq, Afghanistan, Guantánamo Bay, Cuba, and the Horn of Africa; "man[ning] air defense batteries in [Washington, DC] and [the] ballistic missile interceptor site in Alaska"; carrying out "peacekeeping operations in the [Balkans] and the Sinai";[5] and working alongside the

---

[4] 10 U.S.C. §10102.
[5] Prepared combined witness statement of Lieutenant General H Steven Blum, Chief, National Guard Bureau; Lieutenant General Clyde A. Vaughn, Director, Army National Guard; and Major General Charles Ickes II, Acting Director, Air National Guard, before the Senate Appropriations Committee Subcommittee on Defense, Hearing on National Guard and Reserve Posture, April 26, 2006 (www.ngb.army.mil/media/transcripts/ngb_written_testimony.doc), p. 11.

Border Patrol in "Operation Jump Start."[6] Overall, as shown in Figure 4, the Army National Guard provides 38 percent of the total Army force structure.

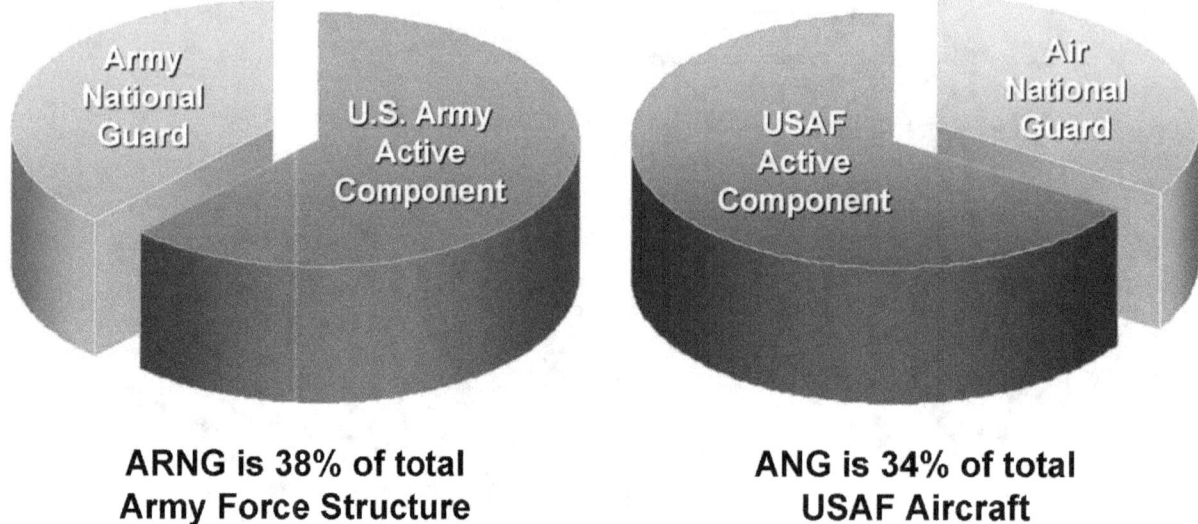

**ARNG is 38% of total
Army Force Structure**

**ANG is 34% of total
USAF Aircraft**

Source: National Guard Bureau Overview briefing to House Defense Appropriations Subcommittee staff, January 9, 2007, slide 17.

Figure 4. National Guard Force Structure Contribution

The Air National Guard supports domestic and overseas missions through the use of tankers, airlift aircraft, fighters, air defense, and JSTARS (the Joint Surveillance Target Attack Radar System). At this time, Air National Guard members fly air sovereignty missions over America's cities, serve in state rapid reaction forces, and "provide extensive [homeland security capabilities] with…communications, ground transportation, and chemical-biological-radiological detection units."[7] The men and women of the Air Guard also serve in Air Guard RED HORSE (Rapid Engineer Deployable Heavy Operational Repair Squadron Engineer) teams and EMEDS (Expeditionary Medical Support), "both of which proved extremely valuable during Hurricane Katrina."[8] As also shown in Figure 4, the number of Air National Guard aircraft represents 34 percent of the total number of Air Force aircraft.

Each state has at least one weapons of mass destruction civil support team (WMD-CST). As Guard witnesses explained to Congress, "The WMD-CSTs are joint units, consisting of both Army and Air Guard personnel. [This gives] each state and territory the capability of rapidly assisting civil authorities in detecting and responding to a WMD attack."[9]

---

[6] "Fact Sheet: Operation Jump Start: Acting Now to Secure the Border," White House Office of the Press Secretary, August 3, 2006 (www.whitehouse.gov/news/releases/2006/08/20060803-7.html).

[7] Prepared witness statement of Lieutenant General Blum, Lieutenant General Vaughn, and Major General Ickes II, pp. 11, 13.

[8] Prepared witness statement of Lieutenant General Blum, Lieutenant General Vaughn, and Major General Ickes II, p. 13.

[9] Prepared witness statement of Lieutenant General Blum, Lieutenant General Vaughn, and Major General Ickes II, p. 13.

In addition to these WMD-CSTs, the Army and Air National Guard have developed, funded, and manned 12 regional chemical, biological, radiological, nuclear, or high-yield explosive (CBRNE) Enhanced Response Force Packages (CERFPs). These units are capable of providing mass casualty decontamination, medical treatment, security, and urban search and extraction in contaminated environments.[10]

Figures 5 and 6 graphically depict the National Guard's contributions to the nation's defense and security around the world.

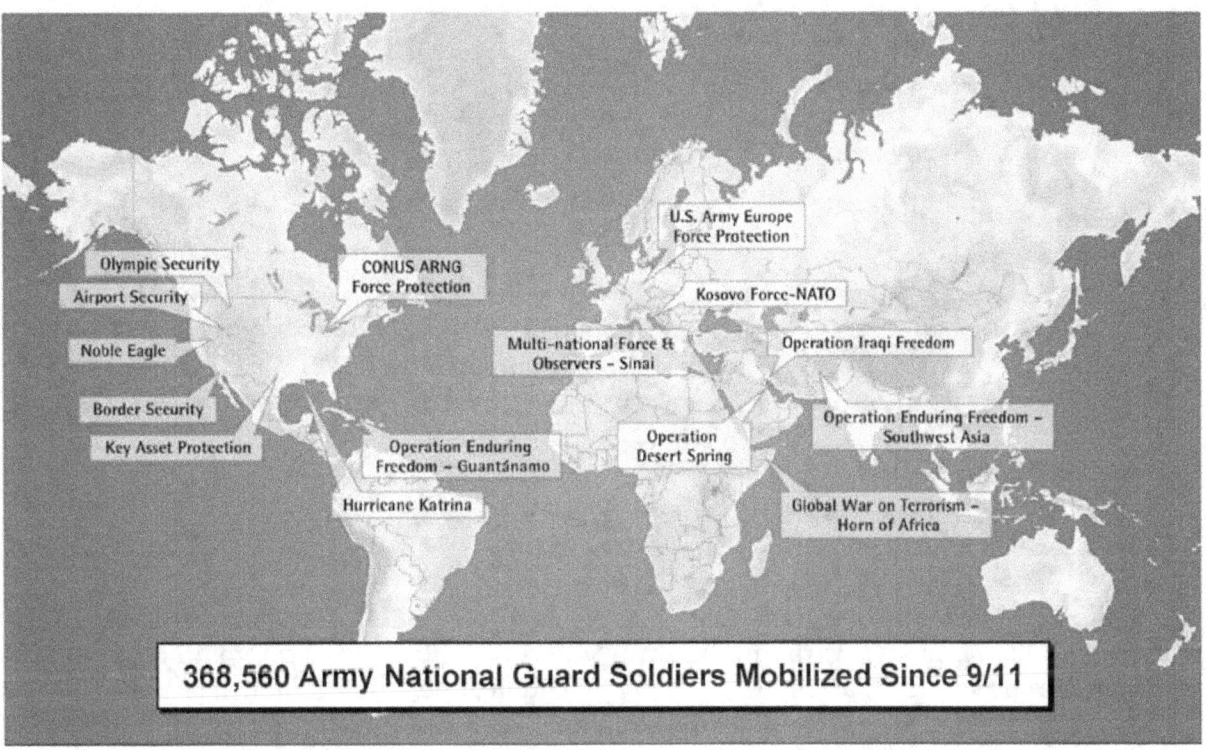

Source: National Guard, "2007 Posture Statement," January 2007, p. 12.

Figure 5. ARNG Contributions Worldwide
(as of FY 2007)

---

[10] Prepared witness statement of Lieutenant General Blum, Lieutenant General Vaughn, and Major General Ickes II, p. 13.

Source: National Guard, "2007 Posture Statement," January 2007, p. 19.

**Figure 6. ANG Contributions Worldwide
(as of FY 2007)**

Given the wide range of missions that they perform, augmenting the ability of the active force to participate in any warfight, the Army and Air National Guard remain cost-effective for their parent services, as Figure 7 shows. To date, the Commission has not seen any credible analysis that would counter the long-held conviction that the Guard and Reserve components are a bargain for the taxpayer.

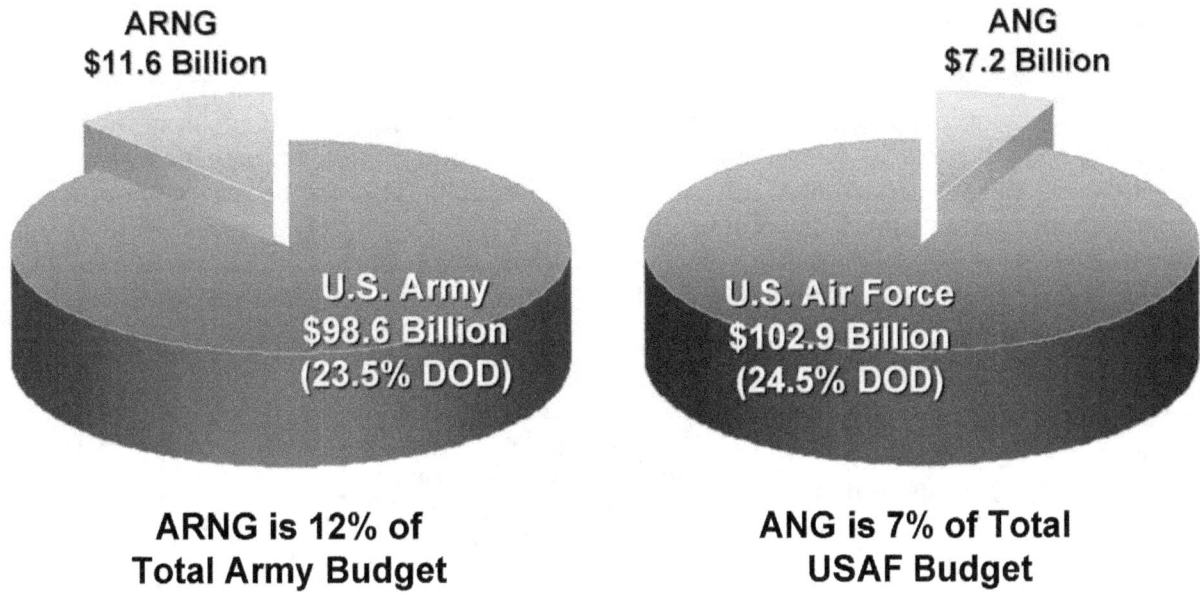

Source: National Guard Bureau Overview briefing to House Defense Appropriations Subcommittee staff, January 9, 2007, slide 17.

Figure 7. National Guard Share of Budget

INCREASED OPERATIONAL UTILIZATION

Following the force drawdown after the Vietnam War, the nation's military forces were structured for the continuing Cold War against Soviet and other Communist expansionism that had determined U.S. military and foreign policy since the late 1940s. The United States maintained a large active duty military presence in Europe as a NATO first responder to the threat of a large number of armored Soviet divisions. Backing up the active forces stationed both overseas and in the United States was a sizable strategic reserve force, including reserve component combat divisions, that would augment and reinforce—after a lengthy train-up period.

From the end of the Korean War in 1953 until 1990, reservists were involuntarily activated for federal service only three times: 148,034 reservists, for the Berlin Crisis from 1961 to 1962; 14,200, for the Cuban Missile Crisis in 1962; and 37,643, for the Vietnam War and USS *Pueblo* crisis from 1968 to 1969. In comparison, 857,877 reservists were involuntarily activated for the Korean War.[11]

Reserve utilization began to change, however, with the involuntary reserve call-up for Operations Desert Shield and Desert Storm in 1990–91 that affected 238,729 reservists. Additional involuntary activations continued throughout the 1990s and into the new century for Haiti, Bosnia, Kosovo, and the low-intensity conflict in Iraq;[12] they culminated with Operation Noble Eagle, Operation Enduring Freedom, and Operation Iraqi Freedom,

---

[11] Lawrence Kapp, *Reserve Component Personnel Issues: Questions and Answers*, CRS Report RL30802 (updated January 18, 2006), p. 8.
[12] Kapp, *Reserve Component Personnel Issues*, pp. 8–9.

which involved the involuntary activation of more than 590,000 reserve component members.[13]

Although the reserve component presence in Iraq has decreased from its peak of more than 40 percent of the force in 2004,[14] the overall reserve contribution in both peacetime and contingency operations remains quite high (see Figure 8). The use of reserve component personnel increased from 12.7 million duty days in fiscal year 2001 to 68.3 million duty days in fiscal year 2005. For reasons discussed later in this report, the Commission believes that the force cannot be sustained over the long term at this level of utilization.

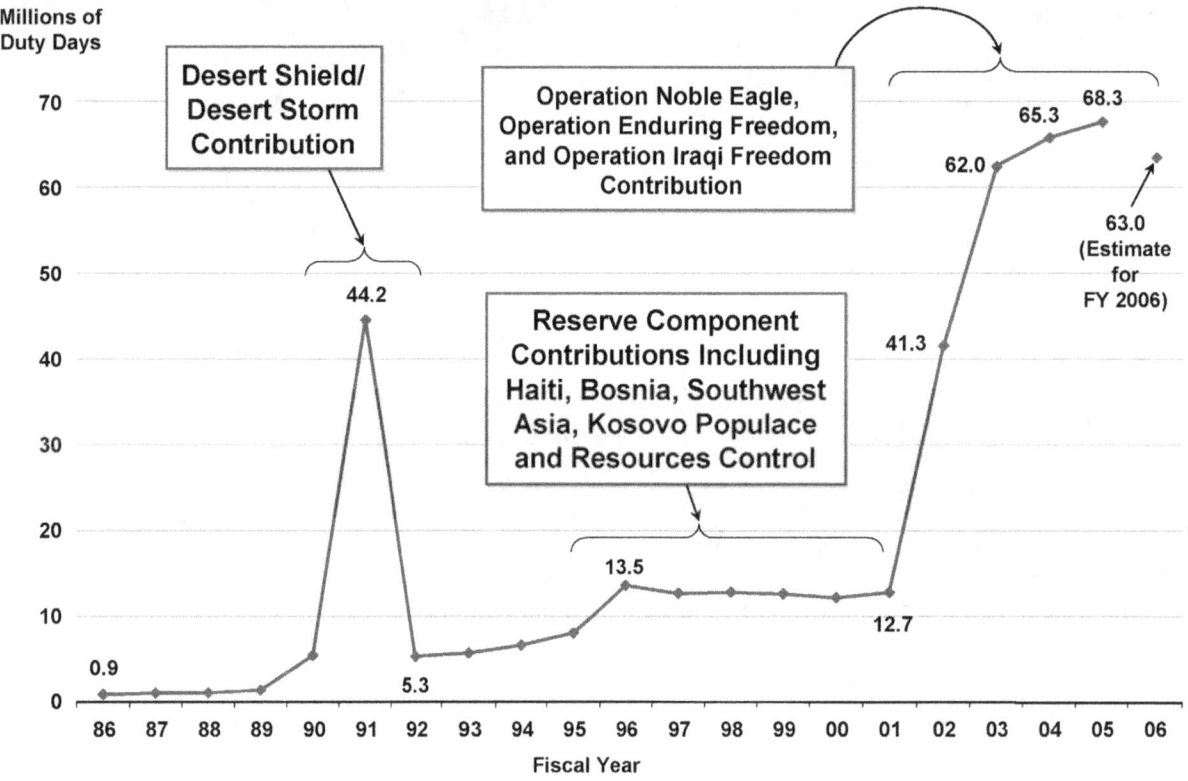

Source: Briefing prepared for the Secretary of Defense (SecDef) by the OASD-RA, January 2007, slide 3.

Figure 8. DOD Reserve Contributions in Both Peacetime and Contingency Operations

---

[13] Office of the Secretary of Defense, Services Daily Mobilization Report, February 10, 2007.

[14] Congressman Duncan Hunter, Chairman, House Armed Services Committee, opening statement at hearing on Army and Marine Corps Troop Rotations for Operation Iraqi Freedom 3 and Operation Enduring Freedom 6 and the Mobilization of the Individual Ready Reserve, Operations and Reconstruction Efforts in Iraq, House Armed Services Committee, July 7, 2004, 108th Congress, 2nd sess., p. 702; Assistant Secretary of Defense for Reserve Affairs Thomas F. Hall, FY2007 Posture Statement before the Senate Armed Services Committee Subcommittee on Personnel, March 30, 2006, p. 6.

Cross-Leveling

The reliance on the reserve components was succinctly summarized by the Department of Defense in its fiscal year 2002 Emergency Supplemental Request to Congress: "Today, the DOD cannot implement the National Security Strategy without National Guard and Reserve forces. During the past several years, a smaller Total Force has led to an increased role for the Reserve Components. The National Guard and Reserve members are full-fledged members of the nation's defense team, and sustained military operations cannot succeed without their support and participation."[15] In mobilizing the reserve components, DOD has attempted to reconcile competing readiness and personnel requirements in such a manner as to create an unsustainable process of forming units. Taken together, the implementation of the President's Partial Mobilization Authority, which capped mobilization at 24 months cumulative; DOD's policy of one-time-only involuntary mobilization; the reliance on volunteerism; and a mismatch between the reserve components' end-strength and organizational structure have forced the Army and Marine Corps to cobble together reserve fighting units by using individual volunteers borrowed from other units around the country. This practice, known as *cross-leveling*, has deleterious effects on unit cohesion, training, and readiness and on the ability of the reserve components to provide support to the families of mobilized reservists. One battalion commander testified before the Commission that "cross leveling is evil."[16]

In testimony before the House Appropriations Subcommittee on Defense, Lieutenant General H Steven Blum, Chief of the National Guard Bureau, used the example of the 162nd Infantry Brigade of the Oregon Army National Guard to illustrate the harmful effects of these practices: "When one battalion from the 162nd Infantry was alerted for an overseas mission, volunteers from the other two battalions jumped into the deploying one. Months later, a second battalion received a mission. By the time the third battalion received its mission to fight in Iraq, there were few soldiers still in it—they had been piecemealed away. If all three battalions had a predictable schedule this could have been avoided."[17]

Reserve component units were brought up to strength with individual volunteers from other units rather than with the Individual Ready Reserve, which was established to meet just such requirements. Policy guidance from the Under Secretary of Defense for Personnel and Readiness directed, "Involuntarily recal[l] the Individual Ready Reserve only after considering Selected Reserve members and volunteers."[18] When he was Chief of the Army Reserve, Lieutenant General James R. Helmly charged that such policies, which emphasized individual voluntary mobilizations over the existing Army Reserve unit structure,

---

[15] Department of Defense, "FY 2002 Supplemental Request to Continue the Global War on Terrorism," March 2002, p. 6.

[16] Lieutenant Colonel Mark Smith, USMCR, testimony before the CNGR, Hearing on Readiness: Battalion Commanders, Recently Returned from Iraq and Afghanistan, transcript of September 21, 2006, hearing (www.cngr.gov/hearing918-21/transcript4.pdf), p. 42.

[17] Lieutenant General Blum, testimony before the House Committee on Appropriations Subcommittee on Defense, January 18, 2007, pp. 5–6.

[18] Under Secretary of Defense, Personnel and Readiness memo to Secretary of Defense, "Force Deployment Rules for Operations Iraqi Freedom and Enduring Freedom," July 30, 2004.

"threaten to distort the very nature of service in the Reserve Components."[19] When asked by the Commission about the use of cross-leveling, Under Secretary of Defense for Personnel and Readiness David S. C. Chu explained that the issue results from "a difference in perspective between the operational chain of authority in the military service and the personnel community."[20]

During its hearings and investigations, the Commission has received compelling evidence about the large number of units from which soldiers have had to be drawn in order to make a single unit deployable. General Robert Magnus, Assistant Commandant of the Marine Corps, described to the Commission how the First Battalion, Twenty-Fifth Marines (1/25) was sourced: "261 Reserve Marines from 2/25 and Headquarters Company, 25th Marines had to be activated to fully man 1/25, thereby requiring essentially two battalions worth of [U]SMCR Marines to make one that can activate and deploy at strength." General Magnus recognized that "this causes cascading negative effects on sourcing future OIF [Operation Iraqi Freedom] requirements," as providing marines to the deploying battalion delayed reconstitution of the 2/25 for more than a year.[21] Another such example comes from the 756th Transportation Company of the California Army National Guard, which was mobilized on July 26, 2005. Of the 170 individual mobilization requirements, only 7 were available within the company; 163 had to be cross-leveled into the unit. Soldiers came from 65 units and 49 locations. More than 100 soldiers needed additional qualification training in their military occupational specialty.[22]

The negative impacts of cross-leveling are significant. Cross-leveled units take a longer time to train for deployment and have less unit cohesion, and unit members' families are less able to reach out to family support services, which may only be available several states away. In testimony before the Commission, General Peter J. Schoomaker, the Army Chief of Staff, urged the Department of Defense to put an end to the policies that drive cross-leveling,[23] and Secretary of Defense Robert Gates has taken steps toward stopping this practice. In a memorandum issued in January 2007, Secretary Gates limited the involuntary mobilization period to a maximum one year at any one time but permitted service discretion to "exclude individual skill training required for deployment, and post-mobilization leave" from this period. The memo further prescribed that the "planning objective for involuntary mobilization of Guard/Reserve units will remain a one year mobilized to five years demobilized ratio" and directed that a new compensation program be established to incentivize both active and reserve component service members for more frequent deployment.[24] The degree to which the Secretary's guidance is successfully implemented could have a major impact on both recruiting and retention.

---

[19] Lieutenant General Helmly, memorandum to the Army Chief of Staff, "Readiness of the United States Army Reserve," December 20, 2004.

[20] Under Secretary Chu, testimony before the CNGR, Hearing on Proposed Changes to the National Guard, transcript of December 13, 2006, hearing (www.cngr.gov/hearing121314/1213cngr-panel1.pdf), p. 9.

[21] General Magnus, prepared witness statement before the CNGR, Hearing on Roles and Mission of the Guard and Reserves, March 9, 2006 (www.cngr.gov/hearing308-9/Magnus.pdf), p. 15.

[22] FORSCOM Mobilization Conference, September 27, 2006, slide 29.

[23] General Schoomaker, testimony before the CNGR, Hearing on Proposed Changes to the National Guard, transcript of December 14, 2006, hearing (www.cngr.gov/hearing121314/1214cngr-panel2.pdf), pp. 13–15.

[24] Defense Secretary Robert Gates, memorandum, "Utilization of the Total Force," January 19, 2007.

Cross-leveling to equip units for training and deployment has similar adverse impacts and is driven by the same causes as personnel cross-leveling, with the addition of two significant factors. First, many of the systems in the inventory of the reserve components are older and sometimes outdated items that are not deployable to Iraq or Afghanistan. Second, much of the modern equipment that they possess is left in theater for the use of follow-on units, further degrading unit readiness at home.[25]

Figure 9a reveals the extent of cross-leveling within the Army National Guard. Figure 9b represents the number of National Guard units, by year, required to contribute equipment to fill the needs of one deploying unit. The Commission views the reliance on cross-leveling as a key indicator of the status of the reserve components. This reliance reveals whether the reserve components are organized to meet their evolving mission requirements and whether DOD is recognizing the existing reserve component structure when it seeks to mobilize its reserve. The Commission notes the new Secretary of Defense's memorandum, which is an initial attempt to mitigate the impact of cross-leveling. The Commission will closely monitor the implementation of the Secretary's policy change and will further address this issue in its final report on reserve component mobilization policy.

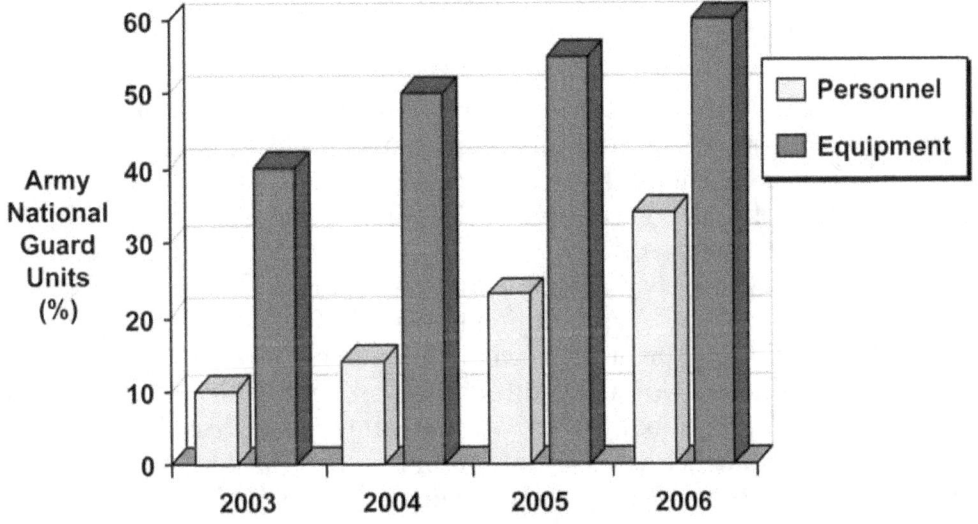

Note: Equipment includes items from National Guard and other Army and theater sources.
Source: Staff analysis of data provided by National Guard Bureau, Readiness and Logistics Divisions, January 2007.

Figure 9a. Average Percent Cross-Leveled to Build Deployable Army Guard Unit

---

[25] Janet St. Laurent, GAO Director of Defense Capabilities and Management, prepared statement before the CNGR, Hearing on National Guard and Reserve Issues, September 21, 2006 (www.cngr.gov/hearing918-21/ReserveCommissiontestimonyGAO.pdf), p. 6.

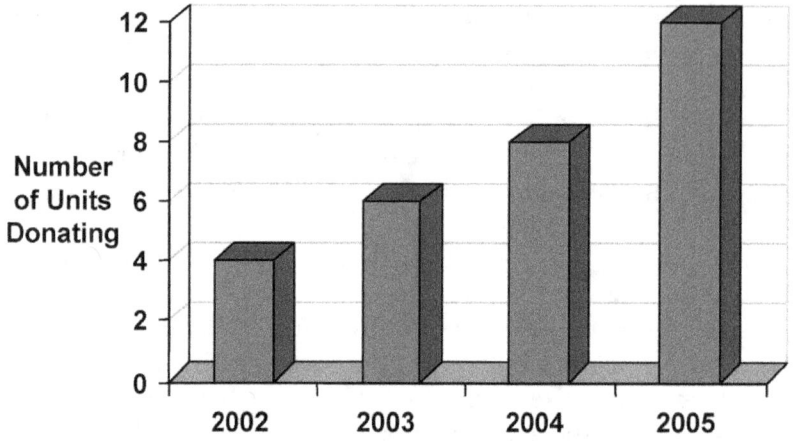

Note: Average Number of Army National Guard Units Contributing Equipment to Fill One Deploying Unit
Source: Data provided by National Guard Bureau Logistics Division, January 2007.

Figure 9b. Average Number of Army National Guard Units Contributing Equipment to Fill One Deploying Unit

RECRUITING AND RETENTION

Historically, the reserve components have recruited heavily from individuals with previous active duty service—"prior service" recruits—who have already acquired military skills and training. This pattern is particularly strong in the air and naval components and less marked in the ground force components (particularly the Marine Corps Reserve). As Table 1 makes clear, over the past decade, from fiscal year 1997 to fiscal year 2006, all the DOD reserve components have seen a decline in the proportion of prior service enlistments. In several cases, including the Army National Guard, the decline is by more than 20 percentage points. The share of prior service enlistments has steadily decreased in the Army National Guard from almost two out of three in fiscal year 1997 to just over one out of three last year. For the Air National Guard, while the figures are less dramatic, the share of prior service enlistments has decreased from more than two out of three in fiscal year 1997 to only one out of two in fiscal year 2006. The Department's stop-loss policies, the desire of service members leaving active duty not to participate and be subject to future deployments, and the smaller size of the overall force to draw from have resulted in fewer prior service enlistments in all reserve components. Prior service personnel are very desirable from the perspective of both capabilities and cost, as they are already highly trained and experienced.

Army National Guard	61.1	53.4	54.3	48.4	46.6	48.1	44.9	44.3	44.9	38.5
Army Reserve	59.3	59.7	56.9	53.5	39.8	46.7	46.0	50.1	45.9	51.9
Air National Guard	68.7	60.7	58.7	52.3	46.9	48.9	47.0	49.0	53.1	54.2
Air Force Reserve	N/A	82.7	82.4	77.6	71.7	61.7	60.7	65.5	76.2	69.7
Navy Reserve	100.0	N/A	85.3	80.7	81.7	67.6	60.9	76.5	63.8	64.6
Marine Corps Reserve	50.4	40.5	38.2	35.3	35.2	41.5	25.0	25.3	29.0	27.0
Fiscal Year	97	98	99	00	01	02	03	04	05	06

Source: Derived from Reserve Component (Selected Reserve) Enlisted Recruiting data provided by the Office of the Deputy Assistant Secretary of Defense for Reserve Affairs (Manpower and Personnel), October 27, 2006.

Table 1. Prior Service Recruits as Percentage of Total

The level of success or difficulty in recruiting and retention is one indicator of the sustainability of the force, particularly at a time of high operational use. Fiscal year 2005 was a particularly difficult year, as nearly all the reserve components fell short of their recruiting goals: the Army National Guard by 20 percent, Army Reserve by 16 percent, Air National Guard by 14 percent, and Navy Reserve by 15 percent.[26] This decline was reflected in strength levels, with reserve components achieving only 95.2 percent of end-strength attainment, as shown in Figure 10.

---

[26] Recruiting data provided by the Office of the Deputy Assistant Secretary of Defense for Reserve Affairs (Manpower and Personnel), October 27, 2006.

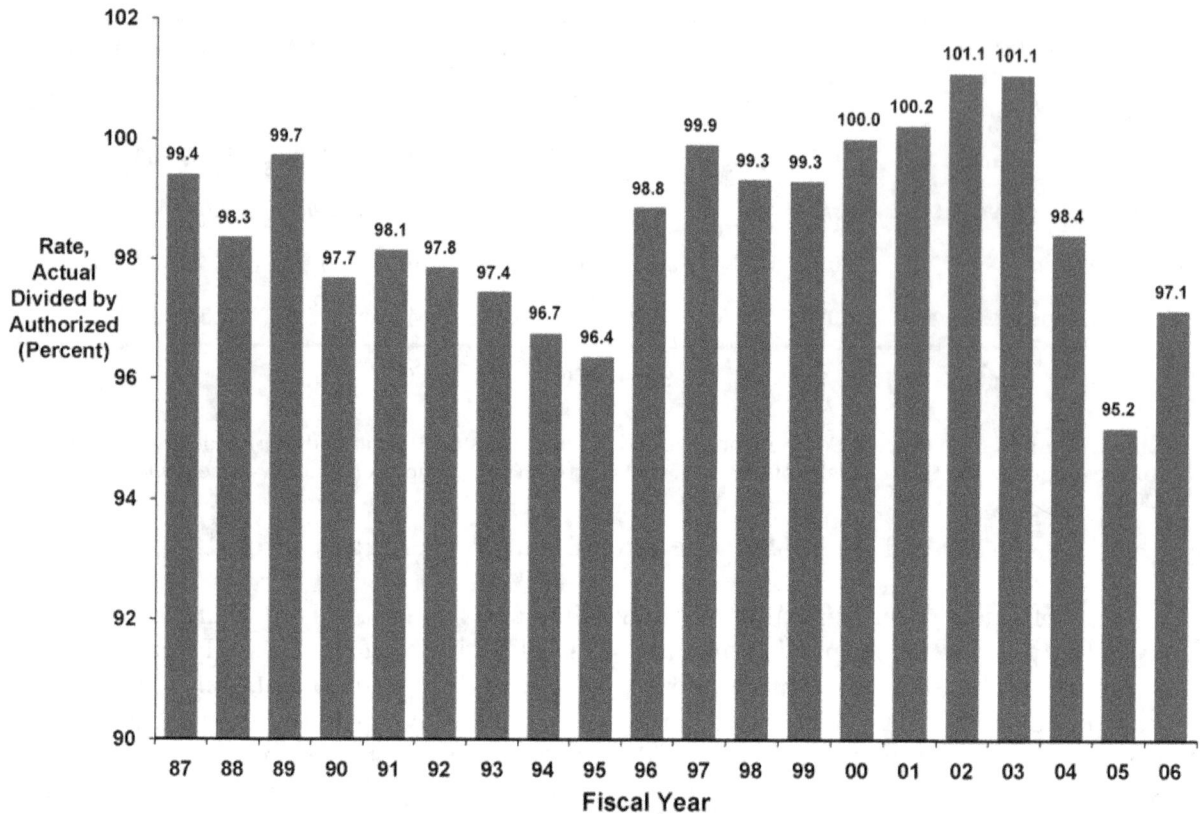

Source: Briefing prepared for the SecDef by the OASD-RA, January 2007, slide 5.

**Figure 10. Selected Reserve End-Strength Achievement Rates
(FY 1987 – FY 2006)**

In addition, the share of enlistees with high school diplomas declined from 92 percent in fiscal year 2004 to 85 percent in fiscal year 2005. DOD-wide, the percentage of reserve component recruits scoring in the top 50 percent on the Armed Forces Qualification Test (AFQT) declined from 70 to 63 percent during the same time period.[27]

Although initial results appeared problematic for fiscal year 2006, all of the reserve components but one achieved at least 95 percent of their recruitment objective. Some components showed considerable improvement from the previous year. The Army National Guard, for example, achieved 99 percent of its objective in fiscal year 2006, compared to 80 percent in fiscal year 2005. But while the Army Reserve achieved 95 percent of its objective, only 59 percent of new recruits scored 50 percent or higher on the AFQT, a decline of 8 percentage points from fiscal year 2005 and 11 percentage points from fiscal year 2004.[28] As discussed below, the recent success in meeting targets came at a price.

Polling data of young people and their influencers suggest that the future for recruitment remains problematic. Twice a year, DOD conducts polls to measure youths' perceptions of

---

[27] Recruiting data provided by the Office of the Deputy Assistant Secretary of Defense for Reserve Affairs (Manpower and Personnel), October 27, 2006.
[28] Recruiting data provided by the Office of the Deputy Assistant Secretary of Defense for Reserve Affairs (Manpower and Personnel), October 27, 2006.

the military and their propensity to enlist. Similarly, on a regular basis DOD also surveys influencers' perceptions and their likelihood to recommend military service to youth.[29] As Figure 11 indicates, the proportion holding a favorable view of the military has continued to decline since November 2001, with the exception of a temporary bump upward in June 2003. An arrow upward or downward indicates a statistically significant change.

Mean Favorability Ratings

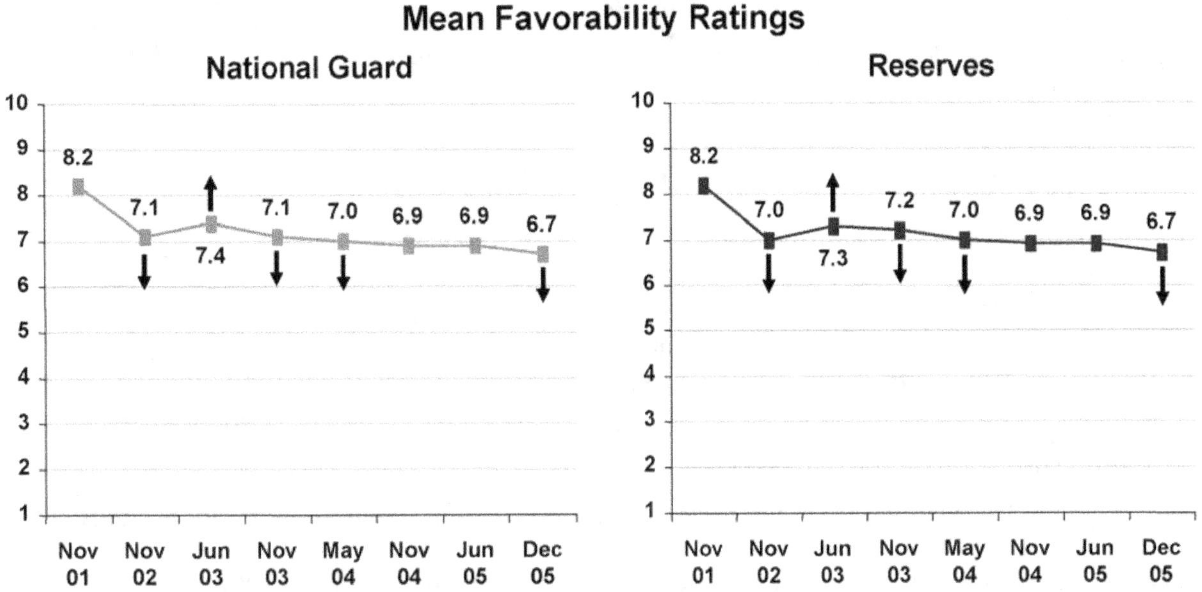

Note: Arrows indicate statistically significant change from previous poll.
Source: Joint Advertising, Market Research and Studies (JAMRS) December 2005 Youth Poll 10 Findings Presentation, slide 7 (available at www.dmren.org).

Figure 11. Favorability of Reserve Components

For influencers, both parents and non-parents, the war on terrorism has had a negative impact, with 59 percent reporting they are less likely to recommend military service—a statistically significant increase from six months before (see Figure 12).

---

[29] Department of Defense, Youth Poll Wave 10—December 2005, Overview Report, JAMRS [Joint Advertising, Market Research and Studies] Report No. 2006-006, July 2006, and Influencer Poll Wave 5—December 2005, JAMRS Report No. 2006-007, June 2006, available at www.dmren.org.

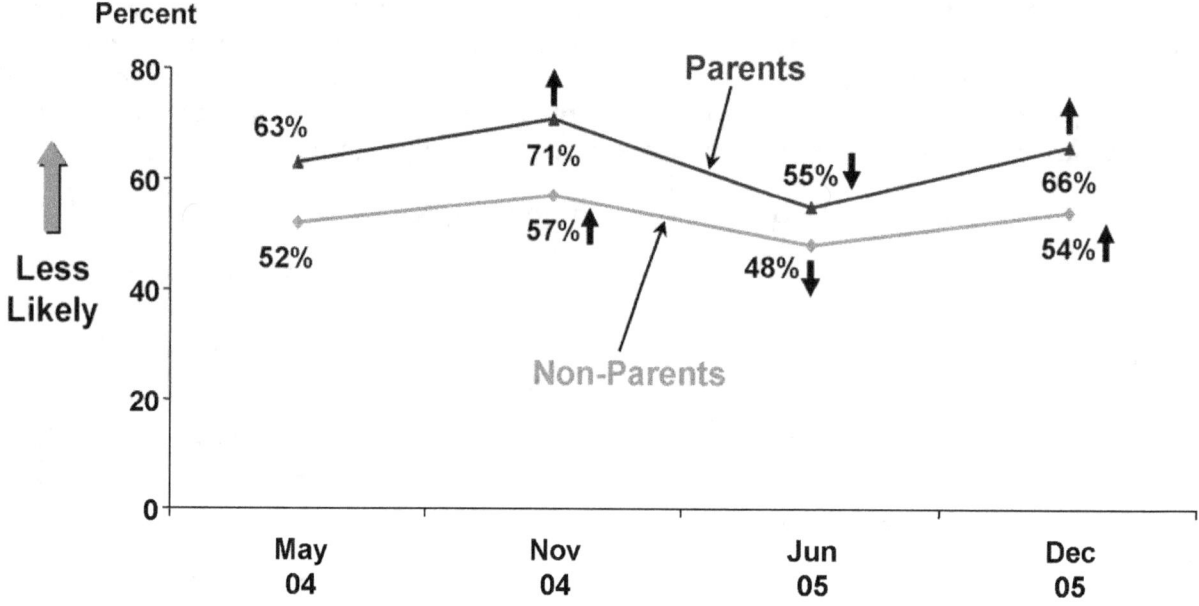

Note: Arrows indicate statistically significant change from previous poll.
Source: JAMRS December 2005 Influencer Poll, slide 16.

Figure 12. The War on Terrorism and Attitudes Toward Military Service

Perhaps the most compelling data, however, come from the June 2006 youth poll, the results of which are graphed in Figure 13. It reveals that the propensity of young men to join the military, which was at 21 percent in 2005, declined sharply to 14 percent in 2006. When the data for young women are included, total youth propensity to enlist declined from 15 to 10 percent.[30]

---

[30] Barbara A. Bicksler and Lisa G. Nolan, "Recruiting an All Volunteer Force: The Need for Sustained Investment in Recruiting Resources," *Policy Perspectives* 1, no. 1 (September 2006): p. 7, fig. 6.

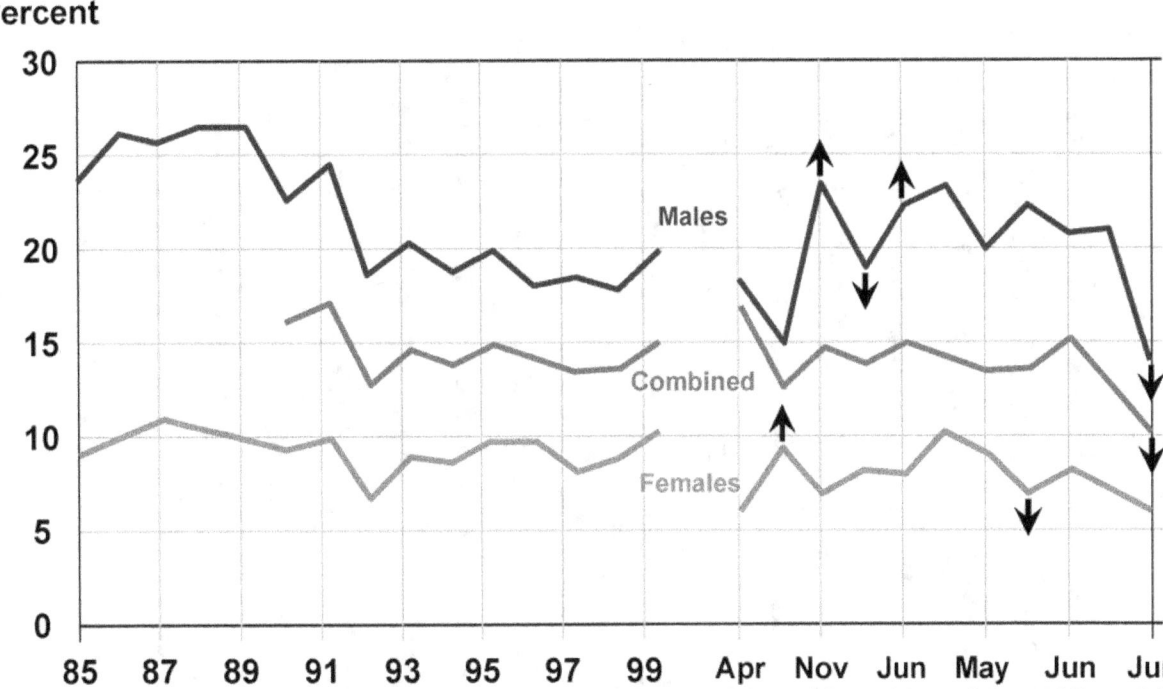

Percent

Note: Arrows indicate statistically significant change from previous poll.
Source: Department of Defense, Youth Attitude Tracking Study, 1985–1999, and Youth Poll, 2001–2006.

Figure 13. Military Propensity of 16- to 24-Year-Olds

Attrition, one of the primary indicators of retention, has remained relatively stable, varying by less than one percentage point since fiscal year 2002. For fiscal year 2006, the reserve component attrition rate was 18.4 percent, the lowest since fiscal year 1991 (see Figure 14). Shortages exist within some specialties and year groups, however, as will be discussed in greater detail in the Commission's final report. But we wish to note briefly the presence here, as in the recruiting survey data, of troubling indicators with respect to future retention trends. The December 2005 Defense Manpower Data Center (DMDC) survey of spouse/significant other favorability to continued participation in the National Guard and Reserves shows a continued downward trend—a 3 percentage point decline from June to December 2005 and an 18 percentage point decline since May 2003 (see Figure 15).

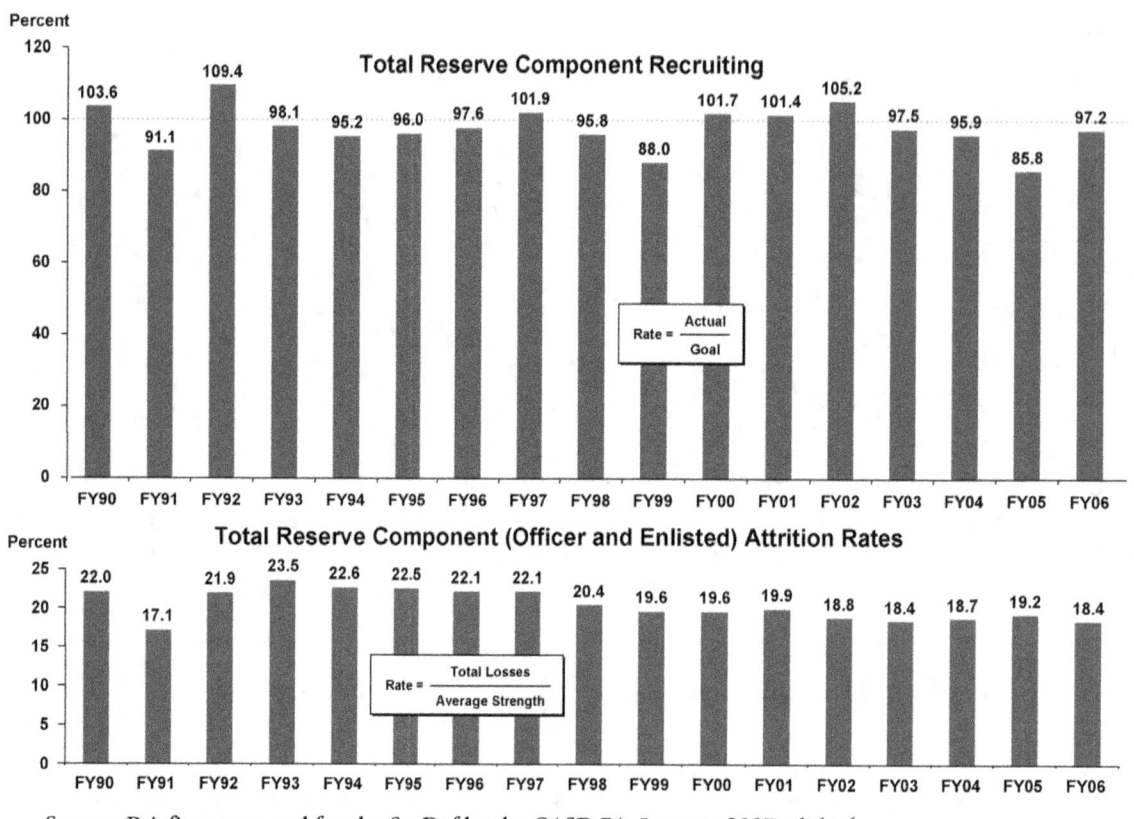

Source: Briefing prepared for the SecDef by the OASD-RA, January 2007, slide 6.

Figure 14. Key Individual Indicators (Gains and Losses)

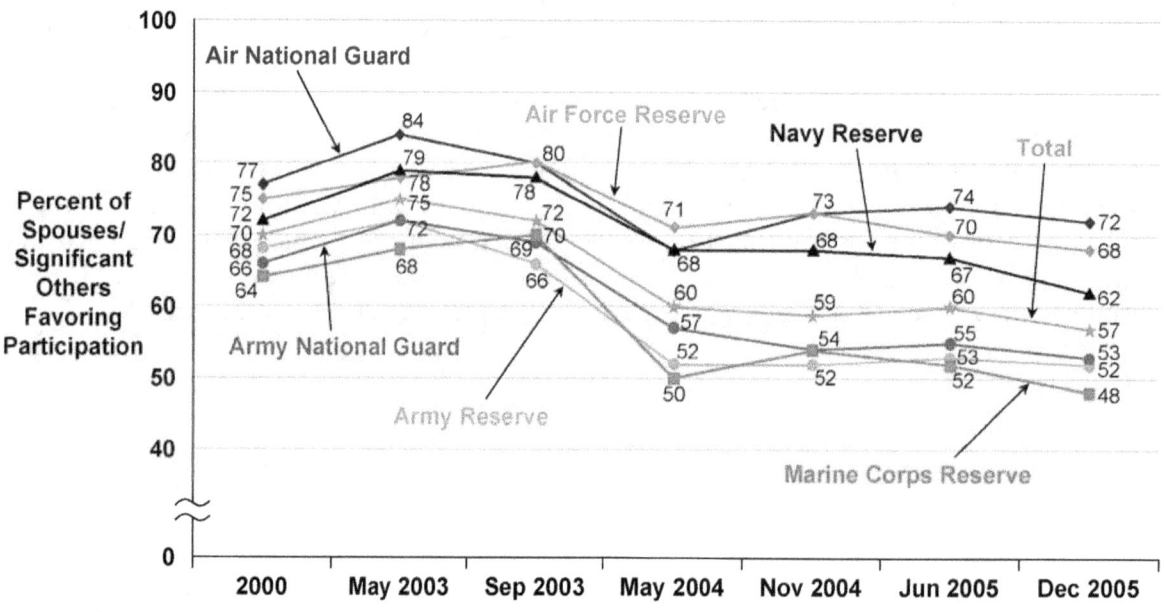

Note: Margins of error range from ±1% to ±4%.
Source: "December 2005 Status of Forces Survey of Reserve Component Members: Leading Indicators," Defense Manpower Data Center Survey Note, No. 2006-003 (April 25, 2006).

Figure 15. Spouse/Significant Other Favorability Toward Participation, by Reserve Component

Similarly, the National Military Family Association's Cycles of Deployment Survey, conducted April–September 2005, reported "that Army National Guard and Reserve families reported the greatest stress concerning deployment length. Their servicemembers typically experience family separations of close to eighteen months[.]…These families are quick to point out they are experiencing the longest family separation of any Service families and that length of these deployments is having a detrimental effect."[31]

As noted previously, recruiting and retention success have come at a price of increasing levels of inducement. In the National Defense Authorization Acts for fiscal years 2003, 2005, and 2006, Congress significantly increased enlistment and affiliation bonuses to $20,000, increased prior service and reenlistment bonuses to $15,000, and also created a new critical skills retention bonus of $100,000 for the reserve components.[32] As Table 2 demonstrates, the Army's expenditures for enlistment and reenlistment bonuses for the active Army, Army National Guard, and Army Reserve have grown significantly.

Fiscal Year	Active Army		Army National Guard		Army Reserve	
	Selective Reenlistment Bonuses	Enlistment Bonuses	Selective Reenlistment Incentive Program	Enlistment Bonuses	Selective Reenlistment Incentive Program	Enlistment Bonuses
2000	105.4	94.9	23.8	20.8	5.5	16.7
2001	112.6	166.2	27.9	60.4	7.6	27.2
2002	127.8	200.7	25.0	61.5	9.9	28.9
2003	102.6	150.3	25.1	63.0	11.0	41.9
2004	142.0	188.1	27.2	77.6	2.7	35.6
2005	505.6	165.9	235.1	138.6	56.0	61.0

Source: CBO, *Recruiting, Retention, and Future Levels of Military Personnel*, CBO Study, Pub. No. 2777 ([Washington, DC:] Congressional Budget Office, 2006), p. 8, table 1-4.

Table 2. Army Spending on Reenlistment and Enlistment Bonuses (Millions of Current Dollars)

Operational tempo also affects employers, the other major influencer of whether service members remain in the reserve component. Many employers have been highly supportive of their National Guard and Reserve employees, but, for others, the absence of employees activated for service has presented a major challenge. As the director of the Congressional Budget Office told Congress,

---

[31] National Military Family Association, "Report on the Cycles of Deployment: An Analysis of Survey Responses from April through September, 2005" (www.dtic.mil/dacowits/docs/apr2006/NMFACyclesofDeployment9.pdf), pp. 7–8.

[32] Public Law 107-314, *National Defense Authorization Act for Fiscal Year 2003*, October 28, 2002, §617; Public Law 108-375, *NDAA for FY05*, October 28, 2004, §§618, 619; Public Law 109-163, *NDAA for FY06*, January 6, 2006, §§631, 633, 634, 640, 641.

Some businesses may absorb the loss of personnel at little cost, but others may experience slowdowns in production, lost sales, or additional expenses as they attempt to compensate for a reservist's absence. A smaller number yet may find that they are unable to operate for lengthy periods—or at all—without their reservist and may experience financial losses or insolvency. Such problems are likely to be more severe for:

- Small businesses that lose essential (key) employees;

- Businesses that require workers with highly specialized skills; and

- Self-employed reservists.[33]

In "Employers More Reluctant to Hire Reservists," published January 19, 2007, in *Navy Times*, the staff writer Karen Jowers cites an informal poll conducted by *Workforce Management* magazine. The Web poll noted, "Last week the Pentagon issued a new rule that extends the limit on the length of time that a member of the National Guard or military reserves can spend on active duty. This move could influence hiring decisions made by employers since the employer may not have a good expectation of how long a citizen soldier in its employ may be gone if called up for active duty. Although there are laws in place to guard against hiring discrimination and other issues regarding members of the National Guard and reserves, violations of these laws can be difficult to prove." The survey then posed the following question: "If you, as an employer, knew that a military reservist or National Guard member could be called up and taken away from their job for an indeterminate amount of time, would you still hire a citizen soldier?"[34] According to *Navy Times*, 51 percent of those who responded to this informal, online poll said that they would not hire the reservist.

Commenting on this poll during a recent hearing before the Senate Committee on Small Business and Entrepreneurship, Theodore L. Daywalt, CEO and President of VetJobs, noted: "These results are indicative of a trend among companies nationally to not want to hire members of the Guard and Reserve due to the extended use by the Department of Defense of their Guard and Reserve employees. The trend to not supporting Guard and Reserve employees is directly correlated to when the term Strategic Reserve was changed to Operational Reserve. If they are operational, they are not really a reserve."[35] The Commission plans to address employer issues in more detail in its final report.

Overall, if the reserve component, including the National Guard, continues its high operational tempo, current indicators cast considerable doubt on the future sustainability of recruiting and retention, even if financial incentives continue to increase.

---

[33] Douglas Holtz-Eakin, Director, Congressional Budget Office, "How Reserve Call-Ups Affect Civilian Employers," prepared statement before the House Subcommittee on Regulatory Reform and Oversight, Committee on Small Business, September 29, 2005 (www.cbo.gov/ftpdocs/66xx/doc6665/09-29-Reservists.pdf), p. 2.

[34] "Hiring National Guard or Military Reservists," *Workforce Management*, at www.workforce.com.

[35] Theodore L. Daywalt, prepared witness statement before the Senate Committee on Small Business and Entrepreneurship, January 31, 2007 (http://sbc.senate.gov/testimony/070131-Daywalt-testimony.pdf), p. 10.

DEFENSE SPENDING AND THE FEDERAL BUDGET

As discussed in following section, the level of total spending by the Department of Defense—and the competition for those often-constrained resources—affects the ability of the reserve components to fulfill mission requirements. This resource competition has become increasingly contentious because of the high rate of equipment utilization in Iraq and Afghanistan for both active and reserve forces and the growing cost to replace that equipment.

It is useful to examine the level of defense spending within the broader context of the federal budget and the overall productivity of the nation's economy, looking not only at the percentage share but also at outlays in current dollars. We see that federal spending on national defense was almost half of all federal spending in 1962. At that time, defense spending represented almost 10 percent of our $567.6 billion gross domestic product (GDP). By the mid-1990s, federal spending on defense represented approximately 16 percent of all federal spending and approximately 3 percent of GDP, as illustrated in Figure 16. Federal spending on defense represented 20 percent of all federal spending and 4.1 percent of our $13,061.1 billion GDP in 2006.

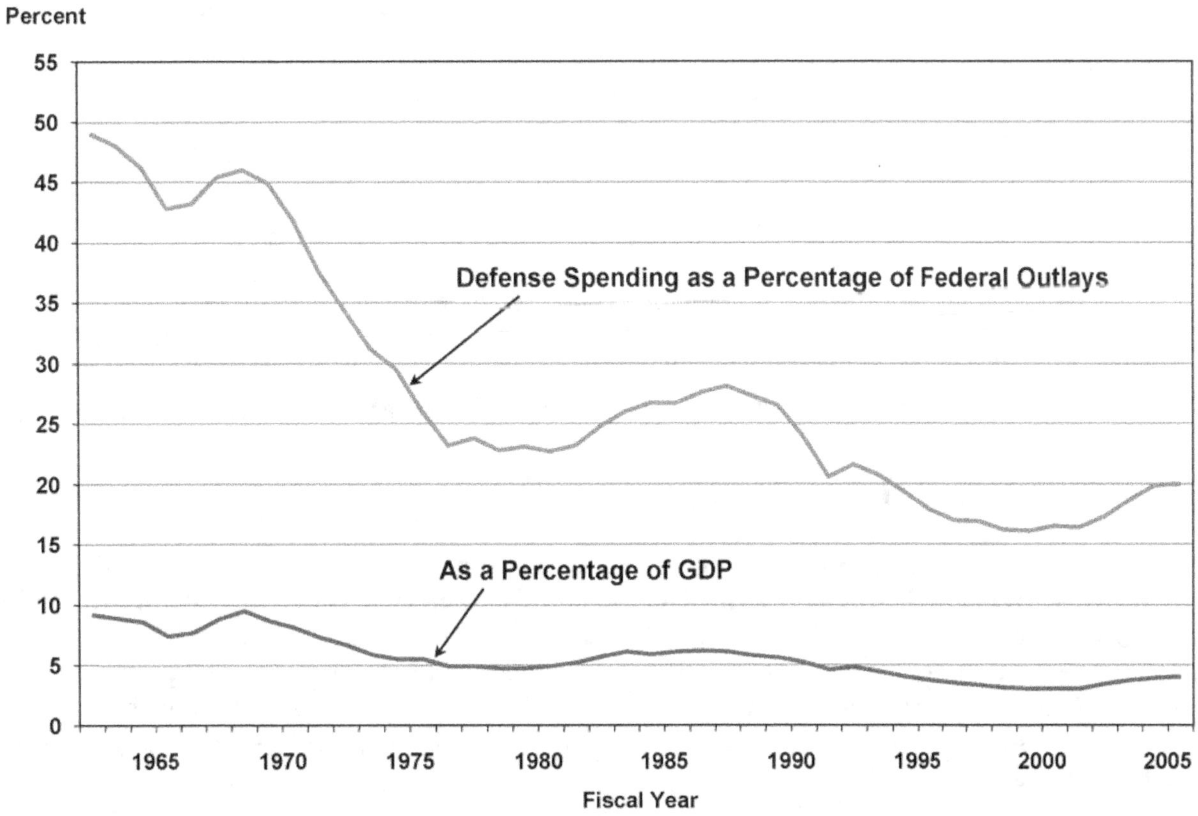

Source: Budget of the United States Government, Fiscal Year 2007, Historical Tables (www.whitehouse.gov/omb/ budget/fy2007/pdf/hist.pdf), pp. 46–54.

Figure 16. National Defense Spending Relative to Federal Outlays and GDP

Figure 17 shows federal spending on national defense in dollar terms instead of percentages. The lower line represents the actual amount of money, in millions of then-year dollars, spent annually on national defense. However, the upper line, which factors in inflation and normalizes the national defense budget to constant 2007 dollars, reveals the post–Cold War decline in the early 1990s and the upward trend over the past several years.

Source: Data from *National Defense Budget Estimate for FY 2007*, Office of the Under Secretary of Defense (Comptroller) (www.dod.mil/comptroller/defbudget/fy2007/fy2007_greenbook.pdf), p. 81; *Budget of the United States Government, Fiscal Year 2007*, pp. 46–54.

Figure 17. U.S. Spending on National Defense (Nominal and Inflation-Adjusted)

PROCUREMENT FUNDING

The Commission heard testimony from the reserve component Chiefs that the funding they received for personnel and operations has generally been adequate, though more would have been welcome.[36] However, funding for equipment has continued at a low level that does not reflect the increased role of the reserve components in undertaking operational missions (such as in Bosnia, Kosovo, Iraq, and Afghanistan) and in supporting their active component (such as providing drill sergeants, conducting exercises, and augmenting headquarters staff).

---

[36] See, e.g., Lieutenant General John Bradley, Chief, United States Air Force Reserve, testimony before CNGR, Hearing on National Guard and Reserve Issues, transcript of July 9, 2006, hearing (www.cngr.gov/July%2019/ transcript 0719.pdf), p. 27, and Lieutenant General H Steven Blum, Chief, National Guard Bureau, prepared statement before CNGR, Hearing on Homeland Defense/Homeland Security, May 3, 2006 (www.cngr.gov/ hearing503-4/Blum.pdf), p. 4.

The Selected Reserve makes up approximately 37 percent of the total force, yet the reserve components receive approximately 3 percent of equipment funding and approximately 8 percent of the DOD budget.[37] The disparity is particularly acute in the Army, where the Army Reserve and Army National Guard constitute 52 percent of the total force but received only 9.3 percent of equipment funding between 2001 and 2006. Congressionally added funds in the National Guard and Reserve Equipment Account (NGREA) amounted to an additional 1.78 percent for Army reserve components during this period.[38]

The shortage of equipment funding extends across all Army components, including the active component. In December 2006, the Commission heard testimony from General Peter J. Schoomaker that Army investment accounts were underfunded by $100 billion; as a result, the Army started the war in Iraq with nearly $56 billion in equipment shortages.[39]

In his testimony before the Commission in January 2007, Lieutenant General Blum emphasized the shortfall in Army equipment funding. He stated: "The units that are over-seas are magnificently equipped. You can't tell the difference—active, guard, reserve — overseas by their equipment....However, having said that, 88 percent of the forces that are back here in the United States are very poorly equipped today in the Army National Guard. And in the Air National Guard, for the last three decades, they have never had a unit below C2 in equipment readiness."[40]

This lack of procurement has created a cycle of steadily increasing need to cross-level equipment to deploying units from non-deployed reserve component units. According to a January 2007 Government Accountability Office report, the National Guard's equipment inventories in the United States have decreased because of overseas operations, particularly in the Army National Guard.[41] While the GAO found that most state National Guard leaders judged that they had adequate resources within their states to respond to typical state missions, these leaders also expressed concerns about having enough equipment to respond to large-scale natural or man-made disasters such as Hurricane Katrina or those described in the Homeland Security Council's National Planning Scenarios. These 15 scenarios, which describe potential catastrophes, are used for planning purposes and to develop an understanding of which capabilities will be required to respond to the disasters.

The GAO found that before current overseas operations began, the majority of the Army National Guard's combat forces were supplied with 65 to 79 percent of their required equipment. As of November 2006, non-deployed Army National Guard forces nationwide still had about 64 percent of the total amount of dual-use equipment they are authorized to

---

[37] Briefing prepared for the Secretary of Defense (SecDef) by the Office of the Assistant Secretary of Defense for Reserve Affairs (OASD-RA), January 2007, slide 2.

[38] Staff analysis of budget documents from Office of the Under Secretary of Defense (Comptroller) (www.dod.mil/comptroller/defbudget/), P1 and P1R documents, fiscal years 2002–07.

[39] General Schoomaker, Chief of Staff, U.S. Army, prepared witness statement before the CNGR, Hearing on Proposed Changes to the National Guard, December 14, 2006 (www.cngr.gov/hearing121314/General%20Schoomaker%2014%20DEC%20Record%20Version.pdf), p. 4.

[40] Lieutenant General Blum, testimony before the CNGR, Hearing on Proposed Changes to the National Guard, transcript of January 31, 2007, hearing (www.cngr.gov/hearing13107/0131cngr-1.pdf), p. 9.

[41] GAO, *Reserve Forces: Actions Needed to Identify National Guard Domestic Equipment Requirements and Readiness*, GAO 07-60 (Report to the Ranking Minority Member, Committee on Oversight and Government Reform, and Ranking Minority Member, Subcommittee on National Security and International Relations, House of Representatives), January 2007, p. 2.

have, including authorized substitute items, based on their warfighting missions. However, inventory levels of the different types of dual-use equipment varied widely, and the average inventory level by type of equipment was roughly 42 percent nationwide.[42]

According to the GAO,

> To improve the equipment readiness of National Guard units, DOD and Congress have several initiatives under way. For example, DOD plans to use $900 million Congress provided in the Department of Defense Appropriations Act for Fiscal Year 2006 to procure equipment for the Army National Guard and Air National Guard that is useful for both warfighting and domestic missions, such as communications gear, tactical vehicles, trucks, and engineering equipment....DOD also plans to use $290 million that Congress provided in the Department of Defense Appropriations Act for Fiscal Year 2007 to procure additional National Guard and Reserve equipment. The conference report accompanying the act states that the conferees intend for $150 million of the $290 million to go toward equipping the National Guard. Furthermore, the conferees directed that $2.94 billion of procurement funds provided in Title IX of the act be available for the Army National Guard and the Army Reserve, and that $500 million of these funds should be used specifically to meet the 10 core capabilities identified by the National Guard Bureau as essential to support domestic missions.[43]

For procurement in future years, the Army has budgeted approximately $21 billion for fiscal years 2005 through 2011 to modernize the Army National Guard ground systems procurement and another $1.9 billion for their aviation systems.[44] These funds are intended to fund dual-use equipment as well as to help fill long-standing equipment shortages, and they represent a fourfold increase in funding over fiscal years 2003–09.

PROGRAM FUNDING IN FUTURE YEARS

Department of Defense Budget Justification Books for Procurement covering the years 1999–2005 reveal that the actual funding in the budget year is sometimes reduced significantly from the amounts identified several years earlier in the program.[45] For example, the fiscal year 2001 budget submission showed that the Army planned to fund $1.346 billion in fiscal year 2004 for Army National Guard procurement. However, according to the fiscal year 2006 budget submission, in fiscal year 2004 the Army actually spent only $578.4 million in the Army National Guard procurement account.

Similarly, the fiscal year 2001 budget projected $1.625 billion to be spent for the Army National Guard in fiscal 2005. However, the fiscal year 2006 budget request showed that

---

[42] GAO, *Reserve Forces*, p. 26.
[43] GAO, *Reserve Forces*, p. 30.
[44] Schoomaker prepared witness statement, pp. 4–5.
[45] Staff analysis of data from the OSD Comptroller Web site (www.dod.mil/comptroller/), Procurement Programs (P1-R) Reserve Components by Fiscal Year.

only $660.9 million was planned for Army National Guard procurement in fiscal year 2005. Figure 18 graphically shows the disparity.

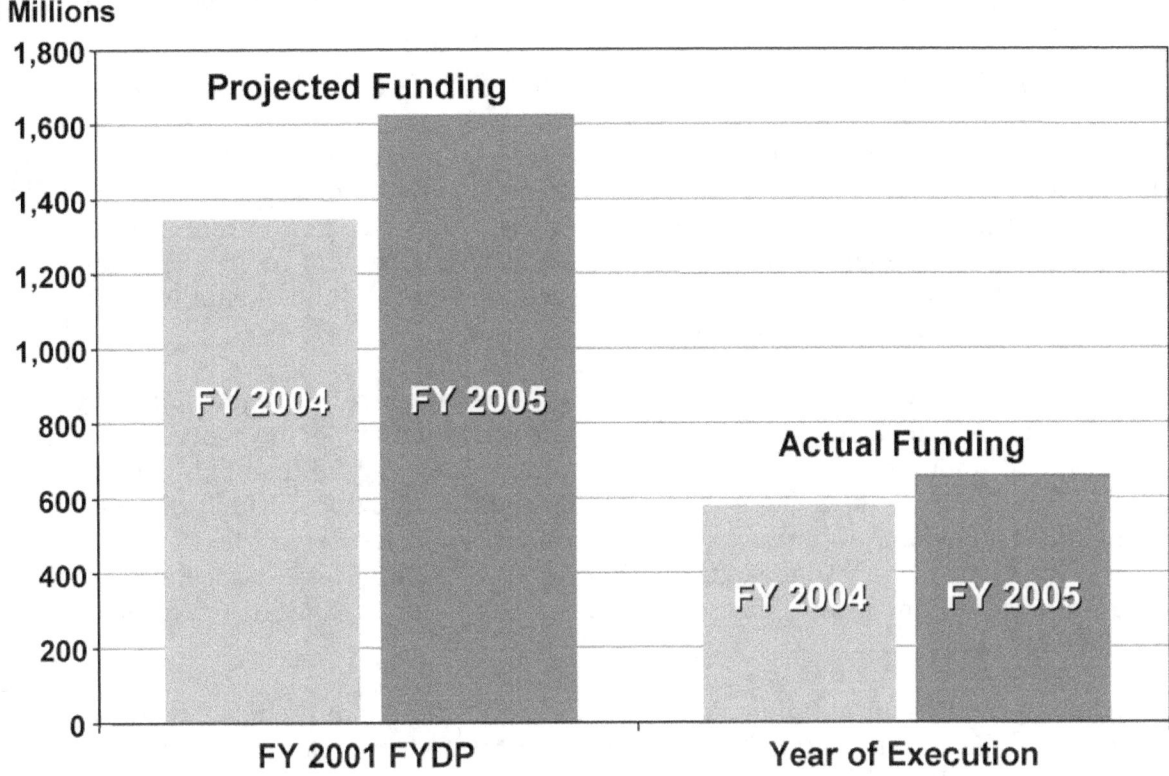

$ Millions

Source: Staff analysis of data from the OSD Comptroller Web site (www.dod.mil/comptroller/), Procurement Programs (P1-R) Reserve Components by Fiscal Year.

**Figure 18. Army National Guard Procurement Budget
(Projections vs. Actual Funding)**

Additional review of the Army National Guard procurement account shows that this difference from programming to budget was atypically extreme in the years 2003–05. Nevertheless, there are examples of procurement reductions in the other reserve components as well. Beyond the budget data, distribution of new equipment will be studied for our final report to determine if equipment intended for reserve component units are diverted to active component organizations. These data raise concern that the amounts the Army has programmed for its reserve components over the years 2008–13 may similarly be reduced as each budget year approaches.

On January 11, 2007, Secretary of Defense Gates announced that he was recommending an end-strength increase of 92,000 personnel in the active Army and Marine Corps over the next five years: 65,000 in the Army and 27,000 in the Marines. The Secretary's proposal would make permanent the temporary increase of 30,000 soldiers and 5,000 marines.[46] In addition, the Secretary recommended an increase of 8,200 in the Army National Guard and

---

[46] DOD News Release, No. 029-07, January 11, 2007 at www.defenselink.mil/Releases/ Release.aspx?ReleaseID =10388.

6,000 in the Army Reserve.[47] These end-strength increases are reflected in the President's budget request for fiscal year 2008.[48] This growth in future end-strength, unless adequately funded in the future, could lead to similar shifting of the approximately $21 billion currently planned for modernizing the Army National Guard to other budget priorities.

OUTDATED LAWS, POLICIES, RULES, AND REGULATIONS

The Commission believes that the state of the reserve components, outlined above, is largely the result of using the National Guard and Reserves operationally under laws, policies, rules, and regulations that were designed to man, train, equip, and mobilize a strategic reserve force. The Department of Defense has declared that the reserve components are operational, yet the framework in which they are used is still fundamentally structured on Cold War notions of infrequent use of a strategic reserve.

The corrosive and ever-growing practice of cross-leveling personnel and equipment to form combat units for deployment is the direct result of employing the reserve components operationally under outdated mobilization laws and Cold War equipping policies. The steady degradation of the readiness of non-deployed Guard units, which diminishes their capabilities to respond to both state and federal emergencies here in the United States, is the product of a pre-9/11 mind-set that support to civil authorities is a secondary capability to be provided on an "as available" basis and of DOD's policy that has resulted from that mind-set.[49]

Antiquated practices for getting reserve component soldiers into the fight, which are based on the "mobilize, train, deploy" construct of a bygone era, add inefficient months to mobilization timelines. These in turn prolong family separations and increase worries about recruiting and retention, as spouses view service in the reserve component in an increasingly negative light.

In his testimony to our Commission in March 2006, Assistant Secretary of Defense for Reserve Affairs Thomas Hall stated, "I might add that good news in this town never quite gets out, but in the past two years there have been 120 provisions in the law that have been changed that affect the Guard and Reserve."[50] But the Commission finds that most of those changes, such as implementation of the "Operational Reserve" duty status category and changes to mobilization authorities under Title 10, merely ease the Department's access to reserve component personnel without addressing the problems outlined above that have been caused by their increasing operational use. The laws, policies, rules, and regulations need to be reformed in order to create a reserve force that is both capable of performing the

---

[47] Department of the Army, "Fiscal Year 2008/2009 Budget Estimates, February 2007, National Guard Personnel, Army" (www.asafm.army.mil/budget/fybm/fy08-09/ngpa.pdf), p. 5; Department of the Army, "Fiscal Year 2008/2009 Budget Estimates, February 2007, Reserve Personnel, Army" (www.asafm.army.mil/budget/ fybm/fy08-09/rpa.pdf), p. 8.

[48] "President Bush's FY 2008 Defense Budget Submission," February 5, 2007, at www.dod.mil/comptroller/defbudget/fy2008/2008_Budget_Rollout_Release.pdf.

[49] See DOD Directive 3025.1, "Military Assistance to Civil Authorities," January 15, 1993: "DoD Components shall not procure or maintain any supplies, materiel, or equipment exclusively for providing MSCA in civil emergencies, unless otherwise directed by the Secretary of Defense" (p. 7).

[50] Assistant Secretary Hall, testimony before the CNGR, Hearing on Roles and Missions, transcript of March 8, 2006, hearing (www.cngr.gov/pdf/0308cngr.pdf), p. 99.

duties our nation desires and expects of it and is sustainable in the long term. The Commission will provide its full assessment and findings and recommendations on the broad scope of these problems in its final report.

Overall, based on its review and analysis of the current state of the National Guard, the Commission makes the following observations:

- The National Guard and Reserves are at a high operational tempo, playing a key role, and performing well, across an array of missions: warfighting, peacekeeping and stability operations, and civil support.

- The practice known as *cross-leveling*, which primarily involves the ground forces, has degraded unit cohesion and, therefore, overall military effectiveness.

- The failure to utilize the Army's Individual Ready Reserve in any meaningful way has contributed to the degree of cross-leveling that has occurred to date.

- Over the past decade, from fiscal year 1997 to fiscal year 2006, the number of prior active duty personnel enlisting in the reserves has steadily decreased in all the reserve components.

- The long-term viability for both recruiting and retention remains highly problematic. Despite an upturn in reserve component recruiting for fiscal year 2006 (reversing a falling trend that had lasted several years), polling data from young people, their parents, and other youth influencers show that favorable attitudes toward military service continue to decline. On the retention side, surveys of spouses in all pay grades and all reserve components show a significant drop in support for reserve service.

- Increasing levels of financial inducements have been necessary to meet recruiting and retention goals for both active and reserve components.

- While the operational tempo of all the reserve components has increased substantially, resourcing has not kept pace.

- The lack of sufficient and ready equipment is a problem common to active and reserve components. In particular, the equipment readiness of the Army National Guard is unacceptable and has reduced the capability of the United States to respond to current and additional major contingencies, foreign and domestic.

- The administration's FY 2008 budget seeks large increases for National Guard equipment. However, DOD historic budget data show that Army plans for projected funding increases for the Army National Guard are not reliably carried through.

- Despite the extraordinarily high operational tempo for the reserve component, many of the underlying laws, regulations, policies, funding mechanisms, pay categories, mobilization processes, and personnel laws have not been modified to support its evolution into an operational force.

In conclusion, DOD has declared that we have an operational reserve without also making the changes necessary to ensure that such a change is sustainable. We believe that the current posture and utilization of the National Guard and Reserve as an "operational reserve" is not sustainable over time, and if not corrected with significant changes to law and policy, the reserve component's ability to serve our nation will diminish.

III. FINDINGS, CONCLUSIONS, AND RECOMMENDATIONS

A. THE DEFENSE DEPARTMENT'S ROLE IN THE HOMELAND

While the National Guard plays a vital role in homeland security, it is not the only element of the Department of Defense to do so. The active and other reserve components also perform important duties, as does the U.S. Northern Command (NORTHCOM). In addition, the Department of Homeland Security and other agencies are deeply involved in maintaining the nation's homeland security. To improve military effectiveness and the role of the National Guard, it is important to understand how all these elements work together to protect the United States domestically.

According to the *National Strategy for Homeland Security*, the Defense Department contributes to homeland security in three ways: military missions overseas, homeland defense, and civil support.[1] Military missions overseas, such as Operation Enduring Freedom, aid homeland security by neutralizing threats where they originate. "Homeland defense" missions involve the "protection of US sovereignty, territory, domestic population, and critical defense infrastructure against external threats or aggression, or other threats as directed by the President."[2] An example of a homeland defense mission is the air defense of U.S. territory against hostile aircraft.[3]

---

[1] *National Strategy for Homeland Security* ([Washington, DC: Office of Homeland Security,] 2002), p. 13.
[2] *Strategy for Homeland Defense and Civil Support* ([Washington, DC: Department of Defense,] 2005), p. 5.
[3] Joint Chiefs of Staff, "Homeland Security," Joint Publication 3-26, August 2, 2005, p. III-4.

Homeland Defense, Homeland Security, and Civil Support

In order to understand how the federal government protects the homeland, it is important to have a clear definition of homeland defense, homeland security, and civil support.

- *Homeland defense is defined as "the protection of U.S. sovereignty, territory, domestic population, and critical defense infrastructure against external threats or aggression, or other threats as directed by the President."[4]*

- *Homeland security is defined as "a concerted national effort to prevent terrorist attacks within the United States, reduce America's vulnerability to terrorism, and minimize the damage and recover from attacks that do occur."[5] The statutory definition of homeland security also includes the "carry[ing] out of all functions of entities transferred to the Department [of Homeland Security], including by acting as a focal point [in handling] natural and man-made crises and emergency planning."[6]*

- *Civil support is defined as "DOD support, including [the use of] federal military forces, the Department's career civilian and contractor personnel, and DOD agency and component assets, for domestic emergencies and for designated law enforcement and other activities."[7]*

The Department of Defense (DOD) takes the lead, assisted by other federal agencies when necessary, for homeland defense missions.[8] In contrast, when carrying out civil support missions, the Defense Department aids other federal agencies carrying out homeland security missions.[9] Examples of civil support missions include support to search-and-rescue missions, support to law enforcement, and assistance in disaster response, such as the military response to Hurricane Katrina.[10]

The Defense Department's role is distinct from that played by the Department of Homeland Security. DHS is the primary agency responsible for "homeland security," which is defined as "a concerted national effort to prevent terrorist attacks within the United States, reduce America's vulnerability to terrorism, and minimize the damage and recover from attacks that do occur."[11] DHS's statutory mission also includes "carry[ing] out all functions of entities transferred to the Department, including by acting as a focal point regarding natural and manmade crises and emergency planning."[12] Three examples of homeland security missions are guarding the border against infiltration by terrorists, securing critical

---

[4] *Strategy for Homeland Defense and Civil Support*, p. 5.
[5] *National Strategy for Homeland Security*, p. 2.
[6] 6 U.S.C. §111(b)(1)(D).
[7] *Strategy for Homeland Defense and Civil Support*, pp. 5–6.
[8] *Strategy for Homeland Defense and Civil Support*, p. 5; Joint Chiefs of Staff, "Homeland Security," p. viii.
[9] *Civil support* (also called *defense support to civil authorities*) has been given a variety of other labels in the past, such as *military assistance to civil authorities* (*Strategy for Homeland Defense and Civil Support*, pp. 5–6; *National Strategy for Homeland Security*, p. 13).
[10] See, e.g., *The Federal Response to Hurricane Katrina: Lessons Learned* ([Washington, DC: The White House,] 2006), p. 54.
[11] *National Strategy for Homeland Security*, p. 2.
[12] 6 U.S.C. §111(b)(1)(D).

infrastructure, and coordinating the government response to a disaster, whether natural or man-made.

Broadly speaking, protecting the people and territory of the United States is the mission of the Department of Defense, the Department of Homeland Security, and the rest of the federal government. Homeland defense, homeland security, and civil support are each part of that broader mission and often overlap with one another. As a result, how a task or mission is defined—whether it is considered to be homeland defense, homeland security, or civil support—generally determines which agency assumes the responsibility for performing that task or mission. Agencies have therefore created definitions that narrow their responsibilities. The resulting "stovepiping" of those responsibilities has detracted from the federal government's ability to protect the people and territory of the United States.

CIVIL SUPPORT AND HOMELAND SECURITY

Currently, the federal official with the responsibility to "identify gaps between federal and state capabilities to prepare for and respond to emergencies" and to recommend programs and activities that could address such gaps is the Secretary of Homeland Security.[13] The basis for this responsibility has been found in Homeland Security Presidential Directive-8 (HSPD-8) and the Homeland Security Act of 2002, although recent legislation appears to have transferred this responsibility to the newly reconfigured Federal Emergency Management Agency (FEMA), an agency under the Department of Homeland Security.[14] Mechanisms used to identify gaps have included the National Preparedness System (NPS), which mandates that the FEMA administrator (acting on behalf of the President) develop an assessment system evaluating the preparedness of the state and federal governments.[15] Preparedness efforts such as this are designed to maximize the nation's ability to respond

---

[13] S. 2658/H.R. 5200 §2(c)(3) §10503a (a)(1); interview with George Foresman, Under Secretary for Preparedness, Department of Homeland Security, November 17, 2006. In response to a question from Chairman Punaro asking who is responsible for establishing requirements for civil support, Under Secretary Foresman stated that the "overall requirements in terms of the national preparedness goal and in terms of our national preparedness structure is a responsibility that's assigned to the Secretary of Homeland Security. But having said that, there are component pieces, such as military support to civil authorities—what we're going to [be] doing [in] the law enforcement arena, the public health arena—that are the domain of the relevant federal agencies who work with their counterparts [in DHS]" (testimony before the CNGR, Hearing on the Proposed Changes to the National Guard, transcript of December 13, 2006, hearing [www.cngr.gov/hearing121314/1213cngr-panel1.pdf], p. 54).

[14] Homeland Security Presidential Directive-8 (December 17, 2003); Public Law 107-296, November 25, 2002; Public Law 109-295, October 4, 2006, §611; 6 U.S.C. §314.

[15] 6 U.S.C. §744. Under Secretary Foresman described the components of the NPS at the Commission's December hearing: "The National Preparedness Goal describes the preparedness end-state that we want. The National Preparedness Goal utilizes and references standard planning tools, that include the National Planning Scenarios, the Universal Task List and the Target Capabilities List. Together these tools provide a consistent way for entities across the Nation to work together to achieve the National Preparedness Goal. The Universal Task List and the Target Capabilities List inform communities and States what they can do to bolster their preparedness by providing guidance on specific tasks and capabilities. The National Planning Scenarios provide a basis for a consistent approach for planning for disasters regardless of the scope and size of the specific scenario" (prepared witness statement before the CNGR, Hearing on Proposed Changes to the National Guard, December 13, 2006 [www.cngr.gov/hearing121314/13DecForesmanCNGRTestimonyFINAL%5B1%5D.pdf], p. 4).

under its emergency response plan, known as the National Response Plan.[16] In addition, DHS has performed the Nationwide Plan Review of 2005–06, in which more than 1,000 emergency management and homeland security officials evaluated over 2,700 emergency operations plans and related documents in 56 states and territories and 75 urban areas over a six-month period.[17] The Commission has found no indication that the National Response Plan, the Nationwide Plan Review, and related preparedness efforts have resulted in additional requirements or funding for DOD.

Under Secretary George Foresman, who heads DHS's Preparedness Directorate, testified at the Commission's December 2006 hearing that the United States has approximately two million state and local first responders, a number roughly comparable to the size of the armed forces. Consistent with the laws and policies enacted following 9/11, DHS has been enhancing the ability of these first responders to operate "across jurisdictional boundaries," significantly increasing the nation's ability to marshal a civilian force to respond to disasters.[18] If successful, this effort should reduce the need to call on DOD for assistance. Nevertheless, in the event of another catastrophe equal to or greater than Hurricane Katrina, DOD will be required to provide civil support on a major scale and therefore must be prepared to do so.

According to the *National Strategy for Homeland Security*, two ways in which the Defense Department contributes to homeland security are domestic missions—homeland defense and civil support.[19] While DOD explicitly trains and equips its forces for homeland defense, it does not do the same for civil support missions, instead relying primarily on "dual-capable forces" for civil support activities.[20] Joint Publication 3-26, "Homeland Security," describes this policy: "The US military organizes, trains, and equips forces primarily to conduct combat operations. Inherent within the combat capabilities of the Services, is the military's ability to rapidly respond to assist civil authorities for domestic emergencies such as disasters, authorized law enforcement, and other activities that exceed the capability of civilian agencies."[21] To put it another way, civil support missions are currently viewed as derivative, or as a "by-product," of training for warfighting.[22]

This policy of treating the capability to perform civil support missions as derivative of the warfighting capability has also shaped how the National Guard is trained and equipped.

---

[16] Homeland Security Presidential Directive-8, §3; Homeland Security Presidential Directive-5 (February 28, 2003).

[17] *Nationwide Plan Review Phase 2 Report* ([Washington DC: Department of Homeland Security,] 2006), pp. vii–ix, 70–78. (This review was separate from that undertaken for the 2006 Homeland Security Grant Awards and had no effect on the awarding of grant money; see DHS, "Fact Sheet: Nationwide Plan Review," June 16, 2006 [www.dhs.gov/xnews/releases/press_release_0928.shtm].)

[18] Under Secretary Foresman, prepared witness statement, pp. 2–3.

[19] *National Strategy for Homeland Security*, p. 13.

[20] *Strategy for Homeland Defense and Civil Support*, pp. 38, 39: "Currently, the Department accounts for homeland defense activities through a variety of disparate programs and funding lines in every Military Department and combatant command and numerous initiatives under the purview of the Office of the Secretary of Defense....DOD will maintain a ready, capable, and agile command and control structure, along with competently trained forces, to assist civilian authorities with catastrophic incident response. However, with the exception of a dedicated command and control element (currently the Joint Task Force–Civil Support) and the National Guard's WMD Civil Support Teams, DOD will continue to rely on dual-capable forces for consequence management and other defense support of civil authorities."

[21] Joint Chiefs of Staff, "Homeland Security," p. IV-2.

[22] CNGR staff meeting with ASD-HD staff, October 24, 2006.

The National Guard, like the active component and other reserve forces, is "trained and equipped primarily for warfighting missions in the forward regions and approaches."[23] But under its state authorities the National Guard is also tasked with being a state's military responder, a key element of state response to emergencies. The National Guard Bureau has attempted to reconcile these two mission sets by identifying the "essential 10" warfighting capabilities inherent in National Guard units for Title 10 missions, but also essential for missions on the homeland.[24]

Securing the homeland is, properly, the Defense Department's top priority. In fact, it is the first strategic objective listed in the current *National Defense Strategy*.[25] As destructive as Hurricane Katrina was, it is all too likely that the nation will have to confront similar, or even larger, catastrophes in the future.[26] Natural disasters can endanger lives and destroy property to an extent that equals or exceeds the damage inflicted by war. Indeed, the Homeland Security Council has developed 15 National Planning Scenarios that contemplate natural and man-made catastrophes with high loss of life. These scenarios are used to develop an understanding of which capabilities will be required to respond to the disasters.[27] One scenario, the detonation of a 10-kiloton improvised nuclear device, would cause hundreds of thousands of casualties and hundreds of billions of dollars in property damage. Another, a biological attack using pneumonic plague, would kill thousands and sicken even more.[28] In addition, the Defense Department's own *Strategy for Homeland Defense and Civil Support* considers the very real possibility of multiple, simultaneous chemical, biological, radiological, nuclear, or high-yield explosive (CBRNE) attacks on the United States.[29] Catastrophes such as these would most likely overwhelm state and local governments' ability to respond, and will require a massive effort by the federal government. As demonstrated by the response to Hurricane Katrina, the United States military's civil support missions will be an indispensable part of this effort. This is not to say that DOD should "become the default manpower resource for other federal agencies or state or local governments" in every disaster.[30] Nor should DOD assume the lead role in disaster response more generally, displacing DHS. The point instead is that DOD can be expected to play a major, and in some scenarios the preeminent, role in responding to catastrophes or

---

[23] *Strategy for Homeland Defense and Civil Support*, p. 35.

[24] National Guard Bureau, Office of Legislative Liaison, "National Guard Equipment Requirements: 'Essential 10' Equipment Requirements for the Global War on Terror," March 16, 2006.

[25] *National Defense Strategy of the United States of America* ([Washington, DC: Department of Defense,] 2005), p. 7; see also *Strategy for Homeland Defense and Civil Support*, p. 35 ("Securing the US homeland is the first among many priorities outlined in the National Defense Strategy").

[26] In his 2007 Annual Threat Assessment, then Director of National Intelligence John Negroponte stated that al Qaeda continues to "plot attacks against our Homeland and other targets with the objective of inflicting mass casualties"; see *Annual Threat Assessment of the Director of National Intelligence* ([Washington, DC: Office of the Director of National Intelligence,] 2007), p. 2.

[27] *National Planning Scenarios* ([Washington, DC: Homeland Security Council,] 2005), p. ii. In its recent report, CSIS noted that DOD has not developed official civil support requirements reflecting the operational challenges posed by these scenarios (Christine E. Wormuth, Michèle A. Flournoy, Patrick T. Henry, and Clark A. Murdock, *The Future of the National Guard and Reserves: The Beyond Goldwater-Nichols Phase III Report* [Washington, DC: Center for Strategic and International Studies, 2006], p. 69).

[28] *National Planning Scenarios*, pp. 1-1, 4-1 to 4-7.

[29] *Strategy for Homeland Defense and Civil Support*, p. 19.

[30] Prepared witness statement of David S. C. Chu, Under Secretary of Defense for Personnel and Readiness, and Thomas F. Hall, Assistant Secretary of Defense for Reserve Affairs, before the Commission on the National Guard and Reserves, Hearing on Proposed Changes to the National Guard, December 13, 2006 (www.cngr.gov/hearing121314/Chu-Hall%20Statement.pdf), p. 11.

other extreme circumstances. This expectation is recognized by the White House's report on the response to Hurricane Katrina, which suggests that the National Response Plan be revised to address circumstances under which it would be necessary for DOD to take the lead in the federal response to a catastrophe.[31]

The Defense Department's position is that civil support is a "lesser included" element of its warfighting capability.[32] According to this view, if DOD is prepared to fight a major war, it is prepared to respond to a disaster or emergency at home. The Commission believes that this position is flawed. Preparing for and responding to emergencies and disasters is not simply a subset of another capability.

> **Finding:** The Department of Defense does not explicitly budget and program for civil support missions because the Department views them as derivative of its wartime missions. This is a flawed assumption.

THE NATIONAL GUARD: STATUS AND COMMAND

Both state and federal military forces may be called on to respond to a disaster.[33] A state's military forces—its National Guard—may respond under the state emergency plan. In fact, the National Guard is often the first (and only) military responder to an event.[34] Such activity occurs under the orders of the governor—the "commander in chief" of National Guard units not in federal service—in accordance with state law. This is called *state active duty* and does not require the approval of the Defense Department. State active duty operations are paid for by the state and may range from such routine operations as providing security following a minor flood to massive operations such as the response to a hurricane. With the approval of the Secretary of Defense, National Guard forces acting under state orders may also be paid for by the federal government under 32 U.S.C. §502(f), a situation often referred to as being in "Title 32" status.[35] For a summary of state and federal roles, see Table 3.

---

[31] "[Recommendation 22:] DOD and DHS should develop recommendations for revision of the NRP to delineate the circumstances, objectives, and limitations of when DOD might temporarily assume the lead for the Federal response to a catastrophic incident. Katrina demonstrated the importance of prior planning for rapid and complex response efforts. DOD should develop plans to lead the Federal response for events of extraordinary scope and nature (*e.g.*, nuclear incident or multiple simultaneous terrorist attacks causing a breakdown in civil society)" (*The Federal Response to Hurricane Katrina: Lessons Learned*, p. 94).

[32] General Peter J. Schoomaker, Chief of Staff, U.S. Army, testimony before the CNGR, Hearing on Proposed Changes to the National Guard, transcript of December 14, 2006, hearing (www.cngr.gov/hearing121314/1214cngr-panel2.pdf), p. 24.

[33] Civil support operations do not solely involve disaster response. They can also include military support to law enforcement agencies, counterterrorism support, counter-drug operations, and other missions where state and local government has been overwhelmed (Joint Chiefs of Staff, "Homeland Security," pp. IV-4–7).

[34] Joint Chiefs of Staff, "Homeland Security," p. II-13.

[35] Steve Bowman, Lawrence Kapp, and Amy Belasco, *Hurricane Katrina: DOD Disaster Response*, CRS Report RL33095 (January 24, 2006), pp. 7–8.

| | State Role | | Federal Role |
	State Funded	Federally Funded	Federally Funded
Command and Control entity	Governor	Governor	President
Mobilization authorities used	In accordance with state law	Title 32 (32 U.S.C. §502(f))	Various Title 10 authorities
Where deployed	In accordance with state law	United States	Worldwide
Mission types	In accordance with state law	Training and other federally authorized missions	Overseas training and as assigned after mobilization
Examples of domestic missions	Forest fires, floods, civil disturbances	Post-9/11 airport security, Hurricane Katrina, southwest border security	Air sovereignty, missile defense, guarding DOD infrastructure
Support law enforcement activities	Yes	Yes	As limited by Posse Comitatus*

* The 1878 Posse Comitatus Act, 18 U.S.C. §1385, prohibits the direct use of federal military troops for domestic civilian law enforcement except where authorized by the Constitution or an act of Congress. This act applies to the Army National Guard and the Air National Guard, which are reserve components of the armed forces under 10 U.S.C. §10101.
Source: GAO analysis (GAO-07-60,p.10)

Table 3. Comparison of National Guard State and Federal Roles

If a state has an insufficient number of National Guard assets to respond to a particular disaster, it may request assistance from other states' National Guards. Such forces operate in state active duty under the command of the requesting state.[36] States are able to use the Emergency Management Assistance Compact (EMAC) to request National Guard forces from other states, but, as the response to Katrina showed, the EMAC process is cumbersome for the large-scale movement of troops. States therefore would be likely to instead rely on the National Guard Bureau (NGB) to coordinate the movement of National Guard forces, as was done in Hurricane Katrina.[37]

Whereas National Guard units in state active duty or Title 32 status can respond to a disaster under state law, federal military forces (including National Guard units placed under federal control) respond in a federal civil support capacity. Under the Stafford Act and the National Response Plan, a state's governor may request assistance from the federal government when the state's (including its local government's) capabilities have been overwhelmed and federal assistance is needed.[38] If the federal government agrees to the request, the federal response will be coordinated by DHS through FEMA.[39] DOD's usual

---

[36] Bowman, Kapp, and Belasco, *Hurricane Katrina: DOD Disaster Response*, p. 8.
[37] Senate Committee on Homeland Security and Governmental Affairs, *Hurricane Katrina: A Nation Still Unprepared*, 109th Cong., 2nd sess., May 2006, pp. 507-8.
[38] 42 U.S.C. §5170; *National Response Plan*, p. 15.
[39] 6 U.S.C. §314; Public Law 109-295, *Department of Homeland Security Appropriations Act for 2007*, October 4, 2006, §611.

role (using Title 10 military forces) is referred to in the 2004 *National Response Plan* as "defense support to civil authorities" (DSCA). When DOD is providing DSCA, it is acting not as the lead responder to a disaster but in support of another agency leading the response.[40]

U.S. Northern Command is the joint command in charge of Title 10 homeland defense and civil support activities.[41] It does not command National Guard forces in state active duty or Title 32 status, but can do so if the President places them under federal control.[42] Like NORTHCOM, the National Guard Bureau does not command National Guard forces in state active duty or Title 32 status. Unlike NORTHCOM, it does not ever command forces. Instead, the NGB's role is to facilitate the execution of domestic missions by National Guard units in Title 32 status.[43] Consequently, NORTHCOM may be thought of as the Title 10 command for homeland defense and civil support, while the NGB may be thought of as the "Title 32 coordinator" for multistate National Guard domestic missions.

Despite the National Guard's vital role in responding to emergencies, it does not appear to have a significant presence at the Department of Homeland Security. At the Commission's January 31, 2007 hearing, Lieutenant General H Steven Blum, Chief of the National Guard Bureau, testified that he had a "very informal relationship" with DHS and "all I have is LNOs [liaison officers] over there and we have to put the LNOs over there at a very second- or third-tier level. There's no flag officers over there....I would think that the National Guard should have a much closer liaison with them, frankly, because they will be the federal lead agency that we would be in support of[.]" He further testified that he had no personnel on the DHS planning staff or in DHS's operations center.[44]

> **Finding:** The Department of Homeland Security does not have a National Guard presence sufficient to promote necessary levels of cooperation.

---

[40] *National Response Plan*, pp. 41–42.

[41] U.S. Southern Command and U.S. Pacific Command play similar roles for those parts of the homeland that fall within their area of operations (Joint Chiefs of Staff, "Homeland Security," pp. II-7–11).

[42] USNORTHCOM Staff Working Paper Executive Summary, "Establishment of National Guard Regional Headquarters to Coordinate Multi State Mission Execution," provided to Commission staff on August 31, 2006.

[43] "National Guard Bureau Joint Staff Manual" [Draft] ([Arlington, VA: National Guard Bureau,] 2004), p. M-8.

[44] Lieutenant General Blum, testimony before the CNGR, Hearing on Proposed Changes to the National Guard, transcript of January 31, 2007, hearing (www.cngr.gov/hearing13107/0131cngr-1.pdf), pp. 26–27.

RESOURCING THE HOMELAND MISSION

The process of identifying requirements for the Department of Defense begins at the highest levels.[45] The National Security Strategy and the strategies derived from it, such as the National Defense Strategy and the National Military Strategy, are the basis for all requirements.[46] Analysis of these strategies informs the development of the Joint Strategic Capabilities Plan (JSCP) and Joint Operating Concepts (JOCs). These documents are the primary source in assigning responsibility for certain capabilities among the combatant commanders, service Chiefs, and defense agencies.[47] In those assignments, they address the missions of the Army and the Air Force and the need for strong homeland defense and civil support capabilities within the Department of Defense. The 2005 *National Defense Strategy of the United States of America* strikes a balance between overseas and domestic requirements and places a high priority on defending the U.S. homeland as the first consideration in the sizing and shaping of United States military forces.[48]

The 2004 *National Military Strategy of the United States of America* describes the interplay between requirements for overseas warfighting and domestic military capabilities:

> Our first line of defense is abroad and includes mutually supporting activities with US allies to counter threats close to their source. Closer to home, the Armed Forces use their capabilities to secure strategic air, land, sea and space approaches to the United States and its territory. When directed, the Armed Forces employ military capabilities at home to protect the nation, the domestic population and critical infrastructure from direct attack. Protecting the United States also requires integrating military capabilities with other government and law enforcement agencies to manage the consequences of an attack or natural disaster.[49]

These strategy documents form the basis for all requirements, including equipment and funding requirements, within the Department of Defense.[50] The transition from policy guidance to operational implementation and requirements definition is best illustrated in the Department of Defense's Joint Operating Concepts. The concepts describe the military capabilities of the joint force required to implement national security objectives in the next

---

[45] Section 529(a)(4) of the National Defense Authorization Act for FY 2007 requires the Commission to report on "The adequacy of the Department of Defense processes for defining the equipment and funding necessary for the National Guard to conduct both its responsibilities under title 10, United States Code, and its responsibilities under title 32 United States Code, including homeland defense and related homeland missions."

[46] Military requirements are "established need[s] justifying the timely allocation of resources to achieve a capability to accomplish approved military objectives, missions, or tasks" (Joint Chiefs of Staff, "Department of Defense Dictionary of Military and Associated Terms," Joint Publication 1-02, April 12, 2001 [as amended through January 5, 2007], p. 340).

[47] Chairman of the Joint Chiefs of Staff Instruction (CJCSI) 3100.01A, "Joint Strategic Planning System," September 12, 2003; "The National Military Strategy is guided by the goals and objectives contained in the President's "National Security Strategy" and serves to implement the Secretary of Defense's "National Defense Strategy of the United States of America" (*National Military Strategy of the United States of America* [Washington, DC: Chairman of the Joint Chiefs of Staff, 2004], p. viii).

[48] *National Defense Strategy of the United States of America* ([Washington, DC: Department of Defense,] 2005), p. 20.

[49] *National Military Strategy of the United States of America* (2004), p. 2.

[50] CJCSI 3100.01A, "Joint Strategic Planning System," pp. A-1 to A-3.

15 to 20 years.[51] The Department is developing a family of four Joint Operating Concepts, now in various stages of development, that demonstrate the full range of capabilities that may be required by the National Guard, both as integral Army and Air Force components and as nonfederalized forces under the control of a governor: (1) deterrence operations; (2) major combat operations; (3) military support to stabilization, security, transition, and reconstruction operations; and (4) homeland defense and civil support.[52] The capabilities required of both the Army and Air National Guard, in their Title 10 warfighting role, are outlined (though not specifically assigned to these components) in the first three concepts. The fourth singles out the National Guard as a unique force, with federal and nonfederal responsibilities and the task of coordinating the activities of military forces in either status when operating in the homeland.[53]

The services, combatant commands, and defense agencies translate the capabilities they require into funding requirements, which are then validated for the resource allocation process. Validation may be accomplished internally by the service. This is the usual method when the requirement is relatively small and not of interest to the joint community.[54] The joint path to requirement validation requires that the sponsor present the requirement to the Joint Requirements Oversight Council (JROC), a group usually consisting of the Chairman or Vice Chairman of the Joint Chiefs of Staff, representatives of the services, and others acting in an advisory capacity.[55] The JROC ensures that the proposed requirement truly addresses an assigned capability, considers joint interests efficiently, and is not redundant with other requirements.

Once a requirement is validated, it must still compete successfully in the resource allocation process to be funded. This process is largely conducted inside the services as each builds its program objective memorandum (POM). The chances of JROC-validated requirements being funded may improve if they are resourced in the service POMs. The Secretary of Defense may direct services to resource certain requirements through the Defense Planning Guidance (DPG), which is also informed by the Chairman's Program Advice (from the Chairman of the Joint Chiefs of Staff). Combatant commanders influence service POMs through their integrated priorities lists (IPLs) reflected in joint programming guidance.[56] After reviewing completed service POMs for conformance to strategic plans, the CJCS sends an assessment to the Secretary of Defense, who may direct changes to the service plans by issuing a program decision memorandum (PDM).[57]

Currently, no one in this process has the responsibility of advocating for funding for homeland security or civil support–related missions. In his testimony to the Commission, Lieutenant General Blum stated that NORTHCOM, in particular, does not regularly advocate requirements for the NGB's Title 32 mission: "NORTHCOM...will not advocate requirements...for the Title 32 piece that the Guard provides....[When] I'm trying to equip or train these CBRNE enhanced response force packages, I run into brick walls...because they say...this is not a Title [10] Army thing, we're not going to pay for this. So now we have

---

[51] DOD, "Strategic Deterrence Joint Operating Concept" (2004), p. 1.
[52] DOD, "Homeland Defense and Civil Support Joint Operating Concept" (draft, 2006).
[53] DOD, "Homeland Defense and Civil Support Joint Operating Concept," pp. 15, 56, 57.
[54] CJCSI 3170.01E, "Joint Capabilities Integration and Development System," May 11, 2005.
[55] CJCSI 5123.01, "Charter of the Joint Requirements Oversight Council," November 9, 2006.
[56] CJCSI 3100.01A, "Joint Strategic Planning System," p. D-4.
[57] CJCSI 3100.01A, "Joint Strategic Planning System," p. D-3.

a capability that the nation is denied because of all of our organizational impediments that we have in the way."[58]

> **Finding:** The commander of U.S. Northern Command does not sufficiently advocate for the full range of civil support requirements affecting the National Guard and Reserves. Neither do the Chiefs or Vice Chiefs of the Army and Air Force.

The National Guard Bureau does not have standing access to the JROC. Its Title 10 warfighting requirements are brought to this process by the appropriate staff of the Army or the Air Force, as the Guard's requirements are subsets of those of the larger total force. Requirements that have unique applicability to the Guard's homeland role, performed in both federal and state status, are more difficult to put before the JROC. The National Guard Bureau has succeeded in gaining access to the JROC only when there has been intense political interest in a certain program or congressional direction to the Department. Several recent examples of unique National Guard requirements that have been validated through the JROC process include

- The equipping of WMD (weapons of mass destruction) civil support teams.

- Communications equipment designed to be compatible with civilian (local, state, and federal) emergency response agencies.

- Command and control organizations for CBRNE incident response, such as U.S. Northern Command's Joint Task Force–Civil Support.[59]

The current planning, programming, budgeting, and execution (PPBES) process does not address resourcing for civil support missions, because requirements for such missions are not generated. Unlike requirements for warfighting, there now exists no official process for generating requirements for civil support missions.[60] As noted above, civil support is currently viewed as a "by-product" or a derivative of the Defense Department's warfighting mission.[61]

Two mechanisms exist that begin to address the lack of a requirements generation process—the Homeland Security Council's 15 "National Planning Scenarios" and the NGB's "essential 10." Nevertheless, within DOD, the definition of a requirement is the

---

[58] Lieutenant General Blum, testimony before the CNGR, Hearing on Proposed Changes to the National Guard, transcript of January 31, 2007, hearing (www.cngr.gov/hearing13107/0131cngr-1.pdf), p. 26.

[59] CNGR staff meeting with National Guard Bureau Joint Staff representatives, November 27, 2006; Lieutenant General H Steven Blum, Chief, National Guard Bureau, letter to Major General Arnold L. Punaro, USMC (ret.), Chairman, CNGR, November 30, 2006, p. 5.

[60] Wormuth et al., *The Future of the National Guard and Reserves*, p. 69.

[61] CNGR staff meeting with ASD-HD staff, October 24, 2006. In a letter to the Commission, the Center for Strategic and International Studies notes that "To the extent that requirements for the Guard's role in MACA/DSCA do exist, it is primarily because Congress ultimately directed DOD to provide funding for such requirements" (John J. Hamre and Christine E. Wormuth, Center for Strategic and International Studies, letter to Major General Arnold L. Punaro, USMC [ret.], Chairman, Commission on the National Guard and Reserves, December 14, 2006, Attachment A, p. 7).

first—and a critical—step in the PPBES cycle. Lieutenant General Blum testified that no mechanism exists for setting civil support requirements, echoing a similar assertion in the National Guard Association of the United States' January 16, 2007, submission to the Commission.[62] The absence of a requirements definition process represents a critical weakness in resourcing for civil support missions.

The Commission is aware of no mechanism to translate the National Response Plan or related preparedness efforts into requirements or additional resources for DOD. Furthermore, during its December 13, 2006, hearing, the Commission repeatedly questioned witnesses from both the Department of Defense and the Department of Homeland Security about how requirements for civil support are developed and who has that responsibility, but was unable to identify the responsible individual or department. During his testimony, in response to a request for a copy of such a requirements document, DHS Under Secretary for Preparedness George Foresman noted: "I think this is a takeaway for us, to sit down with our partners in DOD—Guard, active, Reserve, everybody—to sit down with our partners, look at our requirements generation process and make sure we've got a comparable one, because I can't tell you that there is a document that defines the requirements for the Guard in the context of a homeland defense mission, but I also can't tell you that that there is not."[63] This lack of a requirements generation process is a critical shortfall in the nation's preparedness efforts. Despite a number of changes to law and policy, it is still unclear whether the nation possesses the capabilities necessary to respond to a catastrophic disaster.[64]

> **Finding:** The National Response Plan and related preparedness efforts have not been translated adequately into Department of Defense programming and budgeting requirements.

> **Finding:** The Department of Homeland Security has not identified the requirements that the Department of Defense must meet to adequately perform domestic civil support missions.

Commission research has highlighted the difficulty in tracking Guard and Reserve equipment funding through the lengthy PPBES process, which was developed when the reserve components were a seldom-used strategic reserve. The Commission has received extensive testimony on equipment shortfalls within the reserve components, and Reserve and National Guard proponents believe that there are multiple opportunities for funding originally requested for reserve component equipment to be diverted to other "more pressing" needs.[65] The ability to track such diversions is often limited because of the lack of

---

[62] Lieutenant General Blum, testimony before the CNGR, transcript of January 31, 2007, hearing, p. 34; Major General R. Martin Umbarger, National Guard Association of the United States, letter to Major General Arnold L. Punaro, USMC (ret.), Chairman, CNGR, January 16, 2007, pp. 16–17.

[63] Under Secretary Foresman, testimony before the CNGR, transcript of December 13, 2006, p. 72; see also pp. 40, 54–57, 62, 70–76.

[64] GAO, *Catastrophic Disasters: Enhanced Leadership, Capabilities, and Accountability Will Improve the Effectiveness of the Nation's Preparedness, Response, and Recovery System*, GAO-06-618 (Report to Congressional Committees), September 2006, pp. 37–38.

[65] On equipment shortfalls, see testimony of Janet St. Laurent, Director, Defense Capabilities and Management, Government Accountability Office, before the CNGR, Hearing on National Guard and Reserve Issues, transcript of September 21, 2006, hearing (www.cngr.gov/hearing918-21/transcript4.pdf), pp. 15–17; on diversion of

transparency during the execution phase. Congress partially addresses shortfalls by adding specific items of equipment to a separate National Guard–Reserve equipment account.

The PPBES process is managed within each service through multiple work groups—beginning at the O-3/O-4 level[66] and ending at the service Chief of Staff/military department Secretary level—before the final decision is transmitted to the Office of the Secretary of Defense and then to the Office of Management and Budget for further modifications and fine-tuning. Sponsors of the National Defense Enhancement and National Guard Empowerment Act of 2006 (S. 2658/H.R. 5200) have argued that the interests of the National Guard are not adequately represented at the most senior levels in the decision-making process.[67] Commission research indicates that the reserve components are usually involved at all stages of the internal service/military department process up to the endgame decisions about where cuts must fall.

The Commission concludes that the system of funding and equipping the National Guard under both state and federal status, including homeland-related missions, is inadequate. Because they are not formally established, requirements for homeland security, specifically support to civil authorities, are rarely considered when funding is prioritized. Even though the National Guard is well represented in the process, requirements for the functions that are unique to the Guard in its homeland role have little chance of success in the service and DOD resource allocation processes. Only strong pressure from Congress has in recent cases counteracted this disadvantage. The lack of consideration given these requirements is the result of the Department's policy of viewing civil support as a mission derivative of war-fighting.[68]

> **Finding:** The system for funding and equipping the National Guard under both state and federal status, including for homeland-related missions, is inadequate in that requirements for civil support are rarely considered when Department of Defense funding is prioritized.

> **Finding:** The Department of Defense is not adequately equipping the National Guard for its domestic missions.

---

reserve component equipment, see testimony of Lieutenant General H Steven Blum before the CNGR, Hearing on Homeland Defense/Homeland Security, transcript of May 3, 2006, hearing (www.cngr.gov/hearing503-4/0509natguard2.pdf), p. 39.

[66] Respectively, captain or major in the case of the Army, Air Force, or Marine Corps; lieutenant or lieutenant commander in the case of the Navy.

[67] Senator Leahy, 109th Cong., 2nd sess., *Congressional Record* 152, no. 1 (September 29, 2006): S10808–S10809.

[68] In fact, this reluctance is codified in DOD Directive 3025.1, "Military Support to Civil Authorities (MSCA)," §4.4.8.2, January 15, 1993, which states that "DoD Components shall not procure or maintain any supplies, materiel, or equipment exclusively for providing MSCA in civil emergencies, unless otherwise directed by the Secretary of Defense" (p. 7). The Commission anticipates that if DOD begins to explicitly budget and program for civil support missions, this directive will need to change; it is currently undergoing major revision, but according to the staff of the Assistant Secretary of Defense for Homeland Defense and America's Security Affairs (ASD-HD&ASA), this specific policy is not expected to change).

Conclusion: Although the current Department of Defense Strategy for *Homeland Defense and Civil Support* states that securing the U.S. homeland is "the first among many priorities," the Defense Department in fact has not accepted that this responsibility requires planning, programming, and budgeting for civil support missions.

Recommendation:

1. **The Secretary of Homeland Security, with the assistance of the Secretary of Defense, should generate civil support requirements, which the Department of Defense will be responsible for validating as appropriate. The Department of Defense should include civil support requirements in its programming and budgeting. In a new advisory role, the Chief of the National Guard Bureau should advise the U.S. Northern Command commander, the Secretaries of the Air Force and Army, and, through the Chairman of the Joint Chiefs of Staff, the Secretary of Defense regarding gaps between federal and state emergency response capabilities.**

The Commission believes that the responsibility for identifying and filling gaps in emergency response capabilities should remain in the Department of Homeland Security. As part of this process, DHS should identify the specific gaps that can best be filled by Defense Department civil support activities. It can define these gaps as requirements and submit them to the Department of Defense. DOD would then have the responsibility to validate those requirements it deems appropriate and feed them into the DOD programming and budgeting process.[69]

This proposal would ensure that DHS retains its position as the federal agency responsible for coordinating national preparedness. It would also take advantage of DHS's nationwide perspective on preparedness. In addition, the proposal would make DHS responsible for identifying gaps in capabilities that can best be filled by DOD civil support, while giving DOD the responsibility to determine the best way to fill those gaps once the appropriate requirements have been validated. Thus DOD would have the flexibility to respond to DHS's requirements in a way that prioritizes them appropriately with DOD's other missions.

Recommendation:

2. **The Department of Defense (including combatant commands and the National Guard Bureau) and Department of Homeland Security Headquarters should exchange representatives to improve the knowledge of National Guard and Reserve capabilities; to improve planning, training, and exercising; and to assist the Secretary of Homeland Security with generating requirements for military civil support missions. The Commission recommends that a plan to exchange personnel be developed**

---

[69] The Commission believes that this reallocation of responsibilities will necessitate the revision of DOD Directive 3025.1, "Military Support to Civil Authorities."

and implemented by the Secretary of Defense and the Secretary of Homeland Security within 180 days. The Commission notes the urgency of this recommendation.

Although national guardsmen are placed in DOD's offices responsible for domestic response and as part-time liaisons at the Department of Homeland Security, information sharing is not always coordinated and at times, NORTHCOM and the Bureau are left out of important meetings and deliberations on homeland issues.[70] The Joint Staff currently places a National Guard general officer as director of the Joint Directorate of Military Support office. The Joint Directorate reports through the J-3 to the Chairman of the Joint Chiefs of Staff and serves as a focal point for coordination with combatant commands, the services, and the National Guard. National guardsmen also assist by serving in billets on the staff of the Assistant Secretary of Defense for Homeland Defense and America's Security Affairs (ASD-HD&ASA), but the Joint Staff, ASD-HD&ASA, and DHS lack full-time NORTHCOM representation in critical areas such as planning and exercising.[71]

The Commission believes that DHS would benefit if it were to acquire staff from the NGB and NORTHCOM (and other appropriate combatant commands). By enhancing DHS's insight into the capabilities DOD can bring to support DHS's mission, such staff will greatly improve the federal government's capacity for preparedness and response. This perspective will be especially valuable in assisting DHS in its generation of civil support requirements for DOD. Similarly, assigning DHS personnel to DOD would provide DOD with valuable information on what will be expected of it during civil support missions.

Recommendation:

> **3. The Secretary of Defense and the Secretary of Homeland Security should jointly submit an annual report to Congress on those civil support requirements generated by the Secretary of Homeland Security and those validated as well as funded by the Secretary of Defense, and the Chief of the National Guard Bureau should play a role in the preparation of that report as directed by the Secretary of Defense.**

Proposed section §10503a of S. 2658/H.R. 5200 would give the Chief of the NGB the responsibility to "identify gaps between federal and state capabilities to prepare for and respond to emergencies" and to recommend to the Secretary of Defense National Guard programs and activities to address such gaps.[72] The legislation would also give the NGB a number of new powers to facilitate the filling of those gaps once identified, including validating state civil support requirements.[73] Section 2(b)(4) of the bill amends section 10504 of Title 10, Chapter 1011 (dealing with the National Guard Bureau) to require the CNGB to submit an annual report to Congress on (1) state civil support requirements validated under the CNGB's new responsibilities in new §10503a during the previous fiscal year, (2) the validated civil support requirements for which funding is to be requested in the

---

[70] Memorandum for the Record (MFR), NORAD-NORTHCOM Trip After-Action Report, January 25, 2006; MFR, National Guard Bureau, November 27, 2006.
[71] MFR, Commissioner site visits to DHS Headquarters, April 7 and June 16, 2006.
[72] S. 2658/H.R. 5200 §2(c)(3); see proposed 10 U.S.C. §10503a(a).
[73] S. 2658/H.R. 5200 §2(c)(3); see proposed 10 U.S.C. §10503a(b).

next fiscal year under new §10544, and (3) the validated civil support requirements for which funding will not be requested in the next fiscal year under new §10544.

The Commission's alternative to this proposal would require the Secretary of Homeland Security to generate civil support requirements for the Secretary of Defense. The Secretary of Defense would, in turn, choose which requirements to validate in DOD's budget and programming process. In concert with this alternative to proposed §10503a, the Commission proposes the following reporting requirement. The Secretaries of Homeland Security and Defense should submit a joint report on the civil support requirements generated by DHS for DOD, also specifying which of those requirements DOD chose to validate and which it requested to be funded in its budget. In addition to making more visible DOD's civil support mission and the role DHS sees for DOD, such a report would also force DHS and DOD to work together on a strategy on how best to use DOD's civil support capabilities to strengthen the nation's homeland security efforts. The Chief of the National Guard Bureau should be able to provide substantial input into this report.

Recommendations:

4. **The commander of U.S. Northern Command should advocate for civil support requirements in the Department of Defense's capabilities development, requirements generation and validation, and programming systems. The military services should ensure that civil support requirements are included in their respective budget processes.**

5. **The budget information for National Guard training and equipment for military assistance to civil authorities and other domestic operations should be included in appropriate sections of the Department of the Army and Department of the Air Force budget documents, respectively. There should not be separate budget documents for National Guard training and equipment for military assistance to civil authorities and other domestic operations.**

Section 2(c)(4) of S. 2658/H.R. 5200 would add a new section 10544 to Title 10, Chapter 1013 of the United States Code ("Budget Information and Annual Reports to Congress"). This section would require the budget justification materials submitted to Congress in support of the President's budget to specify separate amounts for training and equipping the National Guard for purposes of civil support and for other domestic operations during the fiscal year. The Commission recommends against this proposal on the grounds that most civil support missions are performed using "dual-use" equipment and that the designation of certain training and equipment as civil support–related would likely be arbitrary and would not help Congress provide meaningful oversight on this matter.

The Commission has recommended instead that DOD explicitly budget and program for civil support. If that recommendation is implemented, budgeting and appropriation will be no different for civil support than for any other DOD mission.

B. The Role of States and Their Governors

As the chief executives of their states, governors are vested with a primary responsibility to protect the life and property of their citizens, and are the senior civilian officials in charge of most emergency preparedness and disaster response efforts in our nation. As the commanders in chief of their respective state National Guard units not in federal status (Title 10), governors have a major interest in how their state National Guard units and personnel are trained, equipped, and utilized. And as commanders in chief, they are responsible for their Guard before and after its use, whether the units are deployed on a state mission, a federal mission, or a combination of both.

America's national military strategy recognizes the key role played by the reserve components of the U.S. military in protecting the homeland. The Defense Department's *Strategy for Homeland Defense and Civil Support* states that the reserve components are especially suited for performing civil support and related domestic missions and recommends a "focused reliance" on them for homeland defense and civil support missions.[1]

Such a focused reliance makes sense given the widespread distribution of reserve forces, particularly the National Guard. The National Guard is located in all 54 states and territories. It is typically a major state emergency responder and a vital part of the state's ability to protect its people and property from disaster and to recover after disaster has struck.[2] Indeed, in many states, the adjutant general, who is in military command of National Guard units in state status, heads the state's emergency response agency.[3]

Along with the other reserve components, the National Guard is forward deployed in 3,200 communities throughout the nation. In addition, it routinely exercises with other state and local first responders, such as police, fire, and emergency medical personnel, and is deeply embedded in communities across the nation.[4] As Major General R. Martin Umbarger, Adjutant General for the State of Indiana, told the Commission, "We know the nation's first responders by name—the police chiefs, the sheriffs, the fire chiefs—the incident commanders."[5] For this reason, the National Response Plan establishes that local and state governments possess the primary responsibility to respond to emergencies, and the federal government is called on only when the event outstrips the resources and capacities of state and local authorities. In most cases, the National Guard is the military's first responder force.

The National Guard is unique in that it serves both state and federal authorities. When in federal (Title 10) status, the Army National Guard acts as a reserve component of the Army, and the Air National Guard is a reserve component of the Air Force, commanded by the President. When in state status, the Army and Air National Guard operates under the orders

---

[1] *Strategy for Homeland Defense and Civil Support* (Washington, DC: Department of Defense, 2005), p. 35.
[2] Joint Chiefs of Staff, "Homeland Security," Joint Publication 3-26, August 2, 2005, pp. II-11 to II-13.
[3] Joint Chiefs of Staff, "Homeland Security," p. II-13.
[4] *Strategy for Homeland Defense and Civil Support*, p. 35.
[5] Major General Umbarger, testimony before the CNGR, Hearing on Proposed Changes to the National Guard, transcript of December 14, 2006, hearing (www.cngr.gov/hearing121314/1214cngr-panel3%20(2).pdf), p. 6.

of the governor. The governor can command Guard troops in either state active duty (paid by the state) or Title 32 (paid by the federal government).[6]

In recent years, the ability of governors to draw on National Guard forces has expanded through the adoption by all states and territories of the Emergency Management Assistance Compact (EMAC), an interstate agreement that allows the governor of one state to send National Guard troops to another state to assist the governor receiving those forces in responding to an emergency. During the response to Hurricane Katrina, approximately 50,000 National Guard troops from 54 states and territories supported Gulf Coast states through EMAC. They were joined by 20,000 federal military personnel.[7]

The dual nature of the National Guard creates tensions between their federal and state commanders. While states are free to provide resources to their National Guard units, most funding for the force comes from the federal government, mainly the U.S. Departments of the Army and Air Force. At the Commission's December hearing, Under Secretary for Personnel and Readiness David S. C. Chu and Assistant Secretary of Defense for Reserve Affairs Thomas F. Hall testified that the federal government pays roughly 90 percent of the annual cost for the National Guard, while the states pay the remaining 10 percent.[8]

Notwithstanding these funding realities, the manning and equipping of the National Guard is of paramount importance to the governors. With the recent major deployments of National Guard units to conflicts in Iraq, Afghanistan, and elsewhere, governors have become increasingly concerned about whether their National Guard forces will be available to respond to emergencies at home. Governors perceive a lack of coordinated planning for the use of nonfederal forces, insufficient coordination of state and federal emergency response capabilities, inadequate funding to re-equip Guard units returning from active duty abroad, a lack of dual-use equipment, and insufficient consultation with governors by the Department of Defense in advance of decisions affecting the National Guard.[9]

Governor Michael F. Easley of North Carolina testified before the Commission about various state missions for which the National Guard has been used in North Carolina, including ice storms and hurricanes. Governor Easley expressed his concern over shortages in National Guard equipment, remarking, "A Guard unit cannot be effective without the right tools." Governor Easley expressed the view that enlarging the federal role for the National Guard would reduce its ability to respond effectively to state missions.[10] Governor Ruth Ann Minner of Delaware testified before the Commission that the Department of

---

[6] National Governors Association, letter to Arnold L. Punaro, Chairman, CNGR, June 15, 2006 (www.cngr.gov/hearing615/NGA--National%20Guard%20Commission%20Statement.pdf), p. 2.

[7] *The Federal Response to Hurricane Katrina: Lessons Learned* ([Washington, DC: The White House,] 2006), p. 43; GAO, *Hurricane Katrina: Better Plans and Exercises Need to Guide the Military's Response to Catastrophic Natural Disasters*, GAO-06-808T (Statement for the Record to the Subcommittee on Terrorism, Unconventional Threats and Capabilities, Committee on Armed Services, House of Representatives), May 2006, pp. [ii], 2, 6.

[8] Under Secretary Chu and Assistant Secretary Hall, testimony before the CNGR, Hearing on Proposed Changes to the National Guard, transcript of December 13, 2006, hearing (www.cngr.gov/ hearing121314/1213cngr-panel1.pdf), p. 37.

[9] National Governors Association, letter to Chairman Punaro, January 26, 2007.

[10] Governor Easley, prepared statement before the CNGR, Hearing on National Guard and Reserve Issues, June 15, 2006 (www.cngr.gov/hearing615/Easley.doc), pp. 2–3.

Defense needs to work with her and other governors in a "collaborative manner to best determine force structure requirements."[11]

Governor George E. Pataki of New York said in a written statement that he has called out the National Guard 49 times since 1995. Although the New York National Guard was able to meet all mission requirements in each instance, at the time of his statement the New York National Guard reported having only 52 percent of critical equipment necessary for state emergencies. Of that, 20 percent was deployed to Iraq or was replaced by substitute equipment. He cited High Mobility Multi-purpose Wheeled Vehicles (Humvees) as an example of the kind of equipment critical to homeland missions, pointing out that the New York National Guard had available only 33 percent of its authorized allocation. Governor Pataki expressed support for integrating the National Guard leadership into force structure planning and decision making in order to address these equipment requirement shortfalls and to generate predictable deployment cycles for National Guard units.[12]

Governor M. Michael Rounds of South Dakota wrote to the Commission expressing his concern about the adequacy of Army National Guard funding and end-strength, the sufficiency of the requirements of U.S. Northern Command (NORTHCOM) for National Guard assets to support homeland defense missions, the adverse effect of Air National Guard force structure cuts, the effects of the Army Force Generation Model, and mobilization issues. Governor Rounds reported that the South Dakota National Guard has more than $20 million worth of equipment in need of replacement.[13]

Governor John H. Lynch of New Hampshire addressed the role of the National Guard in homeland security—an area in which, he noted, the National Guard, not the active component, serves as an operational force. The National Guard works as a "frontline first-responder" in domestic emergencies and therefore "must be the lead military element with command and control authority."[14]

Governor Kathleen Babineaux Blanco of Louisiana, in her letter to the Commission, highlighted the lack of full-time manning for National Guard units, which she said hampers the ability to provide administrative support and equipment maintenance. She identified ongoing equipment shortages in the Louisiana National Guard, including Humvees, helicopters, medium and heavy tactical trucks, and generators, as a major concern. She noted that such equipment is vital to both federal and state service, and recommended that such requirements be fully funded.[15]

Beyond the input that individual governors have provided to the Commission expressing concern about the status of National Guard personnel and equipment, the National Governors Association (NGA) has written repeatedly to the Department of Defense and

---

[11] Governor Minner, prepared witness statement before the CNGR, Hearing on National Guard and Reserve Issues, June 15, 2006 (www.cngr.gov/hearing615/Minner.pdf), p. 3.
[12] Governor Pataki, prepared witness statement before the CNGR, Hearing on National Guard and Reserve Issues, June 15, 2006 (www.cngr.gov/hearing615/Pataki-CNGR%20testimony%20final.pdf), pp. 3–4, 6.
[13] Governor Rounds, letter to Arnold L. Punaro, Chairman, CNGR, April 3, 2006.
[14] Governor Lynch, letter to Arnold L. Punaro, Chairman, CNGR, May 17, 2006.
[15] Governor Blanco, letter to Arnold L. Punaro, Chairman, CNGR, March 30, 2006.

Congress concerning proposals that would affect the National Guard.[16] The NGA has stressed the need for the National Guard to be "properly equipped, efficiently trained, and fully staffed to meet its responsibilities." NGA representatives have called on the Secretary of Defense to "work with the nation's Governors in determining the future role of the Guard in homeland defense and other domestic missions."[17]

In a letter to the Commission dated January 26, 2007, the NGA urged that several fundamental principles guide efforts to enhance the National Guard: (1) the dual mission should be preserved and promoted, (2) the National Guard should receive training and equipment to handle both its state and federal missions, and (3) employers who support National Guard men and women should be supported—for example, through tax relief.[18]

In a letter dated February 5, 2007, to Senators Leahy and Bond, the NGA urged the repeal of Section 1076 of the National Defense Authorization Act (P.L. 109-364), which expanded the President's authority to federalize the National Guard during certain emergencies and disasters. The NGA complains that this portion of the NDAA was drafted "without consultation with governors and without full discussion or debate regarding the ramifications of such a change on domestic emergency response." They also express concern that the provision could cause confusion about who has primary responsibility during a domestic emergency.[19]

The volume, substance, and tenor of the communications between the state governors and the Commission, as well as other evidence, suggest that although consultation between Department of Defense officials and governors on matters related to the National Guard does occur, it is not sufficient.

Under current practice, the states provide input to the Department of Defense about issues affecting the National Guard primarily by communications from the state adjutants general to the Chief of the National Guard Bureau. Lieutenant General H Steven Blum, who, as Chief of the National Guard Bureau, serves as this primary channel of communication, testified that there is no formal mechanism through which governors can consult directly with senior civilian leadership in the Defense Department on matters related to the National Guard's state missions.[20] General Peter Pace, Chairman of the Joint Chiefs of Staff, also commented on the lack of any formal consultation process for governors.[21]

---

[16] National Governors Association, letter to Senators Bill Frist and Harry Reid and to Representatives J. Dennis Hastert and Nancy Pelosi, August 6, 2006. See also Public Law 109-364, *National Defense Authorization Act for Fiscal Year 2007*, October 17, 2006, §1076.

[17] Governor Mike Huckabee and Governor Janet Napolitano, National Governors Association, statement submitted for the record before the CNGR, Hearing on National Guard and Reserves (www.cngr.gov/hearing615/NGA--National%20Guard%20Commission%20Statement.pdf), June 15, 2006, pp. 2, 4.

[18] Governor Michael F. Easley and Governor Mark Sanford, Co-Leads on the National Guard, NGA, letter to Arnold L. Punaro, Chairman, CNGR, January 26, 2007.

[19] National Governors Association, letter to Senators Patrick Leahy and Christopher Bond, February 5, 2007; Lieutenant General H Steven Blum, Chief, National Guard Bureau, testified that this provision was evidence that the Department of Defense has not met governors "halfway" and that its passage "doesn't breed confidence and trust" between governors and DOD (testimony before the CNGR, Hearing on Proposed Changes to the National Guard, transcript of January 31, 2007, hearing [www.cngr.gov/hearing13107/0131cngr-1.pdf], p. 23).

[20] Lieutenant General Blum, testimony, transcript of January 31, 2007, hearing, pp. 23, 31.

[21] General Pace, testimony before the CNGR, Hearing on Proposed Changes to the National Guard, transcript of January 31, 2007, hearing (www.cngr.gov/hearing13107/0131cngr-3.pdf) p. 15.

The size of the Army and Air National Guard as a proportion of the total end-strength of the active and reserve components, and the increasing importance of the National Guard operationally for both overseas and homeland-related missions in today's security environment, means that decisions affecting the force have greater significance than ever before for both the Department of Defense and governors. This reality points to the need for a more formalized arrangement by which governors may interface with executive branch decision makers who ultimately make important decisions with direct implications for state governments.

> **Finding:** Governors do not have a formal mechanism to consult with the Department of Defense on decisions affecting the National Guard of their state, including how the National Guard is organized, manned, trained, equipped, and utilized.

Though not dispersed as extensively as the National Guard, active duty military and other reserve component units and personnel are also located in states and territories across the nation. Like the National Guard, these other federal military components, particularly the reserves, contain capabilities vital to civil support and emergency response, such as military police, chemical decontamination, transportation, and medical units.[22] In fact, General Peter J. Schoomaker, Chief of Staff for the Army, told the Commission that the Army Reserve is the nation's "first Title 10 responder" to disasters and emergencies, echoing the description of the National Guard as the nation's "first military responder."[23] The active components also have numerous capabilities useful in responses to a disaster.

However, unlike the National Guard, neither the federal military reserve units nor the federal active duty military units report to the state's governor; their chain of command ultimately goes to the President. Federal military components also differ from the National Guard because, except in limited circumstances, they respond to a disaster only as part of a federal civil support mission at the request of a lead federal agency, such as the Department of Homeland Security.[24]

Thus, in some scenarios two separate military forces—the state National Guard and the federal military—will be responding to the same disaster under two separate chains of command, one state and one federal. This was the case after Hurricane Katrina, when approximately 20,000 federal military personnel responded to the Gulf Coast commanded by federal military officers in a chain of command through NORTHCOM to the President. At the same time, some 50,000 National Guardsmen in state (Title 32) status deployed to the region pursuant to the Emergency Management Assistance Compact among the states.

---

[22] *Strategy for Homeland Defense and Civil Support*, p. 35.

[23] General Schoomaker, testimony before the Commission on the National Guard and Reserves, Hearing on Proposed Changes to the National Guard, transcript of December 14, 2006, hearing (www.cngr.gov/hearing121314/1214cngr-panel2.pdf), p. 6; Joint Chiefs of Staff, "Homeland Security," p. II-13.

[24] Lieutenant General John. A. Bradley, Chief, Air Force Reserve, and Commander, Air Force Reserve Command, prepared witness statement before the Commission on the National Guard and Reserves, hearing on National Guard and Reserves issues, July 19, 2006 (www.cngr.gov/July%2019/Bradley%20Testimony.doc), pp. 15–17.

One way to enhance the ability to achieve unity of effort in a domestic emergency response is through dual-hatted command. When officers are dual-hatted, they are able to command both Title 10 and Title 32 forces. They exercise command authority over their Title 10 forces in a line of command that runs from the forces, through the officer, and ultimately to the President. Simultaneously, they exercise command authority over their Title 32 forces in a line of command that runs from those forces, through the officer, and ultimately to the governor.

An effort was undertaken during the first week after Hurricane Katrina made landfall to appoint a dual-hatted commander in Louisiana, but these attempts failed. Paul McHale, the Assistant Secretary of Defense for Homeland Defense and America's Security Affairs, later testified that in his view, a dual-hat command—while appropriate for preplanned security events—was not a suitable mechanism to achieve the unity of effort necessary to effectively respond to a major disaster.[25]

According to Lieutenant General Blum, since Hurricane Katrina, every state and territory has established a Joint Force Headquarters, commanded by a National Guard officer, capable of acting as a Joint Interagency Task Force for the purpose of coordinating federal and state military and civilian agency disaster response efforts.[26] While these headquarters could provide the infrastructure to exercise unity of effort, DOD does not have policies, procedures, and plans in place to allow governors to exercise operational control over federal military assets within a state for emergency response purposes.

> **Finding:** There is no established process whereby governors can have operational control over federal military assets within a state to respond to emergencies.

The American people fully expect that all military forces that are available and can help respond to a disaster will do so without unnecessary delays. In time of need, the public, who pays for the military and whom our armed services are pledged to serve, does not care whether the military personnel who come to their aid are active duty or from the National Guard or Reserves.

Conclusion: The priorities of the states and their governors are not adequately considered in the Department of Defense's policy and resourcing decisions related to the National Guard, even though governors are, and likely will continue to be, the leaders of most domestic emergency response efforts involving the National Guard.

---

[25] Assistant Secretary McHale, testimony before the U.S. Senate, Committee on Homeland Security and Governmental Affairs, hearing on Hurricane Katrina and the Defense Department Response, February 9, 2006.
[26] Lieutenant General Blum, testimony before the CNGR, transcript of January 31, 2007, hearing, pp. 43–44.

Recommendation:

6. Congress should establish a bipartisan Council of Governors composed of 10 governors, with bipartisan co-chairs, appointed by the President in consultation with the National Governors Association, to meet and advise the Secretary of Defense, the Secretary of Homeland Security, and the White House Homeland Security Council on matters related to the National Guard and civil support missions. The Council should meet at least semiannually or as otherwise requested by the Secretary of Defense and the Secretary of Homeland Security or the co-chairs.

The Commission's recommendation to create the Council of Governors on the National Guard was undertaken with one overarching goal in mind—to establish a formal and permanent channel of communication through which governors could regularly provide direct input concerning National Guard–related issues, particularly those involving the homeland, to the highest levels of the executive branch.

Outside advice to the Secretaries and the President from governors who have experience with and knowledge of the National Guard, particularly in its state role, should lead to better-informed decisions about the range of National Guard issues that have ramifications for the states. With respect to the Department of Defense, the existence of the Council of Governors should provide the Secretary with a convenient forum through which to receive advice. It also would make governors aware of pending matters affecting the National Guard and the other reserve components, so that claims of surprise and lack of consultation by state authorities in the wake of the public announcement of controversial decisions, including ones related to resourcing and budgeting, should be minimized—itself an important goal to foster public trust.

With respect to the Department of Homeland Security, the Commission believes the Council of Governors would provide a convenient way to inform governors about changes to the National Response Plan and to integrate them into the planning process as necessary. Similarly, the Council of Governors should provide the Homeland Security Council with a convenient, situationally available sounding board as that body pursues the development and implementation of homeland security policies.

The Council of Governors would be modeled structurally after similar high-level advisory bodies, such as the Defense Science Board and Defense Business Board. However, in recognition of the fact that there are 54 state and territorial governors and of their significant responsibilities, the Commission recommends that only 10 governors, no more than 5 of whom should be from the same political party, be appointed to serve on the Council of Governors.

The Commission recommends that the President be responsible for appointing governors to serve on the Council of Governors on the National Guard, in consultation with the National Governors Association. The Commission further recommends that co-chairmen, one from each major political party, be selected by the President. Terms of service would be for two years, but serving governors could be reappointed to additional terms. The Commission recommends that the council meet with the Secretaries of Defense and Homeland Security at least semiannually, more frequently as necessary, subject to the call of either departmental Secretary or the chairmen of the council. The Commission recommends that the Council of Governors meet with the Homeland Security Council at the invitation of the President (who chairs the Homeland Security Council) or at the request of both co-chairs of the Council of Governors. The Commission recommends that the Council of Governors be exempt from the Federal Advisory Committee Act.

The Commission views the Council of Governors as an effective way to give the states, through a representative set of their chief executives, a truly meaningful venue through which to tell the senior leadership of the executive branch about issues of concern related to the National Guard.

Recommendation:

> **7. Laws and procedures should be put into place to enable the President of the United States and a governor to consent in advance that National Guard officers called to federal duty are not relieved of their National Guard state commission, can continue to command National Guard troops, and are exempt from the provisions of the Posse Comitatus Act.**

Presently, a National Guard service member is relieved of duty in the National Guard whenever the service member is placed on Title 10 active duty, except when (1) the service member is an officer, (2) the officer is a commander of a National Guard unit, (3) the President authorizes such service in both duty statuses, and (4) the state or territorial governor consents.[27] DOD has not issued directives or instructions concerning the section of law implementing such "dual-hatting." It has been employed in a few limited instances, such as national political conventions, preplanned security events, and the stand-up of the Joint Surveillance Target Attack Radar System, a mixed active component–National Guard Air Force unit.

The National Defense Authorization Act for Fiscal Year 2007 (Public Law 109-364) requires the Commission to examine the advisability and feasibility of implementing the provisions of section 544 of H.R. 5122, as passed by the House of Representatives in May 2006, which would expand the circumstances in which National Guard officers who have been ordered to active duty may continue to simultaneously perform National Guard duties.

Section 544 would change the law so that any National Guard officer, not just a commander, may remain on duty in the National Guard while serving on federal active duty. Section 544 also would permit the President and the state or territorial governor to give the authorization and consent *in advance* of calling the officer to active duty to allow for the smooth succession of command. Finally, §544 would allow all National Guard officers on federal active duty, not just commanders, to perform any duty authorized by the laws of that officer's state without regard to the Posse Comitatus Act's prohibitions against participation in civilian law enforcement activities.

The Commission recommends that Congress approve the changes made by §544 subject to the following conditions. First, to the extent possible, state and federal authorities should

---

[27] 32 U.S.C. §325.

agree in advance under what circumstances the dual-hatted National Guard officers will be acting under Title 10 authority versus under state authority in carrying out their mission. Second, provision should be made regarding which authority, state or federal, will ordinarily exercise primary military justice jurisdiction. Third, the source of funding should be clear in advance of the activation. Fourth, some mechanism should be in place to account for special pays, promotion eligibility, health care entitlements, and other emoluments of service that may vary according to whether the person is in a state or federal duty status. Finally, it should be clear under what terms consent for the dual status may be withdrawn by federal or state officials.

These changes are consistent with the increasing operational use of the National Guard. As more National Guard units are mobilized and deployed for operational missions, as active and reserve component personnel and units are commingled to meet operational exigencies, and as they operate in mutually supportive state and federal roles in homeland defense and civil support missions, it makes sense to increase the ability and ease with which National Guard officers may command units and operations composed of active component and National Guard personnel.

Recommendation:

8. **As part of Department of Defense efforts to develop plans for consequence management and support to civil authorities that account for state-level activities and incorporate the use of National Guard and Reserve forces as first military responders (see Recommendation 19), the Department of Defense should develop protocols that allow governors to direct the efforts of federal military assets responding to an emergency such as a natural disaster.**

The guiding principle of emergency management doctrine in the United States is that problems should be solved at the lowest level possible. Therefore, unless their use would compromise national security, all military resources that may be needed to respond to a contingency—whether National Guard (in state active duty of Title 32) or active duty or reserve (in Title 10), and whether within the state or in another state—should be included in the state's emergency response planning. As part of that planning, federal and state authorities should develop policies and procedures regarding the nature of the command relationship under which the troops will operate during particular contingencies. These agreements should be entered into before the crisis, rather than in an ad hoc manner while lives and property are at stake—as happened after Hurricane Katrina.

This recommendation requires no changes to existing statutes. Current military doctrine explicitly allows members of the United States armed forces to serve under the operational control of foreign commanders, with the President retaining ultimate command over U.S. forces.[28] If the command relationship with the President can be maintained while American troops are operating under the control of foreign commanders, we see no

---

[28] "In all multinational operations, even when operating under the operational control (OPCON) of a foreign commander, US commanders will maintain the capability to report separately to higher US military authorities in addition to foreign commanders" (Joint Chiefs of Staff, "Joint Operations," Joint Publication 3-0, September 16, 2006, p. II-5).

convincing reason why it cannot be maintained while troops are under the control of a state governor acting through the adjutant general. Governors routinely command National Guard troops from another state in a disaster response. Again, if governors can be trusted to command National Guard soldiers from their own state or from other states, as customarily occurs in disaster response, then they can be trusted to command federal active and reserve component forces as well.

The assignment of active duty personnel to Title 32 National Guard commands is not novel. Federal law specifically authorizes that both enlisted members and commissioned officers may be detailed for duty with a state National Guard.[29] In fact, Title 10 officers detailed in this fashion may accept a commission in the National Guard.[30] Federal forces under the control of a governor would still be subject to the same restrictions placed on the Title 10 military, such as Posse Comitatus law enforcement restrictions.

We are not suggesting that it is necessary for federal military forces to be involved in a response under all circumstances or for all disasters. However, when federal military capabilities are needed to respond to an emergency, their involvement should not alter the fundamental approach to emergency management. The fact that a particular capability needed for the response resides in a federal active duty or reserve unit should not be an impediment to its use to preserve life or property. In most instances, such federal military forces should operate under the direction of state officials.

One way to accomplish such an operation is through the use of dual-hatted commanders, who simultaneously hold ranks in the state National Guard and the federal, Title 10 military. They are therefore able to command both federal and state forces simultaneously.[31] The Commission finds that dual-hatting has been a useful tool in coordinating federal and state civil support missions and, as discussed above, suggests that it be expanded for use in appropriate circumstances.

But dual-hatted command is not a panacea for coordinating federal and state military capabilities in civil support activities. As long as there are two chains of command passing through that one commander—one from the President and one from the governor—there is the potential for confusion and conflict. This reality makes it imperative that state and federal authorities agree in advance about the full range of circumstances under which federal forces would be subject to state control.

Therefore, state and federal officials should plan cooperatively for those situations where federal forces could be under the direction of a governor. This planning requires resolving a number of issues, such as who pays for the use of federal assets in a response and what is the precise nature of the command relationship.

Since the President exercises ultimate federal command authority over federal troops,[32] Title 10 forces cannot be formally turned over to a governor in all respects. However, there are established command relationships that would allow the National Guard officer to

---

[29] 32 U.S.C. §315.
[30] 32 U.S.C. §315.
[31] Joint Chiefs of Staff, "Homeland Security," Joint Publication 3-26, August 2, 2005, p. II-9.
[32] Joint Chiefs of Staff, "Unified Action Armed Forces (UNAAF)," Joint Publication 0-2, July 10, 2001, p. xv.

"command" Title 10 troops with the consent of both the President and the governor. If the President, or the President's designee,[33] agrees to do this, an order would be issued placing the Title 10 forces under the operational or tactical control of the governor.

In a temporary situation such as a disaster response, a military organization could be "attached" to another organization for "operational" or "tactical" purposes, with "administrative control," including disciplinary authority, being retained by the parent organization. Such divisions between operational, tactical, and administrative control are commonplace in the military operating environment. If a Title 32 commander were exercising control over Title 10 forces, this division of authority would avoid having the Title 32 commander exercise disciplinary (Uniform Code of Military Justice) authority over his or her Title 10 subordinates.

Thus, as part of emergency preparedness and response planning efforts, DOD should develop protocols that allow governors to direct the efforts of federal military assets responding to an emergency such as a natural disaster.

---

[33] 3 U.S.C. §301.

C. THE NATIONAL GUARD BUREAU

HISTORY

The constitutional basis for the modern militia system is found in Article I, section 8, of the U.S. Constitution:

> The Congress shall have the power...
>
> [clause 15] To provide for calling forth the Militia to execute the Laws of the Union, suppress Insurrections and repel Invasions;
>
> [clause 16] To provide for organizing, arming, and disciplining, the Militia and for governing such Part of them as may be employed in the Service of the United States, reserving to the States respectively, the Appointment of Officers, and the Authority of training the Militia according to the discipline prescribed by Congress[.]

In the Federal Militia Act of 1792, Congress attempted to codify a national policy regarding the militia. This act established a continuing military census to provide ready reserves that could be called into federal service if the need arose. The law created a uniform age of military obligation and presumed the arrangement of the state militias into organized units.[1] Previously, these militias had operated under the states' complete control.

For more than 100 years the minimalist Militia Act of 1792 governed how the militia was organized. But the emergence of organized reserves as a part of modern warfare in Europe during the second half of the 19th century created pressure for change. The modern National Guard arguably began in 1903 with the passage by Congress of the Militia Act.[2]

The Militia Act divided the class of able-bodied male citizens between the ages of 18 and 45 into an "organized militia," to be known as the National Guard of the several states, and the "reserve militia," which later statutes have termed the "unorganized militia."[3] This law further required the National Guard to conform to the regular Army organizationally and provided that federal funds and regular Army instructors should be used to train its members. In effect, this legislation made the National Guard the reserve component of the Army.

The National Defense Act of 1916 continued the process of increasing federal control over the National Guard. This law required National Guard members to take an oath to the President (as well as to the governor) and provided for more detailed federal regulation and oversight of the state Guards. Section 81 of this law established a Militia Bureau of the War Department under the supervision of the Secretary of War.[4] The National Defense Act of

---

[1] Second Cong., 1st sess. (May 8, 1792), Chapter 33, §1.
[2] The Militia Act of 1903 (57th Cong., 2nd sess. [January 21, 1903], Chapter 196, §3) is commonly known as the Dick Act; it was repealed in 1956.
[3] *Perpich v. Department of Defense*, 496 U.S. 334, 342 n. 11 (1990).
[4] 64th Cong., 1st sess. (June 3, 1916), Chapter 134, §81.

1933 renamed the Militia Bureau the National Guard Bureau (NGB) and laid out the qualifications for the position of its Chief.[5]

Following World War II, Congress passed the National Security Act of 1947. This law abolished the War Department and created the Departments of the Army, Navy, and Air Force. In addition, the act made the National Guard Bureau a joint bureau of the Army and Air Force. The National Guard Bureau was assigned the responsibility of being the channel of communication between these two departments and the several states on matters pertaining to the National Guard.[6] Thus, the National Guard Bureau owes much of its current configuration and responsibilities to this law. Today it remains a joint bureau of the Army and Air Force.[7]

THE NATIONAL GUARD BUREAU'S EVOLVING ROLE

The National Guard Bureau's current responsibilities are contained in its charter, and the contours of the charter are dictated in large measure by statute. Under the Reserve Officers Personnel Management Act (ROPMA) of 1994, the National Guard Bureau Charter is written jointly by the Secretary of the Army and Secretary of the Air Force.[8] Among its key statutory duties defined in 10 U.S.C. §10503 are the responsibility to allocate unit structure, strength authorizations, and resources to the Army and Air National Guard; to prescribe training discipline and requirements; to monitor and assist the states in the organization, maintenance, and operation of National Guard units; to plan and administer the National Guard budget; and to supervise the acquisition, supply, and accounting of federal property issued to the National Guard.[9]

The National Guard Bureau is neither a reserve component nor an operational command. Its chief missions are to participate in the formulation, development, and coordination of programs, policies, and plans pertaining to the Army and Air National Guard; to develop and administer certain operating programs based on guidance from the Army and Air Force; and to participate with and assist the states in the organization, maintenance, and operation of their National Guard units so as to provide trained and equipped units available for service to augment the active Army and Air Force in time of war or emergency.[10]

With the advent of the global war on terror, the NGB has assumed increased responsibilities for domestic homeland-related missions in the wake of the terrorist attacks of September 11, 2001, the NGB coordinated the deployment of 11,000 members of the Army and Air National Guard to assist law enforcement and other federal agencies in securing more than 440 of America's commercial airports.[11]

---

[5] 73rd Cong., 1st sess. (June 15, 1933), Chap. 87, §81.

[6] 80th Cong., 1st sess. (July 26, 1947); see especially Chap. 343, §207.

[7] 10 U.S.C. §10501.

[8] National Guard Bureau Charter, September 1, 1995; reprinted in Appendix 5, below.

[9] 10 U.S.C. §10503(1)–(6).

[10] National Guard Bureau Charter.

[11] Lieutenant General H Steven Blum, Chief, National Guard Bureau, prepared statement before the CNGB, Hearing on Proposed Changes to the National Guard, January 31, 2007 (www.cngr.gov/hearing13107/CNGB%20testimony%20to%20Commission%2031%20Jan%20Record.pdf), p. 5.

Today the NGB provides liaison with every governor—each a state or territorial commander in chief; coordinates National Guard domestic emergency response, homeland defense, and support to homeland security operations nationwide; supports combatant commanders, including the regional combatant commanders, through 54 state partnership programs; administers 54 Joint Force Headquarters, one for each state and territory; and manages the readiness and resourcing of the Army and Air National Guard for the federal Title 10 warfighting mission.[12] The National Guard Bureau also is implementing pilot programs to strengthen the National Guard's ability to respond to events involving weapons of mass destruction and to protect critical infrastructure.[13]

As Lieutenant General H Steven Blum testified before the Commission,

> In the post-9/11 environment, such operations have increased markedly both by States unilaterally and by the increased use of the National Guard in unified state/federal missions like the airport security, G-8 summit, Winter Olympics, Hurricane Katrina response, border security and other domestic operations. The resounding success of these operations in the American homeland has been and will continue to be heavily dependent upon the unique experience of the National Guard in working effectively with elected civilian leaders during emergencies inside the United States— a highly sensitive and politically charged atmosphere. This is the unique and important role of the Chief of the National Guard Bureau in the security environment of America today.[14]

The Chief of the National Guard Bureau possesses detailed knowledge of the status and capabilities of National Guard forces in the states. As noted by Lieutenant General Blum, the National Guard Bureau became the de facto force provider for National Guard forces in the response to Hurricane Katrina and contributed very positively to the overall military response, albeit in a somewhat ad hoc fashion. More than 50,000 Army and Air National Guard troops deployed to Louisiana, Mississippi, Alabama, and Texas.[15]

More recently, the National Guard was directed to assist the U.S. Customs and Border Patrol in "Operation Jump Start." Since June 2006, the NGB has organized the deployment of approximately 6,000 Army and Air National Guard personnel in operations along America's southwest border.[16] The operation once again demonstrates the important role of the NGB in facilitating an interagency response to homeland security requirements.

The increased use of the National Guard for diverse homeland-related operations is likely to continue in the future.[17] However, as discussed earlier in our report, it is difficult to assess

---

[12] Lieutenant General Blum, letter to the Major General Arnold L. Punaro, USMC (ret.), Chairman, CNGR, November 30, 2006, pp. 1–2, 4, 5.

[13] GAO, *Reserve Forces: Actions Needed to Better Prepare the National Guard for Future Overseas and Domestic Missions*, GAO-05-21 (Report to the Chairman, Committee on Government Reform, and Chairman, Subcommittee on National Security, Emerging Threats and International Relations, House of Representatives) November 2004, pp. 27–28.

[14] Lieutenant General Blum, letter to Chairman Punaro, pp. 4–5.

[15] Lieutenant General Blum, prepared statement, p. 8.

[16] Lieutenant General Blum, prepared statement, p. 11.

[17] John J. Hamre and Christine E. Wormuth, Center for Strategic and International Studies, letter to Major General Arnold L. Punaro, USMC (ret.), Chairman, CNGR, December 14, 2006, Attachment A, pp. 2–3.

the National Guard's preparedness to perform future homeland defense and civil support missions because its role in these capacities has not been fully defined, requirements have not been identified, and standards have not been developed against which to measure preparedness.[18]

> **Finding:** Since September 11, 2001, the National Guard Bureau has assumed increased responsibilities for homeland-related missions. This trend will continue in the future.

> **Finding:** The global war against terrorism has placed increased demands on and created new missions for the National Guard to provide forces for both overseas and domestic missions.

In performing its many functions, the National Guard Bureau has maintained informal lines of communication with the offices of the Secretary of Defense, the Joint Staff, and combatant commands such as U.S. Northern Command (NORTHCOM) and Joint Forces Command (JFCOM).[19] However, the existing National Guard Bureau Charter does not formally establish these additional relationships and coordinating responsibilities, which have taken on a substantial proportion of the NGB's time and resources. As a result, and because of other factors described earlier, the current organizational configuration of the NGB is outdated and incomplete.

At the Commission's hearing on January 31, 2007, Lieutenant General Blum explained that the last major change to the National Guard Bureau's charter took place in 1947. Since that time, the Bureau has adapted to changes brought on by major reforms in the Department of Defense, such as the Goldwater-Nichols Department of Defense Reorganization Act of 1986, as well as to the major historical events that have affected the government and the entire country, such as the collapse of the Soviet Union and the terrorist attacks of September 11, 2001.[20]

It is widely known that substantial numbers of National Guard units and personnel have deployed to and continue to serve in Operations Iraqi Freedom and Enduring Freedom. It is also beyond question that the National Guard's homeland-related missions are assuming increasing importance.

Department of Homeland Security Under Secretary for Preparedness George W. Foresman testified before the Commission that "the nature of the asymmetric threat in the 21st century means that we need to have a better capability for protection and prevention missions here at home, missions that can be carried out by the National Guard in support of the civilian community."[21] However, the National Guard Bureau has no formal relation-

---

[18] GAO, *Reserve Forces*, p. 20.

[19] Memorandum for the Record, meeting with the National Guard Bureau staff, October 23, 2006.

[20] Lieutenant General H. Steven Blum, Chief, National Guard Bureau, testimony before the CNGB, Hearing on Proposed Changes to the National Guard, transcript of January 31, 2007, hearing (www.cngr.gov/hearing13107/0131cngr-1.pdf), p. 13.

[21] Under Secretary Foresman, prepared statement before the CNGR, Hearing on Proposed Changes to the National Guard, December 13, 2006 (http://www.cngr.gov/hearing121314/13DecForesmanCNGRTestimonyFINAL%5B1%5D.pdf), p. 3.

ship in law or in charter with the Department of Homeland Security (DHS). Similarly, state and local emergency first responders would like to see improved coordination between federal agencies in meeting homeland security requirements. As Chuck McHugh, the Director of the Arizona Emergency Management Agency, explained to the Commission, when it comes to civilian emergency response working with military assets, "It's all about relationships."[22] The Commission believes that these interactions must be established on a more formal basis to improve cooperation and accountability.

The White House concluded in its 2006 report on the federal response to Hurricane Katrina that the National Guard Bureau needs a defined role in the realm of homeland security; it also concluded that the Department of Defense should ensure that the National Guard focuses on increasing its integration with active duty forces for homeland security plans and activities.[23] The Commission agrees.

> **Finding:** Under its current structure, the National Guard Bureau is not optimized to communicate, collaborate, and coordinate with U.S. Northern Command, the Joint Directorate of Military Support, Joint Forces Command, and the Department of Homeland Security with regard to homeland defense and domestic civil support missions.

> **Finding:** National Guard forces are no longer the Cold War strategic reserve they were when the National Guard Bureau was established. The joint bureau structure of the National Guard Bureau is not sufficiently flexible to adjust to their increased use for domestic and overseas missions.

> **Finding:** The Chief of the National Guard Bureau's detailed understanding of the status and capabilities of National Guard forces would best be utilized by better integrating the Chief and the National Guard Bureau into the workings of U.S. Northern Command, the joint command in charge of most Title 10 homeland defense and civil support activities.

Conclusion: The National Guard Bureau and other elements of the Department of Defense are not properly structured to fully integrate the National Guard into domestic contingency planning, training, exercising, and operations.

---

[22] Chuck McHugh, prepared statement before the CNGR, Hearing on National Guard and Reserve Issues, September 20, 2006 (www.cngr.gov/hearing918-21/McHugh%20CNGR%20Hearing.pdf), p. 1.
[23] *The Federal Response to Hurricane Katrina: Lessons Learned* ([Washington, DC: The White House,] 2006), p. 55.

Recommendation:

> **9.** **The National Guard Bureau should be made a joint activity of the Department of Defense, rather than a joint bureau of the Army and Air Force. This designation should not change the National Guard Bureau's relationship with the Army and Air Force related to Title 10 matters and planning and budgeting for Title 32 mission requirements.**

The Commission researched the organizational, structural, and policy consequences of designating the National Guard Bureau a joint activity of the Department of Defense. No publication or package of authorities describes how to form or design a joint activity, and there is no such formal designation within the Department. Nevertheless, when the term *joint activity* appears, it mainly refers to an organization involving two or more services. Given that the National Guard Bureau routinely interacts not only with two services—chiefly the Army and Air Force—but with a variety of unified commands, the Joint Staff, and the Office of the Secretary of Defense, the National Guard Bureau is a joint activity of the Department of Defense.

Except to the extent discussed below, the Commission does not recommend that designating the National Guard Bureau a joint activity should result in any change in the day-to-day relationship between the Chief of the National Guard Bureau and the Secretaries of the Army and Air Force. However, the Commission recognizes that if this recommendation is adopted, then the process for nominating and selecting the Chief of the National Guard Bureau (CNGB) may likewise need to be modified.

Recommendation:

> **10.** **The statute authorizing the National Guard Bureau Charter should be amended to make the Chief of the National Guard Bureau a senior advisor to the Chairman of the Joint Chiefs of Staff and, through the Chairman, to the Secretary of Defense, for matters pertaining to the National Guard in its nonfederal role. The charter also should be revised to create an advisory relationship between the Chief of the National Guard Bureau and the commanders of the combatant commands for the United States, and between the Chief of the National Guard Bureau and the Department of Homeland Security.**

This recommendation recognizes the increasing importance of the Department of Defense's role in homeland security and homeland defense. Currently, notwithstanding the position of the White House and the Department's own homeland defense strategy,[24] the Department does not adequately make civil support a high-priority mission or resource the reserve components for civil support missions.[25] The Chief of the National Guard Bureau could

---

[24] *The Federal Response to Hurricane Katrina: Lessons Learned*, Appendix A, Recommendations 24 and 27; *Strategy for Homeland Defense and Civil Support* ([Washington, DC: Department of Defense,] 2005), p. 35.

[25] General Peter J. Schoomaker, Chief of Staff, U.S. Army, testimony before the CNGR, Hearing on the Proposed Changes to the National Guard, transcript of the December 14, 2006, hearing (www.cngr.gov/hearing121314/1214cngr-panel2.pd), pp. 24–25. See also GAO, *Hurricane Katrina: Better Plans and Exercises Needed to Guide Military's Response to Catastrophic Natural Disasters*, GAO-06-643 (Statement for the Record to

provide the Chairman and the Secretary valuable advice across a broad spectrum of issues related to the use of non-federalized National Guard forces in these missions. The Commission notes that during its recent hearing, General Peter Pace, Chairman of the Joint Chiefs of Staff, testified that he believes an advisory relationship like that proposed by the Commission is needed and would be beneficial to him in his role as Chairman.[26]

This proposal also recognizes that the Army and Air National Guard's role in responding to domestic contingencies necessarily requires extensive interaction with other organizations within the Department of Defense, particularly U.S. Northern Command and Joint Forces Command, and with DHS, as well as with state and local authorities. Making the Chief of the National Guard Bureau a senior advisor to the Chairman of the Joint Chiefs of Staff for nonfederal National Guard matters would expand access to the CNGB's expertise, would maintain direct reporting, and would mitigate the difficulties inherent in the current structure, which requires the CNGB to work through Army and Air Force channels. The proposed change to the National Guard Bureau's charter would complement the steps taken by the Department of Defense in moving the office of the Director of Military Support to the Joint Staff. This proposal would create a formal mechanism by which the Chief of the National Guard Bureau could provide input to both the Chairman and to the Joint Staff with respect to the National Guard's ability to support homeland-related operational requirements. It would also encourage greater unity of effort between U.S. Northern Command, DHS, and the National Guard units that are employed in responding to domestic contingencies. In the Commission's judgment, this recommendation has the potential to achieve greater efficiency and better advice about the National Guard than the Chairman and Secretary receive under the current organizational construct.

Recommendation:

> **11. The statute authorizing the National Guard Bureau Charter should be amended to include the Bureau's responsibility for "Facilitating and coordinating with other Federal agencies, Combatant Commands, and with the several States on the use of the National Guard not in active Federal service," and other such changes as necessary to implement the spirit and letter of the Commission's recommendations. The National Guard Bureau should not become an operational command.**

The Commission recommends amending the statute authorizing the National Guard Bureau charter to include responsibility for facilitation and coordination with federal agencies, the states, U.S. Northern Command, and Joint Forces Command on the use of nonfederalized National Guard forces for domestic contingency operations, support to civil authorities, and other homeland activities. Although the Commission does not believe that the National Guard Bureau should become an operational command, the Commission believes that it should assign cells of personnel to DHS, NORTHCOM, and JFCOM to assist in operational planning. This recommendation is consistent with the view that a more

---

the Subcommittee on Terrorism, Unconventional Threats and Capabilities, Committee on Armed Services, House of Representatives), May 25, 2006, p. 16.

[26] General Pace, testimony before the CNGR, Hearing on Proposed Changes to the National Guard, transcript of January 31, 2007, hearing (http://www.cngr.gov/hearing13107/0131cngr-3.pdf), p. 11.

integrated relationship between the NGB and these other organizations is necessary in order to ensure better unity of effort in responding to homeland-related contingencies.

The Commission believes that the National Guard Bureau should continue to report to and work with the Secretaries and Chiefs of Staff of the Army and Air Force to facilitate and coordinate the use of National Guard units operating in active federal service under Title 10. Under the Commission's proposal, the National Guard Bureau would still retain its responsibilities to the Army and the Air Force in coordinating the use of national guardsmen when federalized.

Recommendation:

> **12. Immediately after enactment of the statutory changes suggested above, the Secretary of Defense should draft a new charter for the National Guard Bureau, in consultation with the Secretaries of the Army and Air Force and the Chairman of the Joint Chiefs of Staff, reflecting the statutory changes suggested in Recommendations 10 and 11; the charter should be reviewed periodically to ensure that it is updated appropriately.**

The current National Guard Bureau Charter does not reflect some of the key roles and responsibilities that are now within the purview of the National Guard Bureau. For example, the current charter does not reflect the role of the NGB in coordinating the National Guard's activities in drug interdiction, airport security, border security, the State Partnership Program, humanitarian operations, and various homeland security activities. It also does not take into consideration the existence of new unified commands like U.S. Northern Command and new offices such as the Assistant Secretary of Defense for Homeland Defense and America's Security Affairs. The current charter is simply out of date.

The Commission concludes that the National Guard Bureau Charter should reflect the actual and significant responsibilities of the organization. In particular, it is important that the charter speak to the new roles of the National Guard Bureau in the realm of homeland security and to the Chief of the National Guard Bureau's new advisory duties to the Secretary and the Chairman of the Joint Chiefs of Staff. Because many of these responsibilities involve the National Guard's use in its nonfederal status, the Commission believes that the Secretary of Defense, rather than the Secretaries of the Army and Air Force, should have the primary duty to draft an updated charter for the National Guard Bureau.

The Commission concurs with the views on H.R. 5200 and S. 2658 of Lieutenant General Blum, who wrote to the Commission that "it is desirable and should be feasible for a charter to be promulgated by the Secretary of Defense so long as the needs of the two Services remain fully incorporated in the document."[27] The Commission shares this sentiment and also believes the charter should be subject to periodic review to ensure that it is current with Defense Department policy, strategy, requirements, and planning documents.

---

[27] Lieutenant General Blum, letter to Chairman Punaro, p. 6.

Recommendation:

13. The grade of the Chief of the National Guard Bureau should be increased to general, O-10, and the position should be reevaluated periodically to ensure that the duties required to be performed by the CNGB remain commensurate with grade O-10.

The Commission recommends increasing the grade of the Chief of the National Guard Bureau to general based on the changing and expanding responsibilities of the position in this time of war, both those enumerated in the current National Guard Bureau statute and charter and the numerous other duties which should be and are performed but which are not described in the statute or charter. Included among the required responsibilities not in the current statute or charter are a formal relationship between the CNGB and the Joint Staff, the Office of the Secretary of Defense, the unified commands, and other federal agencies on nonfederalized National Guard matters, including planning and coordinating the use of National Guard forces in homeland-related operations and exercises. We base this recommendation on careful analysis of the magnitude and complexity of the combined duties and responsibilities required to be performed, and the significance of the decisions made, by the Chief of the National Guard Bureau.

The duties and responsibilities of the Chief of the National Guard Bureau are not comparable to those of combatant commanders who exercise operational command authority over large numbers of personnel in major geographic areas. Nor are they directly comparable to the duties of the service Chiefs who, with their service Secretaries, are responsible for large budgets and hold ultimate responsibility to organize, man, train, and equip their service members under Title 10.[28]

The Chief of the National Guard Bureau does, however, perform service-chief-like duties simultaneously for the National Guard components of two separate services, a complex task. The CNGB is also the primary liaison between the Department of Defense and governors and adjutants general of all 54 states and territories. These state officials look to the CNGB for guidance about the resources, training, and equipment for their National Guard. In addition, the CNGB serves as the conduit for information from them to DOD officials in the planning, programming, and budgeting processes.

Both the Government Accountability Office and the Federal Research Division of the Library of Congress have examined the requirements associated with general officer positions. The GAO identified 16 different factors used to validate general and flag officer requirements, including the grade and position of superiors and subordinates; the type, scope, and level of function; relations with U.S. and foreign government officials and with the public; the number, type, and value of resources managed; geographical area of responsibility; authority to make decisions and commit resources; the development of policy; and the effect on the prestige of the nation or the armed forces.[29] Similarly, the Federal Research Division analyzed the numbers and typical duties of three- and four-star billets. This study noted that neither the Chairman nor the Joint Chiefs of Staff, whether as

---

[28] See 10 U.S.C. §3033 (for Army Chief of Staff); §8033 (for USAF Chief of Staff).
[29] GAO, *Military Personnel: General and Flag Officer Requirements Are Unclear Based on DOD's 2003 Report to Congress*, GAO-04-488 (Report to Congressional Committees), April 2004, pp. 29–31.

a collective body or as individual service Chiefs, have any command authority over combatant forces. Other four-star positions were assessed in terms of functional responsibilities, complexity of the position, and dual roles.[30] The Commission's review of these studies, including the criteria enumerated in the GAO study in combination with the required responsibilities of the Chief of the National Guard Bureau, supports the conclusion that the position should carry the grade of general.

The Commission agrees with the position of the Chairman of the Joint Chiefs of Staff, expressed during his recent testimony before the Commission, that when the required duties of a general officer equate to those of an O-10, then the position should be so designated.[31] The Commission concludes, based on the duties that the Chief of the National Guard Bureau is required to perform, that the position should be designated an O-10 billet. The Commission recommends that the position of CNGB should be reviewed periodically to ensure that the duties required to be performed remain commensurate with grade of O-10. Furthermore, the Commission recommends that the official qualifications for the position of Chief of the National Guard Bureau reflect the level of experience, expertise, skills, and stature commensurate with the post.

Recommendation:

14. The Chief of the National Guard Bureau should not be a member of the Joint Chiefs of Staff.

The Commission does not recommend that the Chief of the National Guard Bureau be a member of the Joint Chiefs of Staff, on the grounds that the duties of the members of the Joint Chiefs of Staff are greater than those of the Chief of the National Guard Bureau. For example, the Chief of the National Guard Bureau is not responsible for organizing, manning, training, and equipping the National Guard to the same extent as are the service Chiefs of Staff. The qualifications to be selected as a service Chief of Staff also are materially different from and more rigorous than those for selection to be Chief of the National Guard Bureau. Moreover, making the Chief of the National Guard Bureau a member of the Joint Chiefs of Staff would run counter to intra- and inter-service integration and would reverse progress toward jointness and interoperability: making the Chief of the National Guard Bureau a member of the Joint Chiefs of Staff would be fundamentally inconsistent with the status of the Army and Air National Guard as reserve components of the Army and Air Force. Finally, the Commission concludes that this proposal would be counter to the carefully crafted organizational and advisory principles established in the Goldwater-Nichols legislation.

The Commission notes that Lieutenant General Blum, the sitting Chief of the National Guard Bureau, wrote to the Commission: "In practice, the fact that my position is not on the Joint Chiefs of Staff has in no way hindered me from responding to the President's or to the Secretary of Defense's requests for advice....An advisory role [to the JCS] limited to those periods when the Joint Chiefs are deliberating on matters related to the domestic employment of the National Guard under state command for emergencies, homeland

---

[30] Priscilla Offenhauer, "Increasing the Rank of the Chief of the National Guard Bureau," Federal Research Division, Library of Congress (February 2007), pp. 2, 3.
[31] General Pace, transcript of testimony before the CNGR, January 31, 2007, pp. 6–7.

defense and support for homeland security operations and other National Guard–specific matters, might be a more practical and appropriate reform."[32]

Department of Defense civilian and military leaders have recommended against placing the CNGB on the JCS. When asked about this issue by members of Congress, Deputy Secretary of Defense Gordon England said, "I believe it is a negative effect, rather than a positive effect. Organizationally, I think it sounds good, but it is not a good integrating approach."[33] In his testimony before the Commission, General Pace concurred: "We spent 20-plus years, first kicking and dragging our feet and then embracing jointness, as directed by the Goldwater-Nichols Act, all to get one Army, one Navy, one Air Force, one Marine Corps, one Joint Force. If you make this individual a member of the Joint Chiefs, you create two Armies and two Air Forces. You're going absolutely 100 percent counter to the thrust of Goldwater-Nichols and you will do major damage to the synergy we've gotten."[34]

John J. Hamre and Christine Wormuth of the Center for Strategic and International Studies informed the Commission: "The Chief of the National Guard Bureau should not be made a member of the Joint Chiefs of Staff....Elevating the Chief, NGB to the Joint Chiefs...[would] risk sending the message that the National Guard is a separate military service, and it is not. If implemented,...[this] could undermine efforts to further integrate the National Guard, particularly the Army Guard, into the Army and Air Force and exacerbate longstanding AC-RC cultural tensions."[35] The Commission concurs and therefore recommends against this provision of the National Guard Empowerment Act.

Recommendation:

15. The current position of Assistant to the Chairman of the Joint Chiefs of Staff for National Guard Matters should not be eliminated.

The Commission does not recommend that the position of Assistant to the Joint Chiefs of Staff for National Guard Matters be eliminated, regardless of the ultimate disposition of the companion proposal in the National Guard Empowerment Act to make the Chief of the National Guard Bureau the principal advisor to the Secretary of Defense and Chairman of the Joint Chiefs of Staff. As described above, the Commission recommends that the National Guard Bureau charter be revised to make the Chief of the National Guard Bureau a senior advisor to the Chairman of the Joint Chiefs of Staff and, through him, to the Secretary of Defense, with respect to the nonfederal aspects of the National Guard. Nevertheless, the Commission believes that the position of the Assistant to the Chairman of the Joint Chiefs of Staff for National Guard Matters (ACJCS-NGM) should not be eliminated.

The Commission recommends keeping the position of ACJCS-NGM intact because of its importance to the decisions made by the CJCS and by the Joint Staff generally. The Chiefs of the Army Reserve, Naval Reserve, and Air Force Reserve, as well as the Director of the

---

[32] Lieutenant General Blum, letter to Chairman Punaro, November 30, 2006, p. 4.

[33] Deputy Secretary England, transcript of testimony before the House Armed Services Committee, Hearing on National Guard Enhancement, June 13, 2006, p. 24.

[34] General Pace, transcript of testimony before the CNGR, January 31, 2007, p. 28.

[35] Hamre and Wormuth, letter to Chairman Punaro, December 14, 2006, Attachment A, p. 1.

Air National Guard and a representative from the Coast Guard Reserve, unanimously favor retaining the current functioning of the ACJCS-NGM and ACJCS-RM. All agreed that the existing system was working well and that no changes were necessary.[36] Lieutenant General Blum wrote: "It is my view that the current position of Assistant to the Chairman for National Guard matters should not be eliminated under any circumstances. This position provides invaluable coordination capabilities to the Chairman and the Joint staff and is not in any way a substitute for a more formal relationship between the Chief of the National Guard Bureau and the Chairman of the Joint Chiefs of Staff. Further, the position [of ACJCS-NGM] is now and would remain an essential aid to the Chairman even if such a relationship were to be formalized."[37]

General Peter Pace, Chairman of the Joint Chiefs of Staff, testified before the Commission:

> I value both of them [the ACJCS-NGM and the Assistant to the Chairman of the Joint Chiefs of Staff for Reserve Matters] very much and I would not want to lose those members of my staff, even though I do want to have the chief of the National Guard Bureau be an advisor to me. There's a difference. There's a staff function—I've got a J-1 who helps me with personnel and a J-2 who helps me with intelligence. That does not mean that they're doing the J-1 business of the services or that they're doing the intel business of the CIA, for example. But they're helping me, from a staff level, focus on my own attention on the issues that are important and helping me develop opinions and the like, which is different than advice on how to properly employ, utilize, man, equip the Guard and Reserve.
>
> From where I stand, both are needed. Keep what you've given me and add the advisor role to the chief of the National Guard to be my advisor and, through me, to be an advisor to the secretary of Defense.[38]

The Commission concludes that the Assistant to the Chairman of the Joint Chiefs for National Guard Matters serves important functions as a conduit of information about the National Guard to the Joint Staff, a monitor of Joint Staff activities for the National Guard, and a coordinator and liaison between the National Guard and the Joint Staff. In view of the virtually unanimous support for retaining the position voiced by those best situated to assess its value, the Commission recommends against its abolition.

---

[36] Lieutenant General Jack Stultz, Chief, USAR, Questions for the Record (QFR) answers submitted to the CNGR, December 4, 2006, p. 21; Vice Admiral John G. Cotton, Chief, USNR, QFR answers submitted September 26, 2006, p. 17; Lieutenant General John A. Bradley, Chief, USAFR, QFR answers submitted December 7, 2006, p. 31; Lieutenant General Craig R. McKinley, DANG, QFR answers submitted August 10, 2006, p. 12; Rear Admiral John C. Acton, USCGR, QFR answers submitted December 7, 2006, p. 21.

[37] Lieutenant General Blum, letter to Chairman Punaro, pp. 8–9.

[38] General Pace, transcript of testimony before the CNGR, January 31, 2007, p. 12.

D. U.S. NORTHERN COMMAND

U.S. Northern Command (NORTHCOM) is the unified command with primary responsibility for homeland defense and civil support missions.[1] Joint Publication 3-26, "Homeland Security," describes its mission as conducting "operations to deter, prevent, and defeat threats and aggression aimed at the United States, its territories, and interests within the assigned area of responsibility (AOR) and as directed by the President or SecDef [Secretary of Defense], provide military assistance to civil authorities including [consequence management] operations. USNORTHCOM embodies the principles of unity of effort and unity of command as the single, responsible, designated DOD [Department of Defense] commander for overall command and control of DOD support to civil authorities within the USNORTHCOM AOR."[2] NORTHCOM views homeland defense, but not civil support, as its primary mission.[3]

Under existing procedures, if a major crisis occurs in a state where both federal and nonfederal (National Guard under state control) forces provide civil support, military assistance is coordinated at the federal level in two ways. NORTHCOM controls the movement of Title 10 active and reserve forces into the state and maintains command and control over them. Simultaneously, the National Guard Bureau (NGB) coordinates the movement of National Guard forces in Title 32 status; but once in state, they are commanded by the governor.[4] Consequently, there are two separate entities coordinating, communicating, and organizing the large-scale movement of military forces. As the White House report and the two congressional reports on Hurricane Katrina make clear, this arrangement is fraught with the potential for confusion and error. All three reports indicate that despite heroic efforts on the parts of the NGB and NORTHCOM, National Guard and Title 10 military deployments were not well-coordinated.[5]

> **Finding:** The commander of U.S. Northern Command is responsible for the planning, exercising, and command and control

---

[1] U.S. Southern Command and U.S. Pacific Command play similar roles for those parts of the homeland that fall within their area of operations (Joint Chiefs of Staff, "Homeland Security," Joint Publication 3-26, August 2, 2005, pp. II-7 to II-11).

[2] Joint Chiefs of Staff, "Homeland Security," pp. vii–viii.

[3] "As we act to support civil authorities in responding to natural disasters, we never lose focus on our primary mission of homeland defense" (Lieutenant General Joseph R. Inge, Deputy Commander, U.S. Northern Command, prepared witness statement before the Senate Armed Services Committee Subcommittee on Emerging Threats and Capabilities, hearing on the roles and missions of the Department of Defense regarding homeland defense and support to civil authorities in review of the Defense Authorization Request for Fiscal Year 2007 and the Future Years Defense Program, March 10, 2006 [http://armed-services.senate.gov/statemnt/2006/March/Inge%2003-10-06.pdf], p. 6).

[4] "National Guard Bureau Joint Staff Manual" [Draft] ([Arlington, VA: National Guard Bureau,] 2004), p. M-8. States would also be able to use the Emergency Management Assistance Compact (EMAC) to obtain National Guardsmen from other states. But as the response to Katrina showed, the EMAC process is unworkable for the large-scale movement of troops; states therefore would be likely to rely instead on the NGB to coordinate the movement of troops (Senate Committee on Homeland Security and Governmental Affairs, *Hurricane Katrina: A Nation Still Unprepared*, 109th Cong., 2nd sess., May 2006, pp. 507–8).

[5] Senate Committee on Homeland Security and Governmental Affairs, *Hurricane Katrina: A Nation Still Unprepared*, p. 512; House Select Bipartisan Committee to Investigate the Preparation for and Response to Hurricane Katrina, *A Failure of Initiative: Final Report of the Select Bipartisan Committee to Investigate the Preparation for and Response to Hurricane Katrina*, 109th Cong., 2nd sess., February 2006, pp. 218–19; *The Federal Response to Hurricane Katrina: Lessons Learned* ([Washington, DC: The White House,] 2006), p. 43.

of assigned and apportioned Title 10 forces in response to a domestic emergency. The National Guard Bureau coordinates the movement of nonfederalized National Guard forces. This arrangement can impair the coordination of the military response to disaster.

The *Strategy for Homeland Defense and Civil Support* recognizes that there should be a "focused reliance" on the reserve components for homeland defense and civil support activities.[6] Admiral Keating, NORTHCOM's current commander, noted that there are a number of advantages that national guardsmen bring to disaster response beyond providing the bulk of the forces, including their experience in working with first responders and their familiarity with local conditions.[7] In fact, the National Guard can be expected to make up most of the forces responding to a disaster. For example, the National Guard provided 70 percent of the military force for Hurricane Katrina.[8] Reserve components are forward deployed and placed in every state and large city in America, and thus they would be the most logical first choice to react swiftly to a local disaster. Yet just 69 of the 850 military billets at NORTHCOM—only 8 percent—are currently active Guard and Reserve. Of those 69, only 39—less than 5 percent of the 850 billets—are Army and Air National Guardsmen.[9] There is one senior billet filled by a national guardsman, the Chief of Staff position, but the senior staff are primarily active duty officers or civilians with little experience and knowledge of the reserve forces that will be called on to deal with a domestic incident. U.S. Northern Command Headquarters would benefit from greater access to the knowledge and experience of full-time reserve members. Admiral Keating himself reported that during the response to Hurricane Katrina he had little sense of National Guard capabilities beyond the number of troops being deployed.[10]

Like other regional unified commands, NORTHCOM is supported by service components. Two of NORTHCOM's four service component headquarters are organized, led, and manned by active duty Title 10 forces without the benefit of reserve force expertise. At present, the Air Force service component of NORTHCOM (AFNORTH) is composed of approximately 68 percent Active Guard and Reserve (AGR), while the Army's (ARNORTH) and Navy's (NAVNORTH) service components of NORTHCOM are primarily staffed by active component personnel.[11] In contrast, the Marine Corps combines "Marine Forces Reserve" and "Marine Forces North" duties in one commander and staff in order "to leverage one of the great strengths of the Reserve: its close contact with communities all across the United States," as well as to make "efficient and effective use of headquarters personnel, while at the same time increasing the Marine Corps ability to support Northern

---

[6] *Strategy for Homeland Defense and Civil Support* ([Washington, DC: Department of Defense,] 2005), p. 35.

[7] House Select Bipartisan Committee to Investigate the Preparation for and Response to Hurricane Katrina, *A Failure of Initiative*, pp. 222–23.

[8] Paul McHale, Assistant Secretary of Defense for Homeland Defense, prepared witness statement before the CNGR, Hearing on Homeland Defense/Homeland Security, May 3, 2006 (www.cngr.gov/hearing503-4/McHale.pdf), p. 6.

[9] NORTHCOM e-mail to CNGR staff, December 7, 2006.

[10] Senate Committee on Homeland Security and Governmental Affairs, *Hurricane Katrina: A Nation Still Unprepared*, p. 497.

[11] E-mail from AFNORTH Public Affairs, November 18, 2006; Memorandum for the Record (MFR), telephone conversation of CNGR staff with Northern Command J-1 Lieutenant Colonel Gene Smith, September 27, 2006; MFR, telephone conversation of CNGR staff with ARNORTH, February 9, 2006.

Command."[12] Combining the reserve forces staffs with the service component staffs has reduced manpower requirements and associated costs for the Marine Corps.

As discussed in section A above, the Department of Defense has not explicitly budgeted or programmed for civil support, viewing it as derivative of its warfighting capability. This approach has carried over into how NORTHCOM views its mission and is best illustrated by the Commission's previous finding that NORTHCOM does not sufficiently advocate for the full range of civil support requirements affecting the National Guard and Reserves.

> **Finding:** In accordance with Department of Defense policy, U.S. Northern Command's primary mission has been homeland defense, while civil support has been treated as a lesser included mission.

> **Finding:** U.S. Northern Command is staffed predominantly by active duty personnel who are not fully aware of the capabilities that the reserve components can bring to civil support missions.

Conclusion: U.S. Northern Command does not adequately consider and utilize all military components—active and reserve, including the National Guard—in planning, training, and exercising and in the conduct of military operations while in support of a governor, in support of another lead federal agency, or in the defense of America.

To be ready to respond to a catastrophe in the United States, DOD must elevate the importance of civil support and incorporate its importance in all defense strategy and planning documents. Doing so will give NORTHCOM and the NGB the ability to plan for and prioritize civil support appropriately alongside homeland defense and other missions.

Recommendation:

16. **Because U.S. Northern Command is a command with significant responsibility for domestic emergency response and civil support, a majority of U.S. Northern Command's billets, including those for its service components, should be filled by leaders and staff with reserve qualifications and credentials. Job descriptions for senior leaders and other key positions at U.S. Northern Command should contain the requirement of significant Reserve or National Guard experience or service.**

The Commission believes that more must be done to integrate the reserve components into NORTHCOM. Having more national guardsmen fill key leadership positions at NORTHCOM is an essential first step—but only one step. NORTHCOM must incorporate personnel who have greater knowledge of National Guard and Reserve capabilities, strengths, and

---

[12] Lieutenant General Jack W. Bergman, Commander, Marine Forces Reserve, prepared witness statement before the CNGR, Hearing on National Guard and Reserve Issues, July 19, 2006 (www.cngr.gov/July%2019/Bergman%20Testimony.doc), p. 3.

constraints and must assemble a cadre of experts on the intricacies of state and local government, law enforcement, and emergency response. Such knowledge currently resides in the National Guard and Reserves yet remains untapped and unintegrated, in disparate commands. A larger percentage of reservists on the staff and in key leadership positions would provide NORTHCOM with greater insight into the unique skills and strengths available in the reserve forces. Increasing the numbers of members of the National Guard and Reserves within the service components of NORTHCOM would ensure that those preparing and coordinating homeland missions will consider the unique contributions of the reserve component.

Recommendation:

17. Either the officer serving in the position of the commander or the officer serving in the position of deputy commander of U.S. Northern Command should be a National Guard or Reserve officer at all times.

Section 4 of S. 2658/H.R. 5200 proposes a "requirement that the position of Deputy Commander of the United States NORTHCOM be filled by a qualified National Guard Officer" who is eligible for promotion to the grade of lieutenant general. Section 4 further states that the purpose of this requirement "is to ensure that information received from the National Guard Bureau regarding the operation of the National Guard of the several States is integrated into the plans and operations of the United States Northern Command."

The position of deputy commander of each of the combatant commands, with the exception of U.S. European Command, is currently filled by an active component officer in the grade of O-9 (lieutenant general or vice admiral). The process of selecting the deputy commanders begins with a nomination by the respective services; the nomination is then vetted by the Secretary of Defense, Joint Staff, and others, including the combatant commander of the command in question, before being finally forwarded for consideration and approval by the President and Senate. The services have mainly nominated active duty personnel to the senior billets in combatant commands; no national guardsman or reservist has ever been considered for the NORTHCOM senior leader positions.[13] (See section F below on increasing the number of reserve component O-9s.)

Current policy requires senior officers of the grades of O-9 and O-10 to have substantial joint experience; in the past, the career paths of most reserve flag and general officers did not allow them to acquire joint experience. Today many more reservists have gained joint experience, and many have the joint knowledge needed to command in billets such as those at combatant commands, where officers are often required to have some joint knowledge and experience. For example, the special qualifications listed for the NORTHCOM deputy commander position include "possess[ing] knowledge of Joint Service roles and capabilities and knowledge of the Total Force Planning and the ability to work with senior executives in local, state, and federal government."[14] During the four years that NORTHCOM has

---

[13] MFR, Joint Staff Joint General/Flag Officer (G/FO) Matters Office meeting with CNGR staff, October 24, 2006.

[14] NORTHCOM Deputy Commander position description provided to the CNGR, September 19, 2006; see also Chairman of the Joint Chief of Staffs Instruction 1331.01C, "Manpower and Personnel Actions Involving General and Flag Officers," July 7, 2006.

existed, it has been the practice to alternate the services from which the combatant commander and the deputy commander are drawn and to routinely select a National Guard general officer for the position of Chief of Staff of the command. Today, many reservists have the joint experience and qualifications to lead the command and be considered for the two senior command positions.

Recommendation:

18. There should be only one U.S. deputy commander at U.S. Northern Command.

The Commission has been asked by Congress to assess whether U.S. Northern Command's mission is such that it requires two deputy commanders—one specifically designated to oversee National Guard activities.[15]

The Commission investigated the responsibilities of the deputy commander position at NORTHCOM in comparison with other deputy commander positions and found that they were neither so significant nor so complex as to require two individuals to carry them out. Having more National Guard and Reserve experience resident on the senior staff will provide the needed expertise without fracturing the chain of command and dividing responsibilities among flag officers. In addition, the current deputy commander, Lieutenant General Joseph R. Inge, USA, told the Commissioners during a visit to NORTHCOM that he would not know how to employ, nor would there be enough work for, a second deputy commander.[16]

Recommendation:

19. U.S. Northern Command should develop plans for consequence management and support to civil authorities that account for state-level activities and incorporate the use of National Guard and Reserve forces as first military responders.

The Commission has also heard significant concern expressed over inadequate interaction and coordination between NORTHCOM and state entities, including the governor's and the adjutant general's office.[17] Governors and their emergency managers would have greater confidence in NORTHCOM if there were a greater DOD effort to share information with the states, combine exercises, and train jointly. The states must also reach out to federal partners to keep them apprised of new threat developments and any changes to emergency plans, policies, and resources. The states keenly desire information from the military, particularly on matters that specifically affect them. NORTHCOM must be intimately familiar not only with state emergency plans but also with state resources, capabilities, and emergency response activities so that when given a mission in the homeland, it has relationships in place as well as the knowledge and means to bring to bear a seamless and integrated active and reserve military effort.

---

[15] House Report 109-702, on the National Defense Authorization Act for Fiscal Year 2007, 109th Cong., 2nd sess., October 17, 2006, p. 717.

[16] MFR, CNGR visit to U.S. Northern Command, October 5, 2006.

[17] CNGR meeting with National Governor's Association Public Safety Task Force, November 16, 2006.

E. RESERVE POLICY ADVICE

The Commission believes that its assessment of the changes to the National Guard Bureau's role and status within the Department of Defense as proposed by the National Guard Empowerment Act should not be undertaken in isolation. As part of our larger effort, the Commission has been studying organizational structures within the senior levels of the Department that influence the policies and practices governing the reserve components.

The current Reserve Forces Policy Board (RFPB) statute (10 U.S.C. §10301) was enacted in 1999, although the precursor to the board dates to the Truman administration.[1] On October 15, 1947, in Executive Order No. 10007, President Truman directed the Secretary of Defense to take every practicable step for the strengthening of all elements of the reserve components of the United States. Pursuant to this direction, on June 14, 1949, Secretary of Defense Louis Johnson created the Civilian Components Policy Board. Its initial charter stated that "On all matters of major policy so determined by the Chairman, the Board shall make recommendations to the Secretary of Defense."[2] In 1951, Secretary of Defense George C. Marshall created the Reserve Forces Policy Board in lieu of, but with the same membership as, the Civilian Components Policy Board. The board was given the authority to make recommendations for the Secretary of Defense on reserve forces policy matters and to coordinate policies and programs of the reserve forces of the three military departments.[3]

The Armed Forces Reserve Act of 1952 codified a Reserve Forces Policy Board in the Department of Defense.[4] This law made the RFPB, acting through the Assistant Secretary of Defense (Manpower and Personnel), the principal policy advisor to the Secretary of Defense on matters relating to the reserve components.[5] Public Law 98-94 (September 24, 1983) increased the number of Assistant Secretaries of Defense from 7 to 11, including one for reserve affairs. This law also provided that the RFPB would report through the Assistant Secretary of Defense for Reserve Affairs.

Thus, the board predates passage of the Goldwater-Nichols Department of Defense Reorganization Act of 1986 and the creation of the Office of the Under Secretary of Defense for Personnel and Readiness. The RFPB's authorizing statute has not been modified to reflect these changes. As presently constituted, the 24-member RFPB includes a civilian chairman appointed by the Secretary of Defense, the service assistant secretaries for manpower and reserve affairs, and flag and general officers from each of the active and reserve components. The board is served by a staff of 10 people and an executive director. A separate statute (10 U.S.C. §175) simply authorizes the establishment of the RFPB. The

---

[1] In 1947, President Truman ordered the Secretary of Defense to strengthen all elements of the reserve components (Executive Order 10007, October 15, 1948). In response, Secretary of Defense James Forrestal, on June 14, 1949, created the Civilian Components Policy Board as a standing committee to recommend policies and procedures affecting the reserve components (Judith Camarella, memorandum, "Statutory Framework and Historical Development of the RFPB," March 31, 2000, p. 2 n. 9).
[2] Charter for the Civilian Components Policy Board (June 14, 1949).
[3] Department of Defense Directive 20.22-1, June 13, 1951, para. IIIA.
[4] Armed Forces Reserve Act of 1952, §257, codified at 10 U.S.C. §175 (1952 Supp. V).
[5] Armed Forces Reserve Act of 1952, §257.

specifics of the board's constitution, duties, and operation are found in 10 U.S.C. §10301, and DOD Directive 5120.2 provides detailed guidance about its mission and functions.[6]

Subsection (c) of the current statute provides that the board, acting through the Assistant Secretary of Defense for Reserve Affairs (ASD-RA), is the principal policy advisor to the Secretary of Defense on matters relating to the reserve components. A consequence of the board's reporting through the ASD-RA, then reporting through the Under Secretary of Defense for Personnel and Readiness, is that both the assistant secretary and the under secretary can govern and filter advice provided by the board to the Secretary. Section 138(b)(2) of 10 U.S.C. establishes the Office of the Assistant Secretary of Defense for Reserve Affairs and provides that its principal duty is the overall supervision of reserve component affairs of the Department of Defense. In theory, this mandate is not inconsistent with the primary responsibility of the RFPB. In practice, however, there is uncertainty about where primary responsibility really lies for making recommendations to the Secretary of Defense involving reserve component policy issues.

> **Finding:** Statutes establishing the Reserve Forces Policy Board and the Office of the Assistant Secretary of Defense for Reserve Affairs conflict about which organization has the primary responsibility to provide advice to the Department of Defense leadership on National Guard and Reserve matters.

> **Finding:** Uncertainty about which entity has the primary responsibility for making recommendations to the Secretary of Defense involving National Guard and Reserve matters creates conflicting lines of communication and hinders integrated decision making.

Another matter of concern is that with the exception of the civilian chairman, every member of the RFPB is a sitting political appointee in the Department of Defense or a serving military officer. When all who sit on it are a part of the existing decision-making system, a board is less likely to fully consider new ideas, incorporate private-sector best practices, and critically examine present policies. Moreover, it is unrealistic to expect that the service representatives on the board will take a position on policy matters under consideration that is inconsistent with or in advance of the position adopted by their parent service or military department.

At times, the RFPB's effectiveness has further been hindered because of chronic vacancies among its members and the use of surrogates at meetings, decreasing the likelihood of carefully deliberated and meaningful decisions being made.

The Commission has discussed the status of the RFPB with the current and former chairmen of the board, as well as with other stakeholders. The Commission finds a broad consensus that its current structure and operations do not fulfill the intent of the statute. Most recently, Lieutenant General H Steven Blum, Chief of the National Guard Bureau,

---

[6] DOD Directive 5120.2, "Reserve Forces Policy Board," October 13, 1973, reissued August 12, 1985.

testified before the Commission that the RFPB "has been minimized to the point where it is rather ineffective."[7]

> **Finding:** The organization and membership of the Reserve Forces Policy Board and the limits on the topics it may consider prevent decision makers from obtaining the wide range of inputs necessary for them to formulate appropriate and sustainable policies.

The Commission is convinced that the board as presently configured is not functioning effectively. Accordingly, the Commission has determined that it is necessary to reconstitute the Reserve Forces Policy Board, alter its fundamental purpose, and change the way it fits into the Pentagon bureaucracy. The Commission concludes that the RFPB could better evaluate issues and better advise the Secretary of Defense on policy if it were modeled after independent advisory organizations such as the Defense Business Board, Defense Science Board, and Defense Policy Board—which are composed of individuals from outside the Department of Defense.

Conclusion: The Secretary of Defense does not have mechanisms to generate and receive the best possible advice on reserve policy matters. The Reserve Forces Policy Board is not structured to obtain and provide to the Secretary of Defense a wide range of independent advice on National Guard and Reserve matters because of the nature of its membership, and because it is subordinated to other offices within the Office of the Secretary of Defense.

Recommendation:

> **20. To improve the quality and timeliness of independent policy advice to the Secretary of Defense, the Reserve Forces Policy Board statute should be amended to create instead a Reserve Policy Board, composed of 20 members appointed by the Secretary of Defense from outside the Department of Defense. The chairman of the Reserve Policy Board should have extensive knowledge of and experience with the National Guard and Reserves.**

The Commission recommends reconstituting the Reserve Forces Policy Board so that it would be composed of high-level experts from outside the Department of Defense with significant knowledge of and experience with policy matters pertaining to the reserve components. The board would also be renamed the Reserve Policy Board (RPB), consistent with the titles of other current outside advisory boards. This approach is in keeping with the roles now performed by the Defense Business Board, Defense Policy Board, and Defense Science Board; it also would remove ambiguity created by the current statutory charter and the sometimes competing role and practices of the ASD-RA.

---

[7] Lieutenant General Blum, testimony before the CNGR, Hearing on Proposed Changes to the National Guard, January 31, 2007, transcript (www.cngr.gov/hearing13107/0131cngr-1.pdf), p. 30.

The Commission's recommendation to reconstitute the RFPB reflects two guiding principles. First, we believe that the stature and influence of the new RPB must be increased. Revising the charter of the RFPB to make the new body an advisory board composed of outside experts—with a role analogous to that of the Defense Business, Science, and Policy boards—should help achieve this result. The statutory language we propose (in the text box below) is modeled after the statute establishing the Defense Business Board. The new membership criteria should provide the RPB with a broader base of knowledge and experience among its members than exists presently. Outside advice from those having extensive experience with and knowledge of the reserve components should better serve the Secretary of Defense and the reserve components than the advice provided by political appointees and by those who work within the Department of Defense. The new board should be able to take positions and render advice on controversial policies about which no consensus exists inside the Department of Defense.

The second objective was to remove any ambiguity created by the current statutory charter and the sometimes competing statutory mandate of ASD-RA. If the new RPB is made a high-level advisory board whose members are independent of the Department of Defense, it will be clear that the Assistant Secretary of Defense for Reserve Affairs is chiefly responsible inside the Department for the development of policy guidance and the overall supervision of the reserve components.

Accordingly, the Commission recommends that the existing authorizing statute of the RFPB (10 U.S.C. §10301) be revised to

- Rename the RFPB the Reserve Policy Board (RPB).

- Expand the purview of the RPB to include providing independent advice and recommendations on strategies, policies, and practices designed to improve and enhance the capabilities, efficiency, and effectiveness of the reserve components.

- Have the RPB report through the Deputy Secretary of Defense rather than through the Assistant Secretary of Defense for Reserve Affairs, thereby affording the RPB access to the highest levels of the Department of Defense and increasing its ability to influence policy decisions that affect the reserve components.

- Change the constitution of the RPB to include 20 members appointed by the Secretary of Defense from civilian life, rather than individuals currently serving in the Department of Defense.

- Provide for renewable, two-year terms of service.

- Require that persons selected for board membership have records of significant knowledge, expertise, and achievement in fields that touch on national security and reserve component issues.

- Require that the person selected as chairman have extensive knowledge of and expertise with the reserve components, including the National Guard.

- Designate the Under Secretary of Defense for Personnel and Readiness to provide logistical support to the RPB, much as the Defense Science Board uses the Under Secretary of Defense for Acquisition, Technology, and Logistics for support.

- Provide that the RPB may act on matters referred by the Secretary of Defense, the chairman, or on any matter raised by a board member.

- Require the RPB to periodically meet with members of the reserve components in order to help ensure currency of knowledge about the state of the reserve components.

The Commission also recommends an amendment to section 113(c)(2) of Title 10. This section currently requires the Secretary of Defense to include a separate report from the RFPB in his annual report to the President and Congress. The Commission's amendment would instead make the inclusion of matters from the new RPB discretionary.[8]

---

[8] New language proposed by the CNGR: "At the same time the Secretary submits the annual report under paragraph (1), the Secretary may include in the report to the President and Congress additional matters from the Reserve Policy Board on the reserve programs or activities of the Department of Defense."

The Commission suggests the following language in changing section 10301 of Title 10, United States Code:

Sec. 10301. Reserve Policy Board

(a) There is in the Office of the Secretary of Defense a Reserve Policy Board. The Board shall provide the Secretary of Defense, through the Deputy Secretary of Defense, independent advice and recommendations on strategies, policies, and practices designed to improve and enhance the capabilities, efficiency, and effectiveness of the reserve components of the United States.

(b) The Board shall consist of twenty members appointed from civilian life by the Secretary of Defense. The Secretary shall designate the chairman and a vice chairman of the Board. Members of the Board shall be appointed without regard to political affiliation, shall be appointed for two-year, renewable terms, and shall have a proven record of high-level achievement in a national security–related field that includes matters pertaining to the reserve components of the United States.

(c) Members of the Board shall be selected on the basis of knowledge, expertise, or achievement in the following areas:

> *(1) the reserve components of the United States;*
>
> *(2) the national security and national military strategies of the United States;*
>
> *(3) the roles and missions of the active and reserve components of the United States Armed Forces;*
>
> *(4) the organization, force structure, and force mix of the United States Armed Forces;*
>
> *(5) Acquisition, research and development, military operations, or personnel and compensation programs, policies and activities of the Department of Defense; and*
>
> *(6) Homeland defense and support to civil authorities.*

(d) The chairman shall be selected on the basis of extensive knowledge, expertise, or achievement with respect to the reserve components of the United States, including the National Guard.

(e) The Under Secretary of Defense for Personnel and Readiness shall provide an executive director and the necessary support staff to manage the activities of the Board in consultation with the chairman.

(f) The Board shall act on those matters referred to it by the Secretary or the Chairman and, in addition, on any matter raised by a member of the Board. As a part of its duties, the Board shall periodically meet with members of the reserve components of the United States.

F. RESERVE COMPONENT OFFICER PROMOTION

An important aspect of enhancing the National Guard to ensure military effectiveness is to ensure that reserve component officers have the opportunity to gain both joint duty experience and joint professional military education in order to be competitive for promotion to senior positions, including combatant commanders and senior joint and service positions.

As prescribed by chapter 36 of Title 10, United States Code, general and flag officers are recommended by promotion selection boards to the permanent grades of O-7 and O-8,[1] subject to subsequent Senate confirmation. Appointments to the grades of O-9 and O-10[2] are temporary and predicated on the President's appointing an officer, with the advice and consent of the Senate, to a position designated as a position of importance and responsibility in accordance with 10 U.S.C. §601. When an officer is recommended to the President for initial appointment as an O-9 or O-10, the Chairman of the Joint Chiefs of Staff must submit an evaluation to the Secretary of Defense of that officer's performance as a member of the Joint Staff and in other joint duty assignments.

Chapter 38 of Title 10, United States Code, prescribes the joint officer management policies enacted by the Goldwater-Nichols Department of Defense Reorganization Act of 1986. This legislation provided a framework for developing active component joint specialty officers, including the joint duty assignment and joint professional military education requirements for promotion to flag and general officer rank on the active duty list.

Section 666 of Title 10, United States Code, states that "The Secretary of Defense shall establish personnel policies emphasizing education and experience in joint matters for reserve officers not on the active-duty list. Such policies shall, to the extent practicable for the reserve components, be similar to the policies provided by this chapter." This vision laid out by the Goldwater-Nichols Act 20 years ago has not yet been realized in the reserve components.[3]

Section 531 of the National Defense Authorization Act for Fiscal Year 2005 required the Secretary of Defense to develop a strategic plan for joint officer management and joint professional military education that links joint officer development to accomplishing the overall missions and goals of the Department of Defense. Also included was a requirement that joint officer development for officers on the reserve active status list be incorporated into the strategic plan.[4] In its initial report, the House Armed Services Committee noted that multiple proposals had been received from DOD over the past several years to "change

---

[1] Respectively, brigadier general in the case of the Army, Air Force, or Marine Corps and rear admiral (lower half) in the case of the Navy; major general in the case of the Army, Air Force, or Marine Corps and rear admiral (upper half) in the case of the Navy.

[2] Respectively, lieutenant general in the case of the Army, Air Force, or Marine Corps and vice admiral in the case of the Navy; general in the case of the Army, Air Force, or Marine Corps and admiral in the case of the Navy.

[3] Lieutenant General H Steven Blum, Chief of the National Guard Bureau, testimony before the CNGR, Hearing on Proposed Changes to the National Guard, transcript of January 31, 2007, hearing (www.cngr.gov/hearing13107/0131cngr-1.pdf), p. 14; Department of Defense Instruction 1215.20, "RC Joint Officer Management Program," September 12, 2002, p. 2.

[4] Public Law 108-375, October 28, 2004.

significant aspects" of the Goldwater-Nichols joint officer framework, but it judged that these proposals lacked a "coherent, comprehensive context."[5]

Following the submission of DOD's strategic plan in April 2006,[6] Congress in the National Defense Authorization Act for Fiscal Year 2007 modified the joint officer management provisions of the Goldwater-Nichols Act to reflect that plan's recommendations. The effective date of the changes is October 1, 2007. In the meantime, DOD was directed to submit a plan for implementing a joint officer management system not later than March 31, 2007.[7]

The changes proposed in the strategic plan and the resultant legislation focus on developing an alternative path to jointness by creating a multilevel joint qualification system that captures all joint experiences; the new path should rely on "a capabilities-based system in which experience, education, and performance are evaluated in an officer's progress to higher levels of qualification," as the statement of managers' language accompanying §516 put it.[8] The amendments to 10 U.S.C. §661, contained in §516, direct the Secretary of Defense to "establish different levels of joint qualification, as well as criteria for qualification at each level." In its March 31, 2007, implementation plan, DOD is expected to flesh out the requirements for these multiple levels, including joint education and joint experience.

In its strategic plan, DOD stressed that the nature of "joint matters" had changed significantly in the 20 years since the enactment of the Goldwater-Nichols legislation, pointing out that the "military is increasingly required to operate in multi-service, interagency environments to conduct and sustain operations across a greater variety of domains." The report also noted the growing role of multinational coalitions and the new way that military forces are aligned and deployed, with joint task forces forming "the tip of the spear."[9] In contrast, the original Goldwater-Nichols Act focused on officers serving a three-year tour in a joint duty assignment list billet.

The changed focus of the department's strategic plan is reflected in the revised definition of *joint matters* in 10 U.S.C. §668, as amended by §519. Under current law, until October 1, 2007, joint matters are limited to "the integrated employment of land, sea, and air forces, including matters related to (1) national military strategy, (2) strategic planning and contingency planning, and (3) command and control of combat operations under unified command."

As amended, *joint matters* "means matters related to the achievement of unified action by *multiple military forces* in operations conducted across domains such as land, sea, or air, in space, or in the information environment." Moreover, two new categories are added to the three previously listed: (4) "national security planning with other departments and agencies of the United States" and (5) "combined operations with military forces of allied nations."

---

[5] House Report 108-491, on the National Defense Authorization Act for Fiscal Year 2005, 108th Cong., 2nd sess., May 14, 2004, §531, p. 318.

[6] Department of Defense, *Strategic Plan for Joint Officer Management and Joint Professional Military Education*, April 3, 2006.

[7] Public Law 109-364, October 17, 2006, §§516–519.

[8] House Report 109-702, on the National Defense Authorization Act for Fiscal Year 2007, 109th Cong., 2nd sess., October 17, 2006, p. 712.

[9] DOD, *Strategic Plan*, pp. 9–10.

Multiple military forces "refers to forces that involve participants from the armed forces and one or more of the following: (A) other departments and agencies of the United States, (B) the military forces or agencies of other countries, and (C) non-governmental persons or entities."[10] This change should significantly expand reserve component officers' opportunities to accrue joint duty credit.

The Goldwater-Nichols Amendments in the National Defense Authorization Act for Fiscal Year 2007 should set the stage for wider eligibility of reserve component officers. DOD's March 31, 2007, implementation plan will be the key determining factor. How, to take one example, will service in an in-theater wartime joint task force billet be treated in comparison to a longer peacetime assignment in a joint duty assignment billet on the Joint Staff? This determination will be particularly important for reserve component officers who may be unable to undertake a three-year Joint Staff tour, but may have served a shorter time on one or more in-theater joint task forces. DOD's *Strategic Plan* provides some indication that greater flexibility is likely:

> [C]urrent time requirements necessitate an intricate system of waivers with a one-size fits all approach. However, the law does not adequately address the exceptional experience gained in intensive or focused contingency operations staffs and the majority of combat joint assignments merit consideration equal to a full JDA [joint duty assignment] experience as we know it today. The same argument can be applied to many one-year remote joint tours demonstrating the same level of intensity. Again, we should recognize and track levels of joint qualifications based on demonstrated competency and successful completion of tours in joint intensive environments versus simply fulfilling arbitrary tour lengths.[11]

> **Finding:** Reserve component officers often serve in a joint environment in positions for which they currently do not receive joint duty credit.

In addition to implementing these Goldwater-Nichols changes, the Department of Defense must also find ways to expand the pool of combatant command, Joint Staff, and critical service staff positions available to or specifically designated for reserve component general and flag officers. In 1999, Congress exempted up to 10 one- and two-star general and flag officer positions, to be designated for reserve component officers by the Chairman of the Joint Chiefs of Staff, from counting against statutory ceilings on the number and grade distribution of general and flag officers.[12] The statute further directs that these "Chairman's 10" positions on the staffs of combatant commanders are to be considered joint duty assignment positions for purposes of Goldwater-Nichols.[13] Congressional intent was clearly expressed in the accompanying Senate report: "The Committee continues to seek ways to provide opportunities for reserve component general and flag officers to use their expertise and to gain valuable experience serving on the staff of a [commander in chief] or other joint

---

[10] Public Law 109-364, §519.
[11] DOD, *Strategic Plan*, p. 16.
[12] Public Law 106-65, *National Defense Authorization Act for Fiscal Year 2000*, October 5, 1999, §553.
[13] House Report 106-301, on the National Defense Authorization Act for Fiscal Year 2000, 106th Cong., 1st sess., August 17, 1999, p. 737.

duty positions. The recommended provision is not intended to be a source of manpower for the active components nor is it intended to be used in cases in which the duties would not provide the reserve general or flag officer significant experience in a joint or critical service staff position."[14]

Carrying out this congressional intent, as expressed in 1999, is even more imperative in the world of today's operational reserve force. The Department has made progress since 1999. General and flag officers from the reserve components are brought on multiyear, full-time duty to serve in meaningful positions in joint commands and organizations. Recent examples include director, U.S. Central Command Deployment Distribution Operations Center in Kuwait; commander, NATO Headquarters in Sarajevo; chief, Office of the Defense Representative in Pakistan; president, Joint Special Operations University; chief of staff, U.S. Transportation Command; vice director for Joint Training, U.S. Joint Forces Command; commander, Joint Task Force Civil Support, U.S. Northern Command; and deputy director, J-4, the Joint Staff. In addition, there are dozens of positions in which reserve component generals can serve on joint staffs in their part-time capacity.

This momentum toward building a highly qualified pool of reserve component one- and two-star generals and admirals with joint experience in command/director positions must continue. The next step is to draw from this pool and promote these individuals to the three-star, and subsequently the four-star, level of responsibility in positions that are filled by active component officers today. During the Commission's January 31, 2007, hearing on the National Guard Empowerment Act legislation, Chairman of the Joint Chiefs of Staff General Peter Pace, USMC, agreed that there are National Guard and Reserve officers today who are qualified for the rank of O-10.[15] The Commission fully concurs with the Chairman's view and believes that there are reserve component general and flag officers fully qualified for four-star rank.

> **Finding:** There are general and flag officers in the National Guard
> and Reserves who are qualified to hold the rank of O-10.

More one- and two-star positions for reserve component officers are needed in joint organizations. Additional opportunities on the Joint Staff, within the Office of the Secretary of Defense, on joint task forces, and at combatant commands and defense agencies will further improve the pool of available candidates. On the Joint Staff, most "J" codes should have a reserve component general officer assigned in an individual mobilization augmentee position. Additionally, primary staff positions (such as the J-3 and J-5) at U.S. Northern Command (NORTHCOM) and Joint Forces Command (JFCOM) should be filled by reserve component officers. In the services, major commands and military departments have many general officer individual mobilization augmentee positions today, but even greater reserve component integration is desirable.

The Department should thoroughly review the developmental experiences needed for officers to serve as the commander at each of the service components to NORTHCOM and

---

[14] Senate Report 106-50, on the National Defense Authorization Act for Fiscal Year 2000, 106th Cong., 1st sess., May 17, 1999, p. 303.

[15] General Pace, testimony at CNGR, Hearing on Proposed Changes to the National Guard, transcript of January 31, 2007, hearing (www.cngr.gov/hearing13107/0131cngr-3.pdf), pp. 7–8.

as the commander and deputy commander of NORTHCOM. On the basis of this review, sufficient one- and two-star general and flag officer positions must be identified that can be filled by both full- and part-time reserve component officers to get this experience. The result would be a considerable number of reserve component officers fully qualified to serve at the three-star level in command of each component of NORTHCOM and as the four-star commander of U.S. Northern Command.

In conclusion, the Commission believes that it is vital to expand the number of reserve component general and flag officers in senior positions at all levels. As part of its assessment of career paths in its final report, the Commission will evaluate both joint professional military education opportunities for reserve component officers and reserve officer career management by the services. Reserve component officers often face many obstacles to obtaining joint professional military education because of limitations on the number of school seats available and the competing demands of their full-time civilian employment.

> **Finding:** Joint Professional Military Education (JPME I & II), required for full joint qualification, is difficult for reservists and national guardsmen to obtain.

> **Finding:** Reserve component members do not have adequate opportunity to gain qualifying joint experience.

> **Finding:** Those reserve component general and flag officers who do not have the opportunity to meet the joint standards imposed by Goldwater-Nichols are often considered less well qualified for senior positions than their active duty counterparts. These reserve component general and flag officers often have valuable civilian experience that is not counted.

> **Finding:** Any attempt to increase the number of reserve component officers serving in joint billets of importance and responsibility must be predicated on increased opportunity, at mid-grade, to gain Joint Professional Military Education and joint experience qualifications. Gradually, all officers should be held to the same standards, although the path to qualifications may vary for reservists.

> **Conclusion: National Guard and Reserve general and flag officers do not have the opportunities to achieve the joint experience and education necessary to be seriously considered for O-9 and O-10 positions. This disparity in opportunity must change. Policies must be put into place that recognize the constraints of a reserve component and provide reserve component personnel adequate opportunities to obtain joint education and joint experience.**

Recommendation:

21. The Department of Defense should modify joint experience qualifications and Joint Professional Military Education delivery methods in ways that significantly enhance the opportunities for reserve component officers. This should include consideration of credit for the quality of reserve component experience, not simply the quantity.

Increasing the opportunities for reserve component members to gain joint qualification and education is critical to their ability to contribute to national defense by developing the skills that a joint environment requires. Paths to joint qualification need to be reasonably accessible to drilling reservists; at the same time, they must provide reservists the same ability to shoulder increasing responsibility as do current programs designed for officers following an active duty career path. Once that goal is reached, reserve component officers should be held to the same standards as those applied to active component officers under Goldwater-Nichols, although the method of attaining those standards may be different. If all officers must meet the same qualifications for promotion to any grade, the legitimacy of the selection of reserve component officers to senior grades and of their nomination to positions of importance and responsibility will be unassailable.

Recommendation:

22. The Department of Defense should strive to ensure that Reserve and National Guard flag and general officers have the opportunity to serve in joint assignments, obtain joint experience, and acquire joint qualifications to compete for promotion to O-9 and O-10 positions, including combatant commanders and senior joint and service positions. Reserve and National Guard flag and general officers should be routinely considered for these positions, a practice that is not now the case.

The Commission strongly supports providing reserve component officers with greater opportunities for promotion to O-9 and O-10 positions of importance and responsibility and believes that in today's operational reserve force, a growing number of officers are serving in billets that should make them increasingly competitive. But the provisions of section 3 of S. 2658/H.R. 5200, though well-intentioned, make no change to the underlying officer promotion statutes. The Commission will closely monitor DOD's March 31, 2007, implementation plan for the recent amendments to Goldwater-Nichols as part of its statutory tasking to assess traditional military career paths for members of the reserve components,[16]

---

[16] Public Law 108-375, §513(c)(2)(I).

and then recommend any further changes, as appropriate, in its January 31, 2008, final report to Congress and the Secretary of Defense. It is important that the implementation plan credit both the quality and quantity of the unique joint experiences of part-time guardsmen and reservists, such as interagency or multinational support and multiservice or joint task force assignments of short duration. The Secretary of Defense should seek to enhance opportunity for all reserve component officers, as well as active component officers, within the total force to achieve education, training, and promotion opportunities. As part of its review, the Commission will also examine the joint duty experience of National Guard officers in operations conducted with state and local governments. The Commission will additionally examine the potential impact of its recommended changes on current statutory ceilings on general and flag officer authorizations.[17]

Recommendation:

23. The President of the United States should not be required to certify that all eligible Reserve Component officers were considered for promotions to the grade of O-9.

Section 3 of S. 2658/H.R. 5200 expresses "the sense of Congress that, whenever officers are considered for promotion to the grade of lieutenant general, or vice admiral in the case of the Navy, on the active duty list, officers of the reserve components of the Armed Forces who are eligible for promotion to such grade should be considered for promotion to such grade." Section 3 proceeds to direct the Secretary of Defense to submit to Congress a proposal to achieve this objective, specifying that the "proposal shall include such recommendations for legislative or administrative action as the Secretary considers appropriate in order to achieve that objective." The President, with each nomination submitted, would further be required to submit a certification "that all reserve officers who were eligible for consideration for promotion to such grade were considered in the making of such nomination."

Section 3 of S. 2658/H.R. 5200 reflects the laudable goal of increasing the opportunity for reserve component officers to be considered for O-9. But the provision addresses neither the underlying officer promotion statutes nor ways to improve the selection rate. Reserve component officers are already eligible for promotion to three-star rank; there is no actual barrier in law or policy to the Secretary of Defense's recommending a reserve component officer to the President for appointment as an O-9 in a position of importance and responsibility. Nevertheless, it is arguably unlikely that the Secretary would make such a recommendation if the officer does not meet the joint duty assignment and joint professional military education requirements of the Goldwater-Nichols Act for initial promotion to general and flag officer rank, even though these requirements formally apply only to officers on the active duty list.

The Commission does not recommend adoption of this section and instead recommends an alternative to achieve the desired goal. The Commission recommends an approach that would ensure that Reserve and Guard flag and general officers have the assignments, joint experience, and qualifications to be seriously considered for O-9 and O-10 positions across

---

[17] 10 U.S.C. §§525 and 526.

the board—including combatant commanders and the most senior joint and service positions, traditionally filled by active duty personnel.

APPENDIX 1

THE PROPOSALS OF THE 2007 NATIONAL DEFENSE AUTHORIZATION ACT AND NATIONAL DEFENSE ENHANCEMENT AND NATIONAL GUARD EMPOWERMENT ACT

The following is a summary of each issue that the Commission on the National Guard and Reserves was directed to assess in the National Defense Authorization Act for Fiscal Year 2007 (Public Law 109-364) and the National Defense Enhancement and National Guard Empowerment Act (S. 2658/H.R. 5200).

Section 529(a)(1) of the National Defense Authorization Act for Fiscal Year 2007 requires the Commission on the National Guard and Reserve to study "the advisability and feasibility of implementing the provisions of S. 2658 and H.R. 5200 of the 109th Congress, as introduced in the Senate and the House of Representatives, respectively, on April 26, 2006."

1. Section 2(a)(1) of S. 2658/H.R. 5200 would amend 10 U.S.C. §10501 by striking "joint bureau of the Department of the Army and the Department of the Air Force" and inserting "joint activity of the Department of Defense."

    The Commission recommends in favor of this proposal. The National Guard Bureau should be made a joint activity of the Department of Defense, rather than remain a joint bureau of the Army and Air Force. This designation should not change the relationship between the National Guard Bureau and the Army and Air Force related to Title 10 matters and to planning and budgeting for Title 32 mission requirements.

2. Section 2(a)(2) of S. 2658/H.R. 5200 would amend 10 U.S.C. §10501(b) by striking "between" and all that follows and inserting "between—

    "(1)(A) the Secretary of Defense, the Joint Chiefs of Staff, and the commanders of the combatant commands of the United States, and (B) the department of the Army and the Department of the Air Force; and

    "(2) the several States."

    The Commission recommends a modification to this proposal. The Commission recommends that the charter of the National Guard Bureau be modified to make the Chief of the National Guard Bureau a senior advisor to the Chairman of the Joint Chiefs of Staff and, through him, to the Secretary of Defense on matters related to the National Guard when not in active federal service. The Commission further recommends that the National Guard Bureau Charter be modified to establish an advisory relationship between the Chief of the National Guard Bureau and the commanders of the combatant commands of the United States, and between the Chief of the National Guard Bureau and the Department of Homeland Security.

3. Section 2(b)(1) of S. 2658/H.R. 5200 would amend 10 U.S.C. §10502(c) by inserting "to the Secretary of Defense, to the Chairman of the Joint Chiefs of Staff," after "principal advisor."

The Commission recommends a modification to this proposal. The Commission recommends that the statute authorizing the National Guard Bureau Charter be amended to provide that the Chief of the National Guard Bureau shall be a senior advisor to the Chairman of the Joint Chiefs of Staff and, through him, to the Secretary of Defense, on matters related to the National Guard when not in active federal service. The Commission further recommends that the National Guard Bureau Charter be modified to establish an advisory relationship between the Chief of the National Guard Bureau and the commanders of the combatant commands of the United States, and between the Chief of the National Guard Bureau and the Department of Homeland Security.

4. Section 2(b)(2) of S. 2658/H.R. 5200 would amend 10 U.S.C. §10502 by redesignating subsection (d) as subsection (e) and inserting new subsection (d):

> "(d) Member of the Joint Chiefs of Staff.—The Chief of the National Guard Bureau shall perform the duties prescribed for him or her as a member of the Joint Chiefs of Staff under section 151 of this title."

The Commission does not recommend that the Chief of the National Guard Bureau be made a member of the Joint Chiefs of Staff, on the grounds that it would be fundamentally inconsistent with the status of the Army and Air National Guard as reserve components of the Army and Air Force. This proposal would run counter to intra- and inter-service integration, would reverse progress toward jointness and interoperability, and would be counter to the organizational and advisory principles of—and a reversal of the significant progress that is the legacy of—the Goldwater-Nichols legislation.

5. Section 2(b)(3) of S. 2658/H.R. 5200 would amend subsection (e) of 10 U.S.C. §10502 (as redesignated by the preceding section) by striking "lieutenant general" and inserting "general."

The Commission recommends in favor of this proposal. When the duties of a general officer equate to those of an O-10, then the position should be so designated. The Commission concludes, on the basis of the duties currently required to be performed by the Chief of the National Guard Bureau, that the position should be designated as an O-10 billet. The Commission recommends that the duties and responsibilities of the position of Chief of the National Guard Bureau should be reevaluated periodically to ensure that the duties required to be performed by the Chief of the National Guard Bureau remain commensurate with grade O-10.

6. Section 2(b)(4) of S. 2658/H.R. 5200 would amend 10 U.S.C. §10504 by adding at the end the following new subsection:

"(c) ANNUAL REPORT ON VALIDATED REQUIREMENTS.—Not later than December 31 of each year, the Chief of the National Guard Bureau shall submit to Congress a report on the following:

> "(1) The requirements validated under section 10503a(b)(1) of this title during the preceding fiscal year.

> "(2) The requirements referred to in paragraph (1) for which funding is to be requested in the next budget for a fiscal year under section 10544 of this title.

"(3) The requirements referred to in paragraph (1) for which funding will not be requested in the next budget for a fiscal year under section 10544 of this title."

The Commission recommends a modification to this proposal. The Commission recommends that the Secretary of Defense and Secretary of Homeland Security should jointly submit an annual report to Congress on those civil support requirements generated by the Department of Homeland Security and those validated and funded by the Department of Defense, and that the Chief of the National Guard Bureau should play a role in the preparation of that report as directed by the Secretary of Defense.

7. Section 2(c)(1) of S. 2658/H.R. 5200 would amend 10 U.S.C. §10503 (relating to the charter of the National Guard Bureau) as follows:

    (A) in the matter preceding paragraph (1), by striking "the Secretary of the Army and the Secretary of the Air Force shall jointly develop" and inserting "The Secretary of Defense, in consultation with the Secretary of the Army and the Secretary of the Air Force, shall develop"; and

    (B) in paragraph (12), by striking "the Secretaries" and inserting "the Secretary of Defense."

The Commission recommends that the Secretary of Defense be responsible for drafting the charter for the National Guard Bureau, in consultation with the Secretaries of the Army and Air Force and the Chairman of the Joint Chiefs of Staff, to accurately reflect the full scope of the Bureau's required duties and activities and that the charter be reviewed periodically to ensure that it is updated appropriately.

8. Section 2(c)(2) of S. 2658/H.R. 5200 would amend 10 U.S.C. §10503 (relating to the charter of the National Guard Bureau) by redesignating paragraph (12), as amended above, as paragraph (13); and by inserting the following new paragraph (12):

    "(12) Facilitating and coordinating with other Federal agencies, and with the several States, the use of National Guard personnel and resources for and in contingency operations, military operations other than war, natural disasters, support of civil authorities, and other circumstances."

The Commission recommends amending the statute authorizing the National Guard Bureau Charter to include facilitation and coordination with federal agencies, the states, Northern Command, and Joint Forces Command on the use of nonfederalized National Guard forces for domestic contingency operations, support to civil authorities, and other homeland activities. The National Guard Bureau should not become an operational command.

9. Section 2(c)(3) of S. 2658/H.R. 5200 would amend Chapter 1011 of Title 10, United States Code, by inserting after section 10503 the following new section:

    "§ 10503a. Functions of National Guard Bureau: military assistance to civil authorities

    "(a) **IDENTIFICATION OF ADDITIONAL NECESSARY ASSISTANCE.**—The Chief of the National Guard Bureau shall—

"(1) identify gaps between Federal and State capabilities to prepare for and respond to emergencies; and

"(2) make recommendations to the Secretary of Defense on programs and activities of the National Guard for military assistance to civil authorities to address such gaps.

"(b) **SCOPE OF RESPONSIBILITIES**.—In meeting the requirements of subsection (a), the Chief of the National Guard Bureau shall, in coordination with the Adjutant Generals of the States, have responsibilities as follows:

"(1) To validate the requirements of the several States and Territories with respect to military assistance to civil authorities.

"(2) To develop doctrine and training requirements relating to the provision of military assistance to civil authorities.

"(3) To acquire equipment, materiel, and other supplies and services for the provision of military assistance to civil authorities.

"(4) To assist the Secretary of Defense in preparing the budget required under section 10544 of this title.

"(5) To administer amounts provided the National Guard for the provision of military assistance to civil authorities.

"(6) To carry out any other responsibility relating to the provision of military assistance to civil authorities as the Secretary of Defense shall specify.

"(c) **ASSISTANCE**.—The Chairman of the Joint Chiefs of Staff shall assist the Chief of the National Guard Bureau in carrying out activities under this section.

"(d) **CONSULTATION**.—The Chief of the National Guard Bureau shall carry out activities under this section in consultation with the Secretary of the Army and the Secretary of the Air Force."

The Commission recommends a modification to this proposal. The Commission recommends that the Secretary of Homeland Security should have the responsibility to define civil support requirements, including those for the Department of Defense. The Secretary of Defense should have the responsibility to determine the best way to meet those requirements deemed valid by the Department through the appropriate procedures. In his new advisory role, the Chief of the National Guard Bureau should advise the commander of Northern Command, the Secretaries of the Air Force and Army, and through the Chairman of the Joint Chiefs of Staff, the Secretary of Defense, regarding how the National Guard may help address gaps between federal and state emergency response capabilities.

10. Section 2(c)(4) of S. 2658/H.R. 5200 would amend Chapter 1013 of Title 10, United States Code, by adding at the end the following new section:

"§ 10544. National Guard training and equipment: budget for military assistance to civil authorities and for other domestic operations

"(a) IN GENERAL.—The budget justification documents materials submitted to Congress in support of the budget of the President for a fiscal year (as submitted with the budget of the President under section 1105(a) of title 31) shall specify separate amounts for training and equipment for the National Guard for purposes of military assistance to civil authorities and for other domestic operations during such fiscal year.

"(b) SCOPE OF FUNDING.—The amounts specified under subsection (a) for a fiscal year shall be sufficient for purposes as follows:

"(1) The development and implementation of doctrine and training requirements applicable to the assistance and operations described in subsection (a) for such fiscal year.

"(2) The acquisition of equipment, materiel, and other supplies and services necessary for the provision of such assistance and such operations in such fiscal year."

The Commission does not recommend this emendation, on the grounds that most civil support missions are performed using "dual-use" equipment and that the designation of certain training and equipment as civil support–related would likely be arbitrary and would not help Congress provide meaningful oversight on this matter. As discussed above, the Commission instead recommends that the Department of Defense explicitly budget and program for civil support, in coordination with the Department of Homeland Security.

11. Section 2(e) of S. 2658/H.R 5200 would amend section 901 of the National Defense Authorization Act for Fiscal Year 1998 (Public Law 105-85) (relating to the positions of Assistant to the Chairman of the Joint Chiefs of Staff for National Guard Matters and for Reserve Matters) to read as follows:

"SEC. 901. ASSISTANT TO THE CHAIRMAN OF THE JOINT CHIEFS OF STAFF FOR RESERVE MATTERS.

"(a) IN GENERAL.—There is within the Joint Staff the position of Assistant to the Chairman of the Joint Chiefs of Staff for Reserve Matters.

"(b) SELECTION.—The Assistant to the Chairman of the Joint Chiefs of Staff for Reserve Matters shall be selected by the Chairman from officers of the Army Reserve, the Navy Reserve, the Marine Corps Reserve, or the Air Force Reserve who—

"(1) are recommended for such selection by the Secretary of the military department concerned;

"(2) have had at least 10 years of commissioned service in their reserve component; and

"(3) are in a grade above colonel or, in the case the Navy Reserve, captain.

"(c) TERM OF OFFICE.—The Assistant to the Chairman of the Joint Chiefs of Staff for Reserve Matters serves at the pleasure of the Chairman for a term of two years and may be continued in that assignment in the same manner, for one additional term. However, in a time of war there is no limit on the number of terms.

"(d) **GRADE**.—The Assistant to the Chairman of the Joint Chiefs of Staff for Reserve Matters while so serving, holds the grade of major general or, in the case of the Navy Reserve, rear admiral. The officer serving in the position shall be considered to be serving in a position external to that officer's Armed Force for purposes of section 721 of title 10, United States Code.

"(e) **DUTIES**.—The Assistant to the Chairman of the Joint Chiefs of Staff for Reserve Matters is an advisor to the Chairman on matters relating to the reserves and performs the duties prescribed for the position by the Chairman.

"(f) **OTHER RESERVE COMPONENT REPRESENTATION ON JOINT STAFF**.—The Secretary of Defense, in consultation with the Chairman of the Joint Chiefs of Staff, shall develop appropriate policy guidance to ensure that, to the maximum extent practicable, the level of reserve component officer representation within the Joint Staff is commensurate with the significant role of the reserve components within the Total Force."

The Commission recommends keeping the position of Assistant to the Chairman of the Joint Chiefs of Staff for National Guard Matters intact because of its importance to the decisions made by the Chairman and by the Joint Staff generally. The Commission concludes that this position serves valuable coordinating and monitoring functions. Moreover, the position can operate as a useful conduit of information and liaison between the Chairman and the National Guard in circumstances not involving the Chief of the National Guard Bureau.

12. Section 3(a) of S. 2658/H.R. 5200 expresses the sense of Congress that whenever officers are considered for promotion to the grade of lieutenant general/vice admiral on the active duty list, officers of the reserve components who are eligible for promotion to such grade should be considered for promotion. Section 3(b) requires the Secretary of Defense to submit to Congress a proposal for mechanisms to achieve the objective specified in subsection (a). Section 3(c) says that the President shall include with each nomination of an officer to the grade of lieutenant general/vice admiral on the active duty list that is submitted to the Senate for consideration a certification that all reserve officers who were eligible for consideration for promotion to that grade were considered in the making of such nomination.

The Commission recommends a modification to this proposal, because it does not believe that requiring the President to certify that all eligible reserve component officers were considered for promotion to O-9 would accomplish the laudable goal of increasing the opportunity for reserve and general flag officers to be selected for positions of importance and responsibility. The Commission instead recommends that the Secretary of Defense create more opportunities for reserve component officers to gain joint experience within the Office of the Secretary of Defense, on the Joint Staff, at combatant commands, and at defense agencies. The Commission further recommends that the Secretary should review and then identify one- and two-star positions for both full- and part-time reserve component officers to obtain joint experience.

13. Section 4(a) of S. 2658/H.R. 5200 would require that the position of deputy commander of United States Northern Command be filled by a qualified officer of the National Guard who is eligible for promotion to the grade of lieutenant general.

    The Commission recommends that either the officer serving in the position of the commander or the officer serving in the position of the deputy commander of U.S. Northern Command should be a National Guard or Reserve officer at all times.

14. Section 529(a)(2) of the National Defense Authorization Act for Fiscal Year 2007 requires the Commission on the National Guard and Reserve to study whether, as an alternative to the provisions of S. 2658/H.R. 5200 that provide for the Chief of the National Guard Bureau to be a member of the Joint Chiefs of Staff and to hold the grade of general, the Chief of the National Guard Bureau should hold the grade of general in the performance of the current duties of that office.

    As described in the full report, on the basis of the duties currently required to be performed by the Chief of the National Guard Bureau in this time of war, the Commission recommends that the Chief of the National Guard Bureau should hold the grade of general. The Commission recommends that the duties and responsibilities of the position of Chief of the National Guard Bureau should be reevaluated periodically to ensure that the duties required to be performed by the Chief of the National Guard Bureau remain commensurate with grade O-10.

15. Section 529(a)(3) of the National Defense Authorization Act for Fiscal Year 2007 requires the Commission to report on the advisability and feasibility of implementing the provisions of section 544 of H.R. 5122 of the 109th Congress, as passed the House of Representatives on May 11, 2006. Section 544 of H.R. 5122 would amend section 325 of Title 32, United States Code. That section presently provides that a National Guard service member is relieved of duty in the National Guard whenever the service member is on federal Title 10 active duty, except when (1) the service member is an officer, (2) the officer is a commander of a National Guard unit, (3) the President authorizes such service in both duty statuses, and (4) the state or territorial governor consents. Section 544 would amend section 325 of Title 32 to provide that any National Guard officer, not just a commander, may not be relieved from duty in the National Guard while serving on federal active duty. Section 544 would permit the President and the governor to give the authorization and consent *in advance* of calling the officer to active duty. Section 544 would also allow so-called dual status National Guard officers on active duty to perform any duty authorized by the laws of that officer's state without regard to the Posse Comitatus Act's prohibitions against participation in civilian law enforcement activities.

    The Commission recommends in favor of this proposal on the grounds that it provides flexibility in the management of mixed component units and is consistent with the greater use of the National Guard and Title 10 forces for domestic missions.

16. Section 529(a)(4) of the National Defense Authorization Act for Fiscal Year 2007 requires the Commission on the National Guard and Reserves to study the adequacy of Department of Defense processes for defining the equipment and funding necessary for the National Guard to conduct its responsibilities under Titles 10 and 32, United States Code, including homeland defense and related homeland missions.

The study shall include consideration of the extent to which those processes should be developed, taking into consideration the views of the Chief of the National Guard Bureau, the 54 adjutants general, and the Directors of the Army and Air National Guard. The study should also consider whether there should be an improved means by which National Guard equipment requirements are validated by the Joint Chiefs of Staff and are considered for funding by the Secretaries of the Army and Air Force.

The current processes for defining funding and equipping requirements are inadequate in that civil support requirements are rarely considered when funding is prioritized. The Secretary of Homeland Security should work with the Secretary of Defense to define and validate homeland-related requirements. The Secretary of Defense should separately budget for homeland-related requirements where those requirements are not subsumed within other funding and equipping requirements related to the Department of Defense's warfighting missions.

17. The Conference Report accompanying the National Defense Authorization Act for Fiscal Year 2007 (House Report 109-702) includes a Joint Explanatory Statement of the Committee of Conference. The joint statement pertaining to section 529 of the bill directs the Commission to evaluate the proposals referred to it, taking into consideration various matters specified in the joint statement. The Commission is asked to consider "Whether the scope and complexities of the duties and responsibilities of the position of Deputy Commander, U.S. Northern Command, require that they be carried out by two officers, each in the grade of O-9, one of whom would be a National Guard officer eligible for promotion to that grade."

The Commission has considered all those matters listed in the Joint Explanatory Statement pertaining to section 529 of the Public Law 109-364. The Commission recommends that there should be only one U.S. deputy commander at U.S. Northern Command.

APPENDIX 2

COMMISSION ON THE NATIONAL GUARD AND RESERVES: AUTHORIZING STATUTES

108th Congress
Public Law 108-375
As amended by
109th Congress
Public Law 109-163, Section 516
And further as amended by:
109th Congress
Public Law 109-364, Section 529

P.L. 108-375, SEC. 513 (AS AMENDED BY P.L. 109-163, SEC. 516). COMMISSION ON THE NATIONAL GUARD AND RESERVES.

(a) ESTABLISHMENT.—There is established in the legislative branch a commission to be known as the 'Commission on the National Guard and Reserves'.

(b) COMPOSITION.—(1) The Commission shall be composed of 13 members appointed as follows:

(A) Three members appointed by the chairman of the Committee on Armed Services of the Senate.

(B) Three members appointed by the chairman of the Committee on Armed Services of the House of Representatives.

(C) Two members appointed by the ranking minority member of the Committee on Armed Services of the Senate.

(D) Two members appointed by the ranking minority member of the Committee on Armed Service of the House of Representatives.

(E) Three members appointed by the Secretary of Defense.

(2) The members of the Commission shall be appointed from among persons who have knowledge and expertise in the following areas:

(A) National security.

(B) Roles and missions of any of the Armed Forces.

(C) The mission, operations, and organization of the National Guard of the United States.

(D) The mission, operations, and organization of the other reserve components of the Armed Forces.

(E) Military readiness of the Armed Forces.

(F) Personnel pay and other forms of compensation.

(G) Other personnel benefits, including health care.

(3) Members of the Commission shall be appointed for the life of the Commission. A vacancy in the membership of the Commission shall not affect the powers of the Commission, but shall be filled in the same manner as the original appointment.

(4) The Secretary of Defense shall designate a member of the Commission to be chairman of the Commission.

(c) DUTIES.—(1) The Commission shall carry out a study of the following matters:

(A) The roles and missions of the National Guard and the other reserve components of the Armed Forces.

(B) The compensation and other benefits, including health care benefits, that are provided for members of the reserve components under the laws of the United States.

(2) In carrying out the study under paragraph (1), the Commission shall do the following:

(A) Assess the current roles and missions of the reserve components and identify appropriate potential future roles and missions for the reserve components.

(B) Assess the capabilities of the reserve components and determine how the units and personnel of the reserve components may be best used to support the military operations of the Armed Forces and the achievement of national security objectives, including homeland defense, of the United States.

(C) Assess the Department of Defense plan for implementation of section 115(b) of title 10, United States Code, as added by section 416(a)(4).

(D) Assess—

(i) the current organization and structure of the National Guard and the other reserve components; and

(ii) the plans of the Department of Defense and the Armed Forces for future organization and structure of the National Guard and the other reserve components.

(E) Assess the manner in which the National Guard and the other reserve components are currently organized and funded for training and identify an organizational and funding structure for training that best supports the achievement of training objectives and operational readiness.

(F) Assess the effectiveness of the policies and programs of the National Guard and the other reserve components for achieving operational readiness and personnel readiness, including medical and personal readiness.

(G) Assess—

(i) the adequacy and appropriateness of the compensation and benefits currently provided for the members of the National Guard and the other reserve components, including the availability of health care benefits and health insurance; and

(ii) the effects of proposed changes in compensation and benefits on military careers in both the regular and the reserve components of the Armed Forces.

(H) Identify various feasible options for improving the compensation and other benefits available to the members of the National Guard and the members of the other reserve components and assess—

(i) the cost-effectiveness of such options; and

(ii) the foreseeable effects of such options on readiness, recruitment, and retention of personnel for careers in the regular and reserve components the Armed Forces.

(I) Assess the traditional military career paths for members of the National Guard and the other reserve components and identify alternative career paths that could enhance professional development.

(J) Assess the adequacy of the funding provided for the National Guard and the other reserve components for several previous fiscal years, including the funding provided for National Guard and reserve component equipment and the funding provided for National Guard and other reserve component personnel in active duty military personnel accounts and reserve military personnel accounts.

(d) FIRST MEETING.—The Commission shall hold its first meeting not later than 30 days after the date on which all members of the Commission have been appointed.

(e) ADMINISTRATIVE AND PROCEDURAL AUTHORITIES.—(1) Sections 955, 956, 957 (other than subsection (f)), 958, and 959 of the National Defense Authorization Act for Fiscal Year 1994 (Public Law 103-160; 10 U.S.C. 111 note) may apply to the Commission, except that—

(A) in applying the first sentence of subsection (a) of section 957 of such Act to the Commission, 'may' shall be substituted for 'shall'; and

(B) in applying subsections (a), (c)(2), and (e) of section 957 of such Act to the Commission, 'level IV of the Executive Schedule' shall be substituted for 'level V of the Executive Schedule'.

(2) The following provisions of law do not apply to the Commission:

(A) Section 3161 of title 5, United States Code.

(B) The Federal Advisory Committee Act (5 U.S.C. App.).

(3) If warranted by circumstances described in subparagraph (A) or (B) of section 8344(i)(1) of title 5, United States Code, or by circumstances described in subparagraph (A) or (B) of section 8468(f)(1) of such title, as applicable, the chairman of the Commission may exercise, with respect to the members of the Commission, the same waiver authority as would be available to the Director of the Office of Personnel Management under such section.

(f) REPORTS.—(1) Not later than three months after the first meeting of the Commission, the Commission shall submit to the Committees on Armed Services of the Senate and the House of Representatives a report setting forth—

(A) a strategic plan for the work of the Commission;

(B) a discussion of the activities of the Commission; and

(C) any initial findings of the Commission.

(2) Not later than January 31, 2008, the Commission shall submit a final report to the committees of Congress referred to in paragraph (1) and to the Secretary of Defense. The final report shall include any recommendations that the Commission determines appropriate, including any recommended legislation, policies, regulations, directives, and practices.

(g) TERMINATION.—The Commission shall terminate 90 days after the date on which the final report is submitted under subsection (f)(2).

(h) ANNUAL REVIEW.—(1) The Secretary of Defense shall annually review the reserve components of the Armed Forces with regard to—

> (A) the roles and missions of the reserve components; and

> (B) the compensation and other benefits, including health care benefits, that are provided for members of the reserve components under the laws of the United States.

(2) The Secretary shall submit a report of the annual review, together with any comments and recommendations that the Secretary considers appropriate, to the Committee on Armed Services of the Senate and the Committee on Armed Services of the House of Representatives.

(3) The first review under paragraph (1) shall take place during fiscal year 2006.

109th Congress
Public Law 109-364, Section 529

SEC. 529. ADDITIONAL MATTERS TO BE REVIEWED BY COMMISSION ON THE NATIONAL GUARD AND RESERVES.

(a) Additional Matters to be Reviewed by Commission—The Commission on the National Guard and Reserves shall include among the matters it studies (in addition to the matters specified in subsection (c) of the commission charter) each of the following:

> (1) NATIONAL GUARD BUREAU ENHANCEMENT PROPOSALS—The advisability and feasibility of implementing the provisions of S. 2658 and H.R. 5200 of the 109th Congress, as introduced in the Senate and the House of Representatives, respectively, on April 26, 2006.

> (2) CHIEF OF NATIONAL GUARD BUREAU—As an alternative to implementation of the provisions of the bills specified in paragraph (1) that provide for the Chief of the National Guard Bureau to be a member of the Joint Chiefs of Staff and to hold the grade of general, the advisability and feasibility of providing for the Chief of the National Guard Bureau to hold the grade of general in the performance of the current duties of that office.

> (3) NATIONAL GUARD OFFICERS AUTHORITY TO COMMAND—The advisability and feasibility of implementing the provisions of section 544 of H.R. 5122 of the 109th Congress, as passed by the House of Representatives on May 11, 2006.

> (4) NATIONAL GUARD EQUIPMENT AND FUNDING REQUIREMENTS—The adequacy of the Department of Defense processes for defining the equipment and funding necessary for the National Guard to conduct both its responsibilities under title 10, United States Code, and its responsibilities under title 32, United States

Code, including homeland defense and related homeland missions, including as part of such study—

> (A) consideration of the extent to which those processes should be developed taking into consideration the views of the Chief of the National Guard Bureau, as well as the views of the 54 Adjutant Generals and the views of the Chiefs of the Army National Guard and the Air Guard; and

> (B) whether there should be an improved means by which National Guard equipment requirements are validated by the Joint Chiefs of Staff and are considered for funding by the Secretaries of the Army and Air Force.

(b) Priority Review and Report—

> (1) **PRIORITY REVIEW**—The Commission on the National Guard and Reserves shall carry out its study of the matters specified in paragraphs (1), (2), and (3) of subsection (a) on a priority basis, with a higher priority for matters under those paragraphs relating to the grade and functions of the Chief of the National Guard Bureau.

> (2) **REPORT**—In addition to the reports required under subsection (f) of the commission charter, the Commission shall submit to the Committee on Armed Services of the Senate and the Committee on Armed Services of the House of Representatives an interim report, not later than March 1, 2007, specifically on the matters covered by paragraph (1). In such report, the Commission shall set forth its findings and any recommendations it considers appropriate with respect to those matters.

(c) Commission Charter Defined—For purposes of this section, the term 'commission charter' means section 513 of the Ronald W. Reagan National Defense Authorization Act for Fiscal Year 2005 (Public Law 108-375; 118 Stat. 1880).

APPENDIX 3

H.R. 5200, THE NATIONAL DEFENSE ENHANCEMENT AND NATIONAL GUARD EMPOWERMENT ACT OF 2006

109th CONGRESS
2d Session
H. R. 5200

To amend title 10, United States Code, to enhance the national defense through empowerment of the Chief of the National Guard Bureau and the enhancement of the functions of the National Guard Bureau, and for other purposes.

IN THE HOUSE OF REPRESENTATIVES

April 26, 2006

Mr. TOM DAVIS of Virginia (for himself, Mr. TAYLOR of Mississippi, Mr. GIBBONS, Mr. HAYES, Mr. WILSON of South Carolina, and Mrs. MILLER of Michigan) introduced the following bill; which was referred to the Committee on Armed Services

---

A BILL

To amend title 10, United States Code, to enhance the national defense through empowerment of the Chief of the National Guard Bureau and the enhancement of the functions of the National Guard Bureau, and for other purposes.

Be it enacted by the Senate and House of Representatives of the United States of America in Congress assembled,

SECTION 1. SHORT TITLE.

This Act may be cited as the `National Defense Enhancement and National Guard Empowerment Act of 2006'.

SEC. 2. EXPANDED AUTHORITY OF CHIEF OF THE NATIONAL GUARD BUREAU AND EXPANDED FUNCTIONS OF THE NATIONAL GUARD BUREAU.

(a) Expanded Authority-
(1) IN GENERAL- Subsection (a) of section 10501 of title 10, United States Code, is amended by striking `joint bureau of the Department of the Army and the Department of the Air Force' and inserting `joint activity of the Department of Defense'.
(2) PURPOSE- Subsection (b) of such section is amended by striking `between' and all that follows and inserting `between--
`(1)(A) the Secretary of Defense, the Joint Chiefs of Staff, and the commanders of the combatant commands for the United States, and (B) the Department of the Army and the Department of the Air Force; and
`(2) the several States.'.

(b) Enhancements of Position of Chief of the National Guard Bureau-

(1) ADVISORY FUNCTION ON NATIONAL GUARD MATTERS- Subsection (c) of section 10502 of title 10, United States Code, is amended by inserting `to the Secretary of Defense, to the Chairman of the Joint Chiefs of Staff,' after `principal advisor'.

(2) MEMBER OF JOINT CHIEFS OF STAFF- (A) Such section is further amended--

(i) by redesignating subsection (d) as subsection (e); and

(ii) by inserting after subsection (c) the following new subsection (d):

`(d) Member of Joint Chiefs of Staff- The Chief of the National Guard Bureau shall perform the duties prescribed for him or her as a member of the Joint Chiefs of Staff under section 151 of this title.'.

(B) Section 151(a) of such title is amended by adding at the end the following new paragraph:

`(7) The Chief of the National Guard Bureau.'.

(3) GRADE- Subsection (e) of such section, as redesignated by paragraph (2)(A)(i) of this subsection, is further amended by striking `lieutenant general' and inserting `general'.

(4) ANNUAL REPORT TO CONGRESS ON VALIDATED REQUIREMENTS- Section 10504 of such title is amended by adding at the end the following new subsection:

`(c) Annual Report on Validated Requirements- Not later than December 31 each year, the Chief of the National Guard Bureau shall submit to Congress a report on the following:

`(1) The requirements validated under section 10503a(b)(1) of this title during the preceding fiscal year.

`(2) The requirements referred to in paragraph (1) for which funding is to be requested in the next budget for a fiscal year under section 10544 of this title.

`(3) The requirements referred to in paragraph (1) for which funding will not be requested in the next budget for a fiscal year under section 10544 of this title.'.

(c) Enhancement of Functions of National Guard Bureau-

(1) DEVELOPMENT OF CHARTER- Section 10503 of title 10, United States Code, is amended--

(A) in the matter preceding paragraph (1), by striking `The Secretary of the Army and the Secretary of the Air Force shall jointly develop' and inserting `The Secretary of Defense, in consultation with the Secretary of the Army and the Secretary of the Air Force, shall develop'; and

(B) in paragraph (12), by striking `the Secretaries' and inserting `the Secretary of Defense'.

(2) ADDITIONAL GENERAL FUNCTIONS- Such section is further amended--

(A) by redesignating paragraph (12), as amended by paragraph (1)(B) of this subsection, as paragraph (13); and

(B) by inserting after paragraph (11) the following new paragraph (12):

`(12) Facilitating and coordinating with other Federal agencies, and with the several States, the use of National Guard personnel and resources for and in contingency operations, military operations other than war, natural disasters, support of civil authorities, and other circumstances.'.

(3) MILITARY ASSISTANCE FOR CIVIL AUTHORITIES- Chapter 1011 of such title is further amended by inserting after section 10503 the following new section:

`Sec. 10503a. Functions of National Guard Bureau: military assistance to civil authorities

`(a) Identification of Additional Necessary Assistance- The Chief of the National Guard Bureau shall--

`(1) identify gaps between Federal and State capabilities to prepare for and respond to emergencies; and

`(2) make recommendations to the Secretary of Defense on programs and activities of the National Guard for military assistance to civil authorities to address such gaps.

`(b) Scope of Responsibilities- In meeting the requirements of subsection (a), the Chief of the National Guard Bureau shall, in coordination with the Adjutant Generals of the States, have responsibilities as follows:

`(1) To validate the requirements of the several States and Territories with respect to military assistance to civil authorities.

`(2) To develop doctrine and training requirements relating to the provision of military assistance to civil authorities.

`(3) To acquire equipment, materiel, and other supplies and services for the provision of military assistance to civil authorities.

`(4) To assist the Secretary of Defense in preparing the budget required under section 10544 of this title.

`(5) To administer amounts provided the National Guard for the provision of military assistance to civil authorities.

`(6) To carry out any other responsibility relating to the provision of military assistance to civil authorities as the Secretary of Defense shall specify.

`(c) Assistance- The Chairman of the Joint Chiefs of Staff shall assist the Chief of the National Guard Bureau in carrying out activities under this section.

`(d) Consultation- The Chief of the National Guard Bureau shall carry out activities under this section in consultation with the Secretary of the Army and the Secretary of the Air Force.'.

(4) BUDGETING FOR TRAINING AND EQUIPMENT FOR MILITARY ASSISTANCE TO CIVIL AUTHORITIES AND OTHER DOMESTIC MISSIONS- Chapter 1013 of title 10, United States Code, is amended by adding at the end the following new section:

`Sec. 10544. National Guard training and equipment: budget for military assistance to civil authorities and for other domestic operations

`(a) In General- The budget justification documents materials submitted to Congress in support of the budget of the President for a fiscal year (as submitted with the budget of the President under section 1105(a) of title 31) shall specify separate amounts for training and equipment for the National Guard for purposes of military assistance to civil authorities and for other domestic operations during such fiscal year.

`(b) Scope of Funding- The amounts specified under subsection (a) for a fiscal year shall be sufficient for purposes as follows:

> `(1) The development and implementation of doctrine and training requirements applicable to the assistance and operations described in subsection (a) for such fiscal year.
>
> `(2) The acquisition of equipment, materiel, and other supplies and services necessary for the provision of such assistance and such operations in such fiscal year.'.
>
> (5) LIMITATION ON INCREASE IN PERSONNEL OF NATIONAL GUARD BUREAU- The Secretary of Defense shall, to the extent practicable, ensure that no additional personnel are assigned to the National Guard Bureau in order to address administrative or other requirements arising out of the amendments made by this subsection.

(d) Conforming and Clerical Amendments-

> (1) CONFORMING AMENDMENT- The heading of section 10503 of such title is amended to read as follows:

`Sec. 10503. Functions of National Guard Bureau: charter'.

> (2) CLERICAL AMENDMENTS- (A) The table of sections at the beginning of chapter 1011 of such title is amended by striking the item relating to section 10503 and inserting the following new items:
> `10503. Functions of National Guard Bureau: charter.
> `10503a. Functions of National Guard Bureau: military assistance to civil authorities.'.
> (B) The table of sections at the beginning of chapter 1013 of such title is amended by adding at the end the following new item:
> `10544. National Guard training and equipment: budget for military assistance to civil authorities and for other domestic operations.'.

(e) Termination of Position of Assistant to Chairman of Joint Chiefs of Staff for National Guard Matters- Section 901 of the National Defense Authorization Act for Fiscal Year 1998 (Public Law 105-85; 111 Stat. 1853; 10 U.S.C. 155 note) is amended to read as follows:

`SEC. 901. Assistant to the Chairman of the Joint Chiefs of Staff for Reserve Matters.

`(a) In General- There is within the Joint Staff the position of Assistant to the Chairman of the Joint Chiefs of Staff for Reserve Matters.

`(b) Selection- The Assistant to the Chairman of the Joint Chiefs of Staff for Reserve Matters shall be selected by the Chairman from officers of the Army Reserve, the Navy Reserve, the Marine Corps Reserve, or the Air Force Reserve who--

`(1) are recommended for such selection by the Secretary of the military department concerned;

`(2) have had at least 10 years of commissioned service in their reserve component; and

`(3) are in a grade above colonel or, in the case the Navy Reserve, captain.

`(c) Term of Office- The Assistant to the Chairman of the Joint Chiefs of Staff for Reserve Matters serves at the pleasure of the Chairman for a term of two years and may be continued in that assignment in the same manner, for one additional term. However, in a time of war there is no limit on the number of terms.

`(d) Grade- The Assistant to the Chairman of the Joint Chiefs of Staff for Reserve Matters while so serving, holds the grade of major general or, in the case of the Navy Reserve, rear admiral. The officer serving in the position shall be considered to be serving in a position external to that officer's Armed Force for purposes of section 721 of title 10, United States Code.

`(e) Duties- The Assistant to the Chairman of the Joint Chiefs of Staff for Reserve Matters is an advisor to the Chairman on matters relating to the reserves and performs the duties prescribed for the position by the Chairman.

`(f) Other Reserve Component Representation on Joint Staff- The Secretary of Defense, in consultation with the Chairman of the Joint Chiefs of Staff, shall develop appropriate policy guidance to ensure that, to the maximum extent practicable, the level of reserve component officer representation within the Joint Staff is commensurate with the significant role of the reserve components within the Total Force.'.

SEC. 3. PROMOTION OF ELIGIBLE RESERVE OFFICERS TO LIEUTENANT GENERAL AND VICE ADMIRAL GRADES ON THE ACTIVE-DUTY LIST.

(a) Sense of Congress- It is the sense of Congress that, whenever officers are considered for promotion to the grade of lieutenant general, or vice admiral in the case of the Navy, on the active duty list, officers of the reserve components of the Armed Forces who are eligible for promotion to such grade should be considered for promotion to such grade.

(b) Proposal- The Secretary of Defense shall submit to Congress a proposal for mechanisms to achieve the objective specified in subsection (a). The proposal shall include such recommendations for legislative or administrative action as the Secretary considers appropriate in order to achieve that objective.

(c) Notice Accompanying Nominations- The President shall include with each nomination of an officer to the grade of lieutenant general, or vice admiral in the case of the Navy, on the active-duty list that is submitted to the Senate for consideration a certification that all reserve officers who were eligible for consideration for promotion to such grade were considered in the making of such nomination.

SEC. 4. REQUIREMENT THAT POSITION OF DEPUTY COMMANDER OF THE UNITED STATES NORTHERN COMMAND BE FILLED BY A QUALIFIED NATIONAL GUARD OFFICER.

(a) In General- The position of Deputy Commander of the United States Northern Command shall be filled by a qualified officer of the National Guard who is eligible for promotion to the grade of lieutenant general.

(b) Purpose- The purpose of the requirement in subsection (a) is to ensure that information received from the National Guard Bureau regarding the operation of the National Guard of the several States is integrated into the plans and operations of the United States Northern Command.

APPENDIX 4

S. 2658, THE NATIONAL DEFENSE ENHANCEMENT AND NATIONAL GUARD EMPOWERMENT ACT OF 2006

109th CONGRESS
2d Session
S. 2658

To amend title 10, United States Code, to enhance the national defense through empowerment of the Chief of the National Guard Bureau and the enhancement of the functions of the National Guard Bureau, and for other purposes.

IN THE SENATE OF THE UNITED STATES

April 26, 2006

Mr. BOND (for himself and Mr. LEAHY) introduced the following bill; which was read twice and referred to the Committee on Armed Services

---

A BILL

To amend title 10, United States Code, to enhance the national defense through empowerment of the Chief of the National Guard Bureau and the enhancement of the functions of the National Guard Bureau, and for other purposes.

Be it enacted by the Senate and House of Representatives of the United States of America in Congress assembled,

SECTION 1. SHORT TITLE.

This Act may be cited as the `National Defense Enhancement and National Guard Empowerment Act of 2006'.

SEC. 2. EXPANDED AUTHORITY OF CHIEF OF THE NATIONAL GUARD BUREAU AND EXPANDED FUNCTIONS OF THE NATIONAL GUARD BUREAU.

(a) Expanded Authority-
    (1) IN GENERAL- Subsection (a) of section 10501 of title 10, United States Code, is amended by striking `joint bureau of the Department of the Army and the Department of the Air Force' and inserting `joint activity of the Department of Defense'.
    (2) PURPOSE- Subsection (b) of such section is amended by striking `between' and all that follows and inserting `between--
    `(1)(A) the Secretary of Defense, the Joint Chiefs of Staff, and the commanders of the combatant commands for the United States, and (B) the Department of the Army and the Department of the Air Force; and
    `(2) the several States.'.
(b) Enhancements of Position of Chief of the National Guard Bureau-

(1) ADVISORY FUNCTION ON NATIONAL GUARD MATTERS- Subsection (c) of section 10502 of title 10, United States Code, is amended by inserting `to the Secretary of Defense, to the Chairman of the Joint Chiefs of Staff,' after `principal advisor'.

(2) MEMBER OF JOINT CHIEFS OF STAFF- (A) Such section is further amended--

    (i) by redesignating subsection (d) as subsection (e); and

    (ii) by inserting after subsection (c) the following new subsection (d):

`(d) Member of Joint Chiefs of Staff- The Chief of the National Guard Bureau shall perform the duties prescribed for him or her as a member of the Joint Chiefs of Staff under section 151 of this title.'.

(B) Section 151(a) of such title is amended by adding at the end the following new paragraph:

`(7) The Chief of the National Guard Bureau.'.

(3) GRADE- Subsection (e) of such section, as redesignated by paragraph (2)(A)(i) of this subsection, is further amended by striking `lieutenant general' and inserting `general'.

(4) ANNUAL REPORT TO CONGRESS ON VALIDATED REQUIREMENTS- Section 10504 of such title is amended by adding at the end the following new subsection:

`(c) Annual Report on Validated Requirements- Not later than December 31 each year, the Chief of the National Guard Bureau shall submit to Congress a report on the following:

`(1) The requirements validated under section 10503a(b)(1) of this title during the preceding fiscal year.

`(2) The requirements referred to in paragraph (1) for which funding is to be requested in the next budget for a fiscal year under section 10544 of this title.

`(3) The requirements referred to in paragraph (1) for which funding will not be requested in the next budget for a fiscal year under section 10544 of this title.'.

(c) Enhancement of Functions of National Guard Bureau-

(1) DEVELOPMENT OF CHARTER- Section 10503 of title 10, United States Code, is amended--

    (A) in the matter preceding paragraph (1), by striking `The Secretary of the Army and the Secretary of the Air Force shall jointly develop' and inserting `The Secretary of Defense, in consultation with the Secretary of the Army and the Secretary of the Air Force, shall develop'; and

    (B) in paragraph (12), by striking `the Secretaries' and inserting `the Secretary of Defense'.

(2) ADDITIONAL GENERAL FUNCTIONS- Such section is further amended--

    (A) by redesignating paragraph (12), as amended by paragraph (1)(B) of this subsection, as paragraph (13); and

    (B) by inserting after paragraph (11) the following new paragraph (12):

`(12) Facilitating and coordinating with other Federal agencies, and with the several States, the use of National Guard personnel and resources for and in contingency operations, military operations other than war, natural disasters, support of civil authorities, and other circumstances.'.

(3) MILITARY ASSISTANCE FOR CIVIL AUTHORITIES- Chapter 1011 of such title is further amended by inserting after section 10503 the following new section:

`Sec. 10503a. Functions of National Guard Bureau: military assistance to civil authorities

`(a) Identification of Additional Necessary Assistance- The Chief of the National Guard Bureau shall--

  `(1) identify gaps between Federal and State capabilities to prepare for and respond to emergencies; and

  `(2) make recommendations to the Secretary of Defense on programs and activities of the National Guard for military assistance to civil authorities to address such gaps.

`(b) Scope of Responsibilities- In meeting the requirements of subsection (a), the Chief of the National Guard Bureau shall, in coordination with the Adjutant Generals of the States, have responsibilities as follows:

  `(1) To validate the requirements of the several States and Territories with respect to military assistance to civil authorities.

  `(2) To develop doctrine and training requirements relating to the provision of military assistance to civil authorities.

  `(3) To acquire equipment, materiel, and other supplies and services for the provision of military assistance to civil authorities.

  `(4) To assist the Secretary of Defense in preparing the budget required under section 10544 of this title.

  `(5) To administer amounts provided the National Guard for the provision of military assistance to civil authorities.

  `(6) To carry out any other responsibility relating to the provision of military assistance to civil authorities as the Secretary of Defense shall specify.

`(c) Assistance- The Chairman of the Joint Chiefs of Staff shall assist the Chief of the National Guard Bureau in carrying out activities under this section.

`(d) Consultation- The Chief of the National Guard Bureau shall carry out activities under this section in consultation with the Secretary of the Army and the Secretary of the Air Force.'.

(4) BUDGETING FOR TRAINING AND EQUIPMENT FOR MILITARY ASSISTANCE TO CIVIL AUTHORITIES AND OTHER DOMESTIC MISSIONS- Chapter 1013 of title 10, United States Code, is amended by adding at the end the following new section:

`Sec. 10544. National Guard training and equipment: budget for military assistance to civil authorities and for other domestic operations

`(a) In General- The budget justification documents materials submitted to Congress in support of the budget of the President for a fiscal year (as submitted with the budget of the President under section 1105(a) of title 31) shall specify separate amounts for training and equipment for the National Guard for purposes of military assistance to civil authorities and for other domestic operations during such fiscal year.

`(b) Scope of Funding- The amounts specified under subsection (a) for a fiscal year shall be sufficient for purposes as follows:

`(1) The development and implementation of doctrine and training requirements applicable to the assistance and operations described in subsection (a) for such fiscal year.

`(2) The acquisition of equipment, materiel, and other supplies and services necessary for the provision of such assistance and such operations in such fiscal year.'.

(5) LIMITATION ON INCREASE IN PERSONNEL OF NATIONAL GUARD BUREAU- The Secretary of Defense shall, to the extent practicable, ensure that no additional personnel are assigned to the National Guard Bureau in order to address administrative or other requirements arising out of the amendments made by this subsection.

(d) Conforming and Clerical Amendments-

(1) CONFORMING AMENDMENT- The heading of section 10503 of such title is amended to read as follows:

`Sec. 10503. Functions of National Guard Bureau: charter'.

(2) CLERICAL AMENDMENTS- (A) The table of sections at the beginning of chapter 1011 of such title is amended by striking the item relating to section 10503 and inserting the following new items:

`10503. Functions of National Guard Bureau: charter.

`10503a. Functions of National Guard Bureau: military assistance to civil authorities.'.

(B) The table of sections at the beginning of chapter 1013 of such title is amended by adding at the end the following new item:

`10544. National Guard training and equipment: budget for military assistance to civil authorities and for other domestic operations.'.

(e) Termination of Position of Assistant to Chairman of Joint Chiefs of Staff for National Guard Matters- Section 901 of the National Defense Authorization Act for Fiscal Year 1998 (Public Law 105-85; 111 Stat. 1853; 10 U.S.C. 155 note) is amended to read as follows:

`Sec. 901. Assistant to the Chairman of the Joint Chiefs of Staff for Reserve Matters.

`(a) In General- There is within the Joint Staff the position of Assistant to the Chairman of the Joint Chiefs of Staff for Reserve Matters.

`(b) Selection- The Assistant to the Chairman of the Joint Chiefs of Staff for Reserve Matters shall be selected by the Chairman from officers of the Army Reserve, the Navy Reserve, the Marine Corps Reserve, or the Air Force Reserve who--

`(1) are recommended for such selection by the Secretary of the military department concerned;

`(2) have had at least 10 years of commissioned service in their reserve component; and

`(3) are in a grade above colonel or, in the case the Navy Reserve, captain.

`(c) Term of Office- The Assistant to the Chairman of the Joint Chiefs of Staff for Reserve Matters serves at the pleasure of the Chairman for a term of two years and may be continued in that assignment in the same manner, for one additional term. However, in a time of war there is no limit on the number of terms.

`(d) Grade- The Assistant to the Chairman of the Joint Chiefs of Staff for Reserve Matters while so serving, holds the grade of major general or, in the case of the Navy Reserve, rear admiral. The officer serving in the position shall be considered to be serving in a position external to that officer's Armed Force for purposes of section 721 of title 10, United States Code.

`(e) Duties- The Assistant to the Chairman of the Joint Chiefs of Staff for Reserve Matters is an advisor to the Chairman on matters relating to the reserves and performs the duties prescribed for the position by the Chairman.

`(f) Other Reserve Component Representation on Joint Staff- The Secretary of Defense, in consultation with the Chairman of the Joint Chiefs of Staff, shall develop appropriate policy guidance to ensure that, to the maximum extent practicable, the level of reserve component officer representation within the Joint Staff is commensurate with the significant role of the reserve components within the Total Force.'.

SEC. 3. PROMOTION OF ELIGIBLE RESERVE OFFICERS TO LIEUTENANT GENERAL AND VICE ADMIRAL GRADES ON THE ACTIVE-DUTY LIST.

(a) Sense of Congress- It is the sense of Congress that, whenever officers are considered for promotion to the grade of lieutenant general, or vice admiral in the case of the Navy, on the active duty list, officers of the reserve components of the Armed Forces who are eligible for promotion to such grade should be considered for promotion to such grade.

(b) Proposal- The Secretary of Defense shall submit to Congress a proposal for mechanisms to achieve the objective specified in subsection (a). The proposal shall include such recommendations for legislative or administrative action as the Secretary considers appropriate in order to achieve that objective.

(c) Notice Accompanying Nominations- The President shall include with each nomination of an officer to the grade of lieutenant general, or vice admiral in the case of the Navy, on the active-duty list that is submitted to the Senate for consideration a certification that all reserve officers who were eligible for consideration for promotion to such grade were considered in the making of such nomination.

SEC. 4. REQUIREMENT THAT POSITION OF DEPUTY COMMANDER OF THE UNITED STATES NORTHERN COMMAND BE FILLED BY A QUALIFIED NATIONAL GUARD OFFICER.

(a) In General- The position of Deputy Commander of the United States Northern Command shall be filled by a qualified officer of the National Guard who is eligible for promotion to the grade of lieutenant general.

(b) Purpose- The purpose of the requirement in subsection (a) is to ensure that information received from the National Guard Bureau regarding the operation of the National Guard of the several States is integrated into the plans and operations of the United States Northern Command.

APPENDIX 5

THE NATIONAL GUARD BUREAU CHARTER

Pursuant to the requirements of Section 10503, Title 10, United States Code, the Secretary of the Army and the Secretary of the Air Force have jointly developed and do hereby prescribe the following Charter for the National Guard Bureau:

NATIONAL GUARD BUREAU CHARTER

Subject to the authority, direction, and control of the Secretary of the Army and the Secretary of the Air Force, subject to sections 3013 and 8013 of Title 10, United States Code, and consistent with approved policies, directives, regulations, and publications of the Army and the Air Force, and subject to inspections in accordance with Section 105 of Title 32, United States Code, the Chief of the National Guard Bureau is responsible for the following functions:

(1) Implementing Departmental guidance on allocation of unit structure, strength authorizations, and other resources to the Army National Guard of the United States and the Air National Guard of the United States.

(2) Prescribing the training discipline and training requirements for the Army National Guard and the Air National Guard and the allocation of Federal funds for the training of the Army National Guard and the Air National Guard.

(3) Ensuring that units and members of the Army National Guard and the Air National Guard are trained by the States in accordance with approved programs and policies of, and guidance from, the Secretary of the Army, the Secretary of the Air Force, and the respective Service Chiefs of Staff.

(4) Monitoring and assisting the States in the organization, maintenance, and operation of National Guard units so as to provide well-trained and well-equipped units capable of augmenting the active forces in time of war or national emergency.

(5) Planning and administering the budgets for the Army National Guard of the United States and the Air National Guard of the United States.

(6) Supervising the acquisition and supply of, and accountability of the States for, Federal property issued to the National Guard through the property and fiscal officers designated, detailed, or appointed under section 708 of Title 32, United States Code.

(7) Granting and withdrawing, in accordance with applicable laws and regulations, Federal recognition of (A) National Guard units, and (B) officers of the National Guard.

(8) Coordinating departmental policies and programs for the employment and use of National Guard technicians under section 709 of Title 32, United States Code.

(9) Supervising and administering the Active Guard and Reserve program as it pertains to the National Guard in accordance with priorities established by the Secretary of the Army and the Secretary of the Air Force.

(10) Issuing, with the coordination and approval of the service concerned, directives, regulations, and publications consistent with approved policies of the Army and Air Force, as appropriate.

(11) Facilitating and supporting the training of members and units of the National Guard to meet State requirements.

(12) Facilitating and coordinating with the Departments of the Army and the Air Force the use of National Guard personnel and resources for contingency operations, Military Operations Other Than War, natural disasters, Military Support to Civil Authorities, and special events.

(13) Ensuring that appointments of all officials and personnel of the National Guard Bureau comply with all applicable Department of the Army and Department of the Air Force personnel and manpower rules and regulations.

(14) Ensuring that, in the performance of their dirties, all officials and personnel of the National Guard Bureau comply fully with applicable Department of the Army and Department of the Air Force policies, directives, publications and legal opinions.

(15) Implementing, with the Chief of the National Guard Bureau as the Responsible Department Official, Title VI of the Civil Rights Act of 1964 and DOD Directive 5500.11, Nondiscrimination in Federally Assisted Programs, as they apply to the Army and Air National Guard.

(16) Such other functions as the Secretaries may prescribe.

(Dated September 1, 1995; published in Army Regulation 130-5/AFMD 10, "Organization and Functions of National Guard Bureau," December 30, 2001, pp. 3–4.)

APPENDIX 6

COMMISSIONERS OF THE COMMISSION ON THE NATIONAL GUARD AND RESERVES

Arnold L. Punaro, Chairman

Chairman Punaro is a retired Marine Corps major general who served as Commanding General of the 4th Marine Division (1997–2000) and Director of Reserve Affairs at Headquarters Marine Corps during the post-9/11 peak reserve mobilization periods. Following active duty service in Vietnam, he was mobilized three times: for Operation Desert Shield in the first Gulf War, to command Joint Task Force Provide Promise (Fwd) in Bosnia and Macedonia, and for Operation Iraqi Freedom in 2003. He worked on Capitol Hill for 24 years for Senator Sam Nunn and served as his staff director of the Senate Armed Services Committee for 14 years. He is currently Executive Vice President of Science Applications International Corporation.

William L. Ball, III

Commissioner Ball is currently Managing Director of The Loeffler Group, a government affairs practice in Washington, DC, and Texas. He also serves as Chairman of the Board of Trustees of the Asia Foundation, an international NGO operating in 18 Asian countries. He served in the Navy for 6 years, followed by 10 years' service on the U.S. Senate staff for Senators Herman Talmadge and John Tower. He joined the Reagan administration in 1985, serving as Assistant Secretary of State for Legislative Affairs, Assistant to the President for Legislative Affairs at the White House, and Secretary of the Navy in 1988–89.

Les Brownlee

Commissioner Brownlee was confirmed as the Under Secretary of the Army in November 2004 and served concurrently as the Acting Secretary of the Army from May 2003 to November 2004. He was appointed by both Senators Strom Thurmond and John Warner to serve as the staff director of the Senate Armed Services Committee. He served two tours in Vietnam and is retired from the United States Army. He is currently President of Les Brownlee & Associates LLC.

Rhett Dawson

Commissioner Dawson is currently President and CEO of the Information Technology Industry Council. He is the former Senior Vice President, Law and Public Policy, for the Potomac Electric Power Company. During the last two years of the Reagan administration, he was an Assistant to the President for Operations. He also served as staff director of the Senate Armed Services Committee. He served on active duty as an ROTC-commissioned Army officer from 1969 to 1972.

Larry K. Eckles

Commissioner Eckles retired as the Assistant Division Commander of the 35th Infantry Division, headquartered at Fort Leavenworth, Kansas, after 37 years of service. He retired with more than 31 years of full-time civil service employment with the Nebraska Army National Guard and has served in numerous positions at state headquarters, including chief of staff of the Nebraska Army National Guard, battalion commander, and director of personnel.

Patricia L. Lewis

Commissioner Lewis served more than 28 years with the federal government, including service with the Senate Armed Services Committee for Chairmen John Warner, Sam Nunn, and Scoop Jackson. Ms. Lewis began her federal career in 1975 with the Department of the Navy and has held positions in Naval Sea Systems Command, the Office of the Navy Comptroller, and the Office of the Secretary of Defense. She is currently a partner with Monfort-Lewis, LLC.

Dan McKinnon

Commissioner McKinnon was founder, Chairman, and CEO of North American Airlines. He undertook special projects for the Director of Central Intelligence and also served as Chairman of the Civil Aeronautics Board, during which time he implemented airline deregulation. He has owned radio stations in San Diego. Early in his career, he spent four years in the United States Navy as an aviator where he set, and holds, the U.S. Navy helicopter peacetime air/sea record of 62 saves.

Wade Rowley

Commissioner Rowley is currently a military border infrastructure construction consultant with the Department of Homeland Security, U.S. Customs and Border Protection. He served more than 23 years with the California Army National Guard and Army Reserves. His last military assignment was with the California Army National Guard, where he served as an engineer officer, company commander, and facility commander for the California National Guard Counterdrug Task Force in support of the U.S. Border Patrol.

James E. Sherrard III

Commissioner Sherrard served as Chief of Air Force Reserve, Headquarters USAF, Washington, DC, and Commander, Air Force Reserve Command, Robins AFB, Georgia, from 1998 to 2004. He is a retired lieutenant general with more than 38 years of commissioned service in the United States Air Force. As Chief of Air Force Reserve and Commander, Air Force Reserve Command, he was responsible for organizing, training, and equipping more than 79,000 military and civil service personnel required to support operations and combat readiness training for 36 flying wings, 14 detached groups, 13 Air Force Reserve installations, three Numbered Air Forces, and the Air Reserve Personnel Center (ARPC). As Chief of Air Force Reserve, he directed and oversaw the mobilization of Air Force Reserve personnel in support of military operations in Kosovo, Afghanistan, and Iraq. During his career, General Sherrard commanded an airlift group, two Air Force Reserve installations, two wings, and two Numbered Air Forces.

Donald L. Stockton

Commissioner Stockton owns and for more than 32 years has operated the Marshfield Drayage Company, a regional trucking company in southwest Missouri. He retired as a lieutenant colonel from the U.S. Air Force Reserves, where he served nearly 30 years. For almost 25 years he commanded various flights and squadrons, was deputy commander for resources, and subsequently was deputy commander for support of the 943rd Airlift Wing at March Air Force Base in California. His last command was with the 934th Maintenance

Squadron, a subordinate unit of the 934th Airlift Wing, Air Force Reserve, in Minneapolis, where he was responsible for the unit's C-130E aircraft and for the training of some 175 reservists. For the Reserve Officers Association of the United States (ROA), he is immediate past national Air Force vice president, a past president, and currently national councilman for the Missouri Department.

E. Gordon Stump

Commissioner Stump retired in January 2003 from his position of Adjutant General and the Director of Military and Veterans Affairs in Michigan after serving for 12 years. He commanded and directed a total of 157 Army and Air National Guard units, two veterans nursing homes, and 12 veterans service organizations. His prior assignments included Squadron Commander 107th TFS and Commander and Deputy Commander of the Headquarters Michigan Air National Guard. He flew 241 combat missions over North and South Vietnam. He also deployed to South Korea during the *Pueblo* crisis. He served as President of the National Guard Association of the United States and as a member of the Reserve Forces Policy Board. Prior to his assignment as Adjutant General, he was Vice President of Automotive Engineering for Uniroyal Goodrich Tire Co. He is currently President of Strategic Defense Associates, LLC.

J. Stanton Thompson

Commissioner Thompson is currently an executive director for the U.S. Department of Agriculture's Farm Service Agency. He is a retired naval rear admiral with more than 35 years of military service. He is the former Special Assistant for Reserve Matters to the Commander, U.S. NORTHCOM and North American Aerospace Command. He also served as a principal advisor to the commander for maritime homeland defense. During his recall to active duty, he provided active duty support to Operation Desert Shield/Desert Storm.

APPENDIX 7

PUBLIC HEARING PANELS TO DATE

HEARING ON PRINCIPLES AND PRIORITIES, ROLES AND MISSIONS

Room 2216, Rayburn House Office Building, Washington, DC

March 8, 2006

9:30 a.m. (IN ORDER OF APPEARANCE)

- Senator Mark Pryor, Co-Chair, Senate Reserve Caucus
- Senator Lindsey Graham, Chairman, Personnel Subcommittee, Senate Armed Services Committee
- Rep. Duncan Hunter, Chairman, House Armed Services Committee
- Senator Kit Bond, Co-Chair, Senate National Guard Caucus
- Senator Patrick Leahy, Co-Chair, Senate National Guard Caucus
- Rep. John McHugh, Chairman, Military Personnel Subcommittee, House Armed Services Committee
- Senator Ben Nelson, Ranking Member, Personnel Subcommittee, Senate Armed Services Committee
- Senator John Warner, Chairman, Senate Armed Services Committee
- Rep. Ike Skelton, Ranking Member, House Armed Services Committee
- Rep. Gene Taylor, Co-Chair, House Guard and Reserve Components Caucus
- Rep. Steve Buyer, Co-Chair, House Guard and Reserve Components Caucus

1:00 p.m.

- Dr. David S. C. Chu, Under Secretary of Defense for Personnel and Readiness
- Lieutenant General Raymond Odierno, Assistant to the Chairman of the Joint Chiefs of Staff

MARCH 9, 2006

9:30 a.m.

- General Richard Cody, Vice Chief of Staff of the U.S. Army
- Admiral Robert Willard, Vice Chief of Naval Operations
- General Robert Magnus, Assistant Commandant of the Marine Corps
- General John D. W. Corley, Vice Chief of Staff of the U. S. Air Force

2:00 p.m.

- Michèle Flournoy, Senior Adviser in the International Security Program at the Center for Strategic & International Studies
- Dr. Andrew Krepinevich, Executive Director of the Center for Strategic and Budgetary Assessments

HEARING ON HOMELAND DEFENSE/HOMELAND SECURITY

National Transportation Safety Board Conference Center

429 L'Enfant Plaza, SW, Washington, DC

May 3, 2006

9:30 a.m.

- Secretary George W. Foresman, Under Secretary for Preparedness, Department of Homeland Security
- Secretary Paul McHale, Assistant Secretary of Defense for Homeland Defense, Department of Defense
- Admiral Timothy J. Keating, USN, Commander, North American Aerospace Defense Command, and Commander, U.S. Northern Command

1:30 p.m.

- Lieutenant General H Steven Blum, USA, Chief, National Guard Bureau
- Major General Roger P. Lempke, ANG, President, Adjutants General Association of the United States, and Adjutant General, State of Nebraska
- Rear Admiral Kenneth T. Venuto, USCG, Assistant Commandant for Human Resources

May 4, 2006

9:30 a.m.

- Honorable John O. Marsh, Jr., Distinguished Professor of Law, George Mason University
- Frank J. Cilluffo, Associate Vice President for Homeland Security, and Director, Homeland Security Policy Institute, The George Washington University
- Dr. James J. Carafano, Senior Research Fellow, Defense and Homeland Security, The Heritage Foundation

HEARING ON NATIONAL GUARD AND RESERVE ISSUES

Rooms 2118 and 2216 Rayburn House Office Building, Washington DC

June 15, 2006

9:00 a.m.

- The Honorable Ruth Ann Minner, Governor of Delaware and Lead Governor on Homeland Security, National Governors Association

11:00 a.m.

- Christine Wormuth, Senior Fellow, Center for Strategic & International Studies

12:45 p.m.

- The Honorable Michael F. Easley, Governor of North Carolina and Lead Governor on the National Guard, National Governors Association

2:00 p.m.

- Michele S. Jones, Command Sergeant Major of the Army Reserve
- John D. Gipe, Command Sergeant Major of the Army National Guard
- Richard A. Smith, Chief Master Sergeant of the Air National Guard
- David R. Pennington, Force Master Chief of the Navy Reserve
- Robin W. Dixon, Sergeant Major of the Marine Corps Reserve
- Jackson A. Winsett, Chief Master Sergeant of the Air Force Reserve
- Jeffrey D. Smith, Reserve Force Master Chief of the U.S. Coast Guard Reserve
- Lawrence W. Holland, Command Sergeant Major for the Assistant Secretary of Defense for Reserve Affairs

HEARING ON NATIONAL GUARD AND RESERVE ISSUES

Iberian Ballroom, La Mansion Del Rio Hotel, San Antonio, TX

July 19, 2006

9:30 a.m.

- Lieutenant General Jack Stultz, Chief of the Army Reserve
- Vice Admiral John Cotton, Chief of the Navy Reserve
- Lieutenant General Jack Bergman, Commander, Marine Forces Reserve
- Lieutenant General John A. Bradley, Chief of the Air Force Reserve
- Lieutenant General Craig R. McKinley, Director, Air National Guard
- Rear Admiral John C. Acton, Deputy LANTAREA Commander for Mobilization and Reserve Affairs and Senior Reserve Officer, U.S. Coast Guard

2:00 p.m.

- Sergeant Allison Kitzerow, Army Reserve
- Sergeant Christopher McWilliams, Army National Guard
- Staff Sergeant Maria Sparks, Air Force Reserve
- Master Sergeant Alphonzo Allen, Air National Guard
- Construction Mechanic Second Class José Quiroz, Navy Reserve
- Corporal Adrian Garza, Marine Corps Reserve
- Chief Petty Officer Douglas Gilmer, Coast Guard Reserve

HEARING ON NATIONAL GUARD AND RESERVE ISSUES

Sims Auditorium, U.S. Navy Fleet Anti-Submarine Warfare Training Center, Point Loma, San Diego, CA

September 20, 2006

9:00 a.m.

- Brigadier General Douglas M. Stone, USMCR, Commanding General, Marine Corps Air Ground Combat Center, Marine Corps Air Ground Task Force Training Command at 29 Palms
- Colonel David L. Blain, USA, Deputy Commander and Chief of Staff, U.S. Army National Training Center at Fort Irwin

10:30 a.m.

- Major Thomas Friloux, ARNG, 3rd Battalion, 156th Infantry, Louisiana Army National Guard
- Major David Owen, USMC, 2nd Battalion, 24th Marine Regiment, 4th Marine Division
- Major Christopher F. Foxx, USAR, Division Maintenance Officer, 108th HQ (DIVIT), Charlotte, NC

1:00 p.m.

- Brigadier General Louis Antonetti, Director, Joint Staff, California National Guard
- Stephen J. Sellers, Regional Administrator, Southern Region, Office of Emergency Services, State of California
- Charles P. McHugh, Assistant Director, Arizona Department of Emergency & Military Affairs, Division of Emergency Management

September 21, 2006

8:30 a.m.

- Lieutenant Colonel Thomas Plunkett, ARNG, 3rd Battalion, 156th Infantry, Louisiana Army National Guard
- Lieutenant Colonel Mark Smith, USMCR, 2nd Battalion, 24th Marine Regiment, 4th Marine Division
- Lieutenant Colonel Thomas Sisinyak, USAR, Commander, 812th Transportation Battalion

- Janet St. Laurent, Director, Defense Capabilities and Management Team, Government Accountability Office

HEARING WITH COMBATANT COMMANDERS

Room 2118, Rayburn House Office Building, Washington, DC

October 5, 2006

9:00 a.m.

- General James L. Jones, USMC, Supreme Allied Commander, Europe (SACEUR) and Commander, United States European Command (COMUSEUCOM)

10:30 a.m.

- General Lance L. Smith, USAF, Commander, U.S. Joint Forces Command/ North Atlantic Treaty Organization and Supreme Allied Commander Transformation

HEARING ON PROPOSED CHANGES TO THE NATIONAL GUARD

Room 2212 and 2216, Rayburn House Office Building, Washington, DC

December 13, 2006

8:00 a.m.

- Dr. David S. C. Chu, Under Secretary of Defense for Personnel and Readiness
- Thomas F. Hall, Assistant Secretary of Defense for Reserve Affairs

10:00 a.m.

- George W. Foresman, Under Secretary for Preparedness, Department of Homeland Security

December 14, 2006

10:30 a.m.

- General Peter J. Schoomaker, Chief of Staff, U.S. Army

11:45 a.m.

- Michael W. Wynne, Secretary of the Air Force
- General T. Michael Moseley, Chief of Staff of the U.S. Air Force

2:00 p.m.

- Major General Frank Vavala, Adjutant General, State of Delaware, and Vice President, Adjutants General Association of the United States
- Major General Raymond F. Rees, Adjutant General, State of Oregon
- Major General R. Martin Umbarger, Adjutant General, State of Indiana, and Chairman, National Guard Association of the United States

HEARING ON PROPOSED CHANGES TO THE NATIONAL GUARD

Room 2212, Rayburn House Office Building, Washington, DC

January 31, 2007

9:00 a.m.

- Lieutenant General H Steven Blum, Chief, National Guard Bureau

11:30 a.m.

- Dr. Francis J. Harvey, Secretary of the Army

2:00 p.m.

- General Peter Pace, USMC, Chairman, Joint Chiefs of Staff

APPENDIX 8

INDIVIDUALS CONSULTED BY THE COMMISSION ON THE NATIONAL GUARD AND RESERVES

Mr. Al Bemis	October 6, 2005	Tysons Corner, VA
Mr. Frederick McKenzie	October 6, 2005	Tysons Corner, VA
Mr. David Smith	October 6, 2005	Tysons Corner, VA
Ms. Cindy Williams	October 13, 2005	Washington, DC
Dr. Curt Gilroy	October 17, 2005	Norfolk, VA
Dr. Lawrence Goldberg	October 17, 2005	Norfolk, VA
Lieutenant General Robert Van Antwerp	October 17, 2005	Norfolk, VA
Dr. James Jay Carafano	October 20, 2005	Washington, DC
Hon. Francis J. Harvey	October 20, 2005	Washington, DC
Senator Kit Bond	November 2, 1005	Washington, DC
Congressman Steve Buyer	November 2, 2005	Washington, DC
Senator Saxby Chambliss	November 2, 2005	Washington, DC
Congressman Duncan Hunter	November 2, 2005	Washington, DC
Congressman Ike Skelton	November 2, 2005	Washington, DC
Congressman Gene Taylor	November 2, 2005	Washington, DC
Senator John Warner	November 2, 2005	Washington, DC
Hon. Thomas Hall	November 3, 2005	Arlington, VA
Vice Admiral Stanley R. Szemborski	November 3, 2005	Arlington, VA
Hon. Kenneth J. Kreig	November 3, 2005	Arlington, VA
Hon. Paul McHale	November 3, 2005	Arlington, VA
Hon. Ryan Henry	November 3, 2005	Arlington, VA
Hon. David S.C. Chu	November 3, 2005	Arlington, VA
Lieutenant General H Steven Blum	November 3, 2005	Arlington, VA
Mr. Michael Shoebridge	November 14, 2005	Washington, DC
Lieutenant General John A. Bradley	November 28, 2005	Arlington, VA
Colonel Gary Crone	November 28, 2005	Arlington, VA
Mr. Michael Dittle	November 28, 2005	Arlington, VA
Brigadier General Rick Ethredge	November 28, 2005	Arlington, VA
Mr. Wayne Gracie	November 28, 2005	Arlington, VA
Major General Jan Blom	December 8, 2005	Washington, DC
Major General Michael W. Davidson	December 8, 2005	Alexandria, VA
Major General Bruce Lawlor	December 8, 2005	Alexandria, VA
Ms. Kirsti Skjerven	December 8, 2005	Washington, DC
Lieutenant Colonel Darlene Hopkins	January 5, 2006	Arlington, VA
Lieutenant Colonel Penelope Speed	January 5, 2006	Arlington, VA

Colonel Edwin Domingo	January 12, 2006	Arlington, VA
Lieutenant Commander Walter Hogan	January 12, 2006	Arlington, VA
Ms. Deborah Bolton	January 24, 2006	Peterson AFB, CO
Lieutenant General Eric "Rick" Findley	January 24, 2006	Peterson AFB, CO
Brigadier General James Hunter	January 24, 2006	Peterson AFB, CO
Mr. Bernd "Bear" McConnell	January 24, 2006	Peterson AFB, CO
Major General Henry Morrow	January 24, 2006	Peterson AFB, CO
Major General Richard Nash	January 24, 2006	Peterson AFB, CO
Major General Robert Ostenberg	January 24, 2006	Peterson AFB, CO
Major General Paul Sullivan	January 24, 2006	Peterson AFB, CO
Colonel Larry Smith	February 8, 2006	Arlington, VA
Mr. Frank Cirillo	February 14, 2006	Arlington, VA
Rear Admiral William D. Sullivan	February 27, 2006	Arlington, VA
Mr. Ryan Fitzgerald	February 28, 2006	Washington, DC
Mr. Nolan Jones	February 28, 2006	Washington, DC
Hon. Dirk Kempthorne	February 28, 2006	Washington, DC
Mr. James McCleskey	February 28, 2006	Washington, DC
Ms. Beth Miller	March 1, 2006	Washington, DC
Mr. David Walker	March 1, 2006	Washington, DC
Lieutenant Colonel Vincent Price	March 1, 2006	Arlington, VA
Major General Michael A. Vane	March 1, 2006	Arlington, VA
Lieutenant Colonel Cedric Wins	March 1, 2006	Arlington, VA
Ms. Michèle Flournoy	March 21, 2006	Washington, DC
Mr. Jack Harrington	March 21, 2006	Washington, DC
Mr. Alex Baird	March 23, 2006	Arlington, VA
Colonel Blaine Coffey	March 23, 2006	Arlington, VA
Colonel Nancy Fortuin	March 23, 2006	Arlington, VA
Hon. Stephen M. Duncan	March 24, 2006	Washington, DC
Colonel Donald Ahern	March 27, 2006	Arlington, VA
Master Sergeant Gloria Burleson	March 27, 2006	Arlington, VA
Colonel Blaine Coffey	March 27, 2006	Arlington, VA
Senior Master Sergeant Miranda Garza	March 27, 2006	Arlington, VA
Mr. Peter Guerrant	March 27, 2006	Arlington, VA
Mr. Edwin Guidroz	March 27, 2006	Arlington, VA
Mr. Thomas McNamara	March 27, 2006	Arlington, VA
Mr. Kevin VonHunke	March 27, 2006	Arlington, VA
Master Sergeant Susan Watson	March 27, 2006	Arlington, VA
Master Sergeant Ramona Whitted	March 27, 2006	Arlington, VA
Mr. Paul Hogan	March 29, 2006	Arlington, VA
Lieutenant Colonel William Birden	March 29, 2006	Arlington, VA
Captain Dale Rausch	April 3, 2006	Sebring, FL

Lieutenant Colonel Trent Dudley	April 4, 2006	Arlington, VA
Lieutenant General Jack W. Bergman	April 6, 2006	Arlington, VA
Lieutenant General H Steven Blum	April 6, 2006	Arlington, VA
Vice Admiral John Cotton	April 6, 2006	Arlington, VA
Brigadier General Rick Etheridge	April 6, 2006	Arlington, VA
Hon. Thomas Hall	April 6, 2006	Arlington, VA
Lieutenant General James Helmly	April 6, 2006	Arlington, VA
Brigadier General Charles Ickes	April 6, 2006	Arlington, VA
Hon. George Foresman	April 7, 2006	Washington, DC
Mr. Casey Hehr	April 7, 2006	Washington, DC
Hon. Michael Jackson	April 7, 2006	Washington, DC
Rear Admiral Timothy S. Sullivan	April 7, 2006	Washington, DC
Mr. Tom Bush	April 7, 2006	Arlington, VA
Hon. Paul McHale	April 7, 2006	Arlington, VA
Mr. Joe Bangal	April 12, 2006	Washington, DC
Mr. Seth Benge	April 14, 2006	Arlington, VA
Mr. Mike Cline	April 14, 2006	Arlington, VA
Mr. David Davidson	April 14, 2006	Arlington, VA
Mr. Bob Fiedler	April 14, 2006	Arlington, VA
Mr. Larry Madison	April 14, 2006	Arlington, VA
Ms. Katy Moakler	April 14, 2006	Arlington, VA
Mr. Bob Norton	April 14, 2006	Arlington, VA
Mr. Ike Puzon	April 14, 2006	Arlington, VA
Mr. Chris Slawinski	April 14, 2006	Arlington, VA
Mr. Seth Benge	April 25, 2006	Arlington, VA
Mr. Mike Cline	April 25, 2006	Arlington, VA
Mr. David Davidson	April 25, 2006	Arlington, VA
Mr. Bob Fiedler	April 25, 2006	Arlington, VA
Brigadier General Richard Green	April 25, 2006	Arlington, VA
Mr. Larry Madison	April 25, 2006	Arlington, VA
Mr. Bob Norton	April 25, 2006	Arlington, VA
Mr. Ike Puzon	April 25, 2006	Arlington, VA
Ms. Joyce Raezer	April 25, 2006	Arlington, VA
Mr. Patrick Reidy	April 25, 2006	Arlington, VA
Mr. Chris Slawinski	April 25, 2006	Arlington, VA
Major General Timothy Lowenberg	May 9, 2006	Arlington, VA
Colonel Jeffrey Mello	May 18, 2006	Arlington, VA
Mr. Tom Boatner	May 26, 2006	Arlington, VA
Mr. Lyle Carlile	May 26, 2006	Arlington, VA
Mr. Tom Dyer	May 26, 2006	Arlington, VA
Mr. Randy Eardley	May 26, 2006	Arlington, VA

Mr. John Fend	May 26, 2006	Arlington, VA
Mr. Tom Frey	May 26, 2006	Arlington, VA
Mr. Doug Shinn	May 26, 2006	Arlington, VA
Mr. Mike Wallace	May 26, 2006	Arlington, VA
Lieutenant Colonel William Birden	May 30, 2006	Arlington, VA
Dr. Denny Eakle	May 30, 2006	Arlington, VA
Hon. Kathleen Babineaux Blanco	May 31, 2006	Baton Rouge, LA
Brigadier General Hunt Downer	May 31, 2006	Baton Rouge, LA
Major General Bennett C. Landreneau	May 31, 2006	Baton Rouge, LA
Mr. Mike Ferron	May 31, 2006	Washington, DC
Mr. Butch Hinton	May 31, 2006	Washington, DC
Ms. Janet St. Laurent	May 31, 2006	Washington, DC
Mr. Derek Stewart	May 31, 2006	Washington, DC
Lieutenant Colonel Mary Henry	June 6, 2006	Arlington, VA
Colonel Jim Glenn	June 6, 2006	Arlington, VA
Captain Kelly Lelito	June 6, 2006	Arlington, VA
Ms. Michèle Flournoy	June 7, 2006	Washington, DC
Lieutenant General James J. Lovelace	June 14, 2006	Arlington, VA
Hon. George Foresman	June 16, 2006	Washington, DC
Mr. Steve Dellaport	June 19, 2006	Arlington, VA
Ms. Mary Dixon	June 19, 2006	Arlington, VA
Ms. Janine Groth	June 19, 2006	Arlington, VA
Brigadier General John Fobian	June 20, 2006	Lackland AFB, TX
Mr. Thomas Helm	June 20, 2006	Lackland AFB, TX
Colonel John Nichols	June 20, 2006	Lackland AFB, TX
Captain Fred Broussard	June 20, 2006	Arlington, VA
Lieutenant Colonel Trent Dudley	June 20, 2006	Arlington, VA
Mr. Victor Macias	June 20, 2006	Arlington, VA
Colonel David Mansfield	June 20, 2006	Arlington, VA
Commander John McCracken	June 20, 2006	Arlington, VA
Colonel Rocky Templon	June 20, 2006	Arlington, VA
Colonel Mark Tracy	June 20, 2006	Arlington, VA
Lieutenant Colonel Todd Wilkinson	June 20, 2006	Arlington, VA
Mr. Jim Fuller	June 27, 2006	Arlington, VA
Mr. Warren Golden	June 27, 2006	Arlington, VA
Mr. Michael Lincecum	June 27, 2006	Arlington, VA
Petty Officer Karen Carlson	July 18, 2006	San Antonio, TX
Petty Officer Stacy Catalano	July 18, 2006	San Antonio, TX
Staff Sergeant Ricky Longoria	July 18, 2006	San Antonio, TX
Master Sergeant Juan Maldonado	July 18, 2006	San Antonio, TX
Master Sergeant Mark Mann	July 18, 2006	San Antonio, TX

Staff Sergeant Timothy O'Neil	July 18, 2006	San Antonio, TX
First Sergeant William Simpson	July 18, 2006	San Antonio, TX
Sergeant First Class Robert Boyer	July 19, 2006	San Antonio, TX
Petty Officer Fidel E. Contreras	July 19, 2006	San Antonio, TX
Technical Sergeant Ruben DeLarosa	July 19, 2006	San Antonio, TX
Staff Sergeant Albert DeLeon	July 19, 2006	San Antonio, TX
Gunnery Sergeant Frank Guajardo	July 19, 2006	San Antonio, TX
Chief Petty Officer Melissa Sharer	July 19, 2006	San Antonio, TX
Major General Allen R. Dehnert	July 20, 2006	Lackland AFB, TX
Brigadier General John Fobian	July 20, 2006	Lackland AFB, TX
Colonel Mike Holloman	July 20, 2006	Lackland AFB, TX
Sergeant Roger Alicea	July 20, 2006	San Antonio, TX
Senior Master Sergeant Dale Berryhill	July 20, 2006	San Antonio, TX
Sergeant Ronald Fore	July 20, 2006	San Antonio, TX
Sergeant Jonathon Jobson	July 20, 2006	San Antonio, TX
Petty Officer David Kelley	July 20, 2006	San Antonio, TX
Chief Petty Officer Linda Laswell	July 20, 2006	San Antonio, TX
Senior Master Sergeant Kenneth Nauert	July 20, 2006	San Antonio, TX
Petty Officer Carlos Nino	July 20, 2006	San Antonio, TX
Master Sergeant Ralph O'Hara	July 20, 2006	San Antonio, TX
Sergeant First Class Trenton Puckett	July 20, 2006	San Antonio, TX
Petty Officer Victor Ramirez	July 20, 2006	San Antonio, TX
Master Sergeant George Reyes	July 20, 2006	San Antonio, TX
Master Sergeant Jose A. Sepulveda	July 20, 2006	San Antonio, TX
Mr. Joe Fengler	August 15, 2006	Washington, DC
Mr. John Davis	August 21, 2006	Arlington, VA
Mr. Dan Else	August 21, 2006	Arlington, VA
Lieutenant Colonel Bob Feidler	August 21, 2006	Arlington, VA
Brigadier General Richard Green	August 21, 2006	Arlington, VA
Mr. Steve Lillie	August 21, 2006	Arlington, VA
Mr. Larry Madison	August 21, 2006	Arlington, VA
Mr. Robert Marshall	August 21, 2006	Arlington, VA
Dr. Jim Martin	August 21, 2006	Arlington, VA
Ms. Kathy Moakler	August 21, 2006	Arlington, VA
Mr. Mike Naylon	August 21, 2006	Arlington, VA
Mr. Bob Norton	August 21, 2006	Arlington, VA
Ms. Molly Ramsdell	August 21, 2006	Arlington, VA
Mr. Pete Verga	August 21, 2006	Arlington, VA
Colonel Ted Mickevicius	August 29, 2006	Arlington, VA
Major Robert Preiss	August 29, 2006	Arlington, VA
Mr. Bruce Hock	August 29, 2006	Washington, DC

Mr. Greg Kiely	August 29, 2006	Washington, DC
Mr. Mike McCord	August 29, 2006	Washington, DC
Mr. D. M. "Dak" Hardwick	September 1, 2006	Arlington, VA
Mr. John Sims	September 1, 2006	Arlington, VA
Mr. Karl Wagner	September 1, 2006	Arlington, VA
Mr. Bob Boggs	September 5, 2006	Peterson AFB, CO
Mr. Barry Cardwell	September 5, 2006	Peterson AFB, CO
Ms. Christie Church	September 5, 2006	Peterson AFB, CO
Captain Bill Cogan	September 5, 2006	Peterson AFB, CO
Colonel Bob Felderman	September 5, 2006	Peterson AFB, CO
Colonel Bill Hill	September 5, 2006	Peterson AFB, CO
Colonel Karin Murphy	September 5, 2006	Peterson AFB, CO
Mr. Matt Musial	September 5, 2006	Peterson AFB, CO
Mr. Jim Weber	September 5, 2006	Peterson AFB, CO
Vice Admiral John Cotton	September 7, 2006	Arlington, VA
Lieutenant Commander Carl Cox	September 7, 2006	Arlington, VA
Rear Admiral Craig McDonald	September 7, 2006	Arlington, VA
Captain Harry Meyers	September 7, 2006	Arlington, VA
Ms. Cindy Butler	September 18, 2006	La Jolla, CA
Mr. Alfonso Carmona	September 18, 2006	La Jolla, CA
Ms. Karen Como	September 18, 2006	La Jolla, CA
Ms. Kathy Dunn	September 18, 2006	La Jolla, CA
Dr. Kevin Gerhart	September 18, 2006	La Jolla, CA
Mr. Michael Kilmer	September 18, 2006	La Jolla, CA
Mr. Clay King	September 18, 2006	La Jolla, CA
Dr. Jacqueline Parthemore	September 18, 2006	La Jolla, CA
Mr. Richard Rodriguez	September 18, 2006	La Jolla, CA
Mr. Gary J. Rossio	September 18, 2006	La Jolla, CA
Mr. Glenn White	September 18, 2006	La Jolla, CA
Rear Admiral Jody Breckinridge	September 18, 2006	San Diego, CA
Petty Officer Trisha Carroll	September 18, 2006	San Diego, CA
Staff Sergeant Victor Castillo	September 18, 2006	San Diego, CA
Staff Sergeant Craig Dockter	September 18, 2006	San Diego, CA
Lieutenant Colonel David Durham	September 18, 2006	San Diego, CA
Staff Sergeant David Fill	September 18, 2006	San Diego, CA
Captain Jody Guidry	September 18, 2006	San Diego, CA
Staff Sergeant Michael Key	September 18, 2006	San Diego, CA
Staff Sergeant Tanya Marie Pablo	September 18, 2006	San Diego, CA
Petty Officer Juan Ramos	September 18, 2006	San Diego, CA
Captain Chip Strangfeld	September 19, 2006	San Diego, CA
Major Keith Vollert	September 19, 2006	San Diego, CA

Captain Timothy Campbell	September 21, 2006	Camp Pendleton, CA
Captain Aaron Duplechin	September 21, 2006	Camp Pendleton, CA
Mr. Jacob Klerman	September 21, 2006	Camp Pendleton, CA
Lieutenant Colonel Sean A. Sullivan	September 21, 2006	Camp Pendleton, CA
Captain B. J. Keepers	September 22, 2006	Coronado, CA
Rear Admiral Jeff Lemmons	September 22, 2006	Coronado, CA
Captain Roger Meek	September 22, 2006	Coronado, CA
Rear Admiral Michael Shatynski	September 22, 2006	Coronado, CA
Commander Ken Wright	September 22, 2006	Coronado, CA
Mr. Matt Schmidt	September 27, 2006	Arlington, VA
Lieutenant Colonel Gene Smith	September 27, 2006	Arlington, VA
Mr. John R. Brinkerhoff	October 5, 2006	Arlington, VA
Ms. Belva Belfour-Nixon	October 18, 2006	Arlington, VA
Brigadier General Michael J. Basla	October 19, 2006	Scott AFB, IL
Captain Joseph Bridge	October 19, 2006	Scott AFB, IL
General Norton Schwartz	October 19, 2006	Scott AFB, IL
Major General Charles Fletcher	October 19, 2006	Scott AFB, IL
Major General William Johnson	October 19, 2006	Scott AFB, IL
Brigadier General James W. Kwiatkowski	October 19, 2006	Scott AFB, IL
Colonel Peter Lennon	October 19, 2006	Scott AFB, IL
Chief Master Sergeant Kenneth McQuiston	October 19, 2006	Scott AFB, IL
Major General Harold Mitchell	October 19, 2006	Scott AFB, IL
Captain David Shiveley	October 19, 2006	Scott AFB, IL
Major General F. Dexter Tutor	October 19, 2006	Scott AFB, IL
Colonel Brian Van Sickel	October 19, 2006	Scott AFB, IL
Captain Bradley Carpenter	October 20, 2006	Scott AFB, IL
Captain Deborah Dombeck	October 20, 2006	Scott AFB, IL
Rear Admiral Raymond English	October 20, 2006	Scott AFB, IL
Lieutenant Colonel Gerald Henry	October 20, 2006	Scott AFB, IL
Colonel Mark Herrick	October 20, 2006	Scott AFB, IL
Colonel Dennis Nebera	October 20, 2006	Scott AFB, IL
Captain Richard Vogel	October 20, 2006	Scott AFB, IL
Ms. Virginia Williamson	October 20, 2006	Scott AFB, IL
Lieutenant Colonel Dan Bader	October 23, 2006	Arlington, VA
Lieutenant Colonel David Boyle	October 23, 2006	Arlington, VA
Mr. George Brock	October 23, 2006	Arlington, VA
Lieutenant Colonel Todd Burton	October 23, 2006	Arlington, VA
Colonel Robert Deforge	October 23, 2006	Arlington, VA
Mr. Dan Donahue	October 23, 2006	Arlington, VA
Mr. Todd Kostelecky	October 23, 2006	Arlington, VA
Colonel Kathleen Patterson	October 23, 2006	Arlington, VA

Ms. Connie Plott	October 23, 2006	Arlington, VA
Lieutenant Colonel Dan Stoneking	October 23, 2006	Arlington, VA
Colonel Pat Tenis	October 23, 2006	Arlington, VA
Colonel Joseph C. Daniel	October 24, 2006	Arlington, VA
Mr. John Hastings	October 24, 2006	Arlington, VA
Mr. John Hathaway	October 24, 2006	Arlington, VA
Mr. Thomas Lacrosse	October 24, 2006	Arlington, VA
Lieutenant Colonel Greg Limberis	October 24, 2006	Arlington, VA
Ms. Terri Reisenfeld	October 24, 2006	Arlington, VA
Mr. John Sims	October 24, 2006	Arlington, VA
Lieutenant Colonel Art Stovall	October 24, 2006	Arlington, VA
Lieutenant Colonel Mark Cogburn	October 27, 2006	Arlington, VA
Colonel Deborah Coley	October 27, 2006	Arlington, VA
Mr. John Davenport	October 27, 2006	Arlington, VA
Colonel John Ellsworth	October 27, 2006	Arlington, VA
Mr. Bob Hollingsworth	October 27, 2006	Arlington, VA
Lieutenant Colonel Carol Leighton	October 27, 2006	Arlington, VA
Major Willis Madden	October 27, 2006	Arlington, VA
Mr. Michael Naylon	October 27, 2006	Arlington, VA
Mr. Terrell Parker	October 27, 2006	Arlington, VA
Lieutenant Colonel Angel Perez	October 27, 2006	Arlington, VA
Ms. Sallie Shaffer	October 27, 2006	Arlington, VA
Mr. Daniel Denning	November 3, 2006	Arlington, VA
Mr. Robert Smiley	November 3, 2006	Arlington, VA
Colonel Doug Curell	November 6, 2006	Arlington, VA
Lieutenant Colonel Kostelecky	November 6, 2006	Arlington, VA
Lieutenant Colonel Greg Riley	November 7, 2006	Arlington, VA
Mr. Allen Tidwell	November 7, 2006	Arlington, VA
Colonel Reginald Geary	November 13, 2006	Arlington, VA
Colonel Lernes "Bear" Herbert	November 13, 2006	Arlington, VA
Lieutenant Colonel Susan Hogg	November 13, 2006	Arlington, VA
Lieutenant Colonel Ken Olivo	November 13, 2006	Arlington, VA
Mr. Dan Kohner	November 14, 2006	Arlington, VA
Mr. Harry Myers	November 14, 2006	Arlington, VA
Lieutenant Colonel Jeffrey Cashman	November 20, 2006	Arlington, VA
Major Robert Preiss	November 20, 2006	Arlington, VA
Rear Admiral Harry Harris	November 21, 2006	Guantánamo Bay, Cuba
Captain Mark Leary	November 21, 2006	Guantánamo Bay, Cuba
Lieutenant Colonel David Boyle	November 27, 2006	Arlington, VA
Mr. Dan Donahue	November 27, 2006	Arlington, VA
Colonel Scott Gorske	November 27, 2006	Arlington, VA

Colonel Ted Mickevicius	November 27, 2006	Arlington, VA
Colonel G. Kevin Thompson	November 27, 2006	Arlington, VA
Hon. William Cohen	November 28, 2006	Washington, DC
Mr. Jacob Klerman	November 28, 2006	Arlington, VA
Mr. Matthew Schmitt	November 28, 2006	Arlington, VA
Mr. Michael Waters	November 28, 2006	Arlington, VA
Mr. Kevin Billings	November 29, 2006	Arlington, VA
Captain Joel Buffardi	November 29, 2006	Arlington, VA
Rear Admiral Christopher J. McMahon	November 29, 2006	Arlington, VA
Captain Eric Wallischeck	November 29, 2006	Arlington, VA
Ms. Leigh Ann Wilson	December 2, 2006	Galax, VA
Colonel Angel Perez	December 4, 2006	Arlington, VA
Brigadier General Richard Sherlock	December 4, 2006	Arlington, VA
Hon. Colin Powell	December 20, 2006	Alexandria, VA
Colonel Russell Stine	December 27, 2006	Arlington, VA
Ms. Garcia Sugioka	February 9, 2007	Arlington, VA

APPENDIX 9

ACRONYMS AND ABBREVIATIONS

ACJCS-NGM	Assistant to the Chairman of the Joint Chiefs of Staff for National Guard Matters
ACJCS-RM	Assistant to the Chairman of the Joint Chiefs of Staff for Reserve Matters
AFNORTH	Air Forces North
AFORGEN	Army Force Generation Model
AFQT	Armed Forces Qualification Test
AFR	Air Force Reserve
AGAUS	Adjutants General Association of the United States
AGR	Active Guard and Reserve
ANG	Air National Guard
AOR	area of responsibility
ARCOM	Army Reserve Command
ARNG	Army National Guard
ARNORTH	Army North
ASD-HD	Assistant Secretary of Defense for Homeland Defense
ASD-HD&ASA	Assistant Secretary of Defense for Homeland Defense and America's Security Affairs
ASD-RA	Assistant Secretary of Defense for Reserve Affairs
BCT	brigade combat team
BRAC	Defense Base Closure and Realignment Commission
CA	civil affairs
CAR	Chief of the Army Reserve
CBP	Customs and Border Protection
CBRNE	chemical, biological, radiological, nuclear, or high-yield explosives
CERFPs	CBRNE enhanced response force packages
CIFC	Combined Intelligence Fusion Center
CJCS	Chairman of the Joint Chiefs of Staff
CNGB	Chief of the National Guard Bureau
CNGR	Commission on the National Guard and Reserves
COCOM	combatant commander
CS	combat support

CSS	combat service support
DHS	Department of Homeland Security
DOD	Department of Defense
DPG	Defense Planning Guidance
DSCA	defense support to civil authorities
EMAC	Emergency Management Assistance Compact
FEMA	Federal Emergency Management Agency
FORSCOM	U.S. Army Forces Command
FYDP	Future Years Defense Program
GAO	Government Accountability Office
GDP	gross domestic product
GWOT	global war on terror
HASC	House Armed Services Committee
HRC	Human Resources Command
HSPD	homeland security presidential directive
IMA	individual mobilization augmentee
IMCOM	Installation Management Command
IPL	integrated priorities list
IRR	Individual Ready Reserve
JCIDS	Joint Capabilities Integration and Development System
JCS	Joint Chiefs of Staff
JFCOM	Joint Forces Command
JOCs	Joint Operating Concepts
JPME	Joint Professional Military Education
JROC	Joint Requirements Oversight Council
JSCP	Joint Strategic Capabilities Plan
JSTARS	Joint Surveillance Target Attack Radar System
JTF	Joint Task Force
MARFORNORTH	Marine Forces North
MSCA	military support to civil authorities
MTOE	Modified Table of Organization and Equipment
NATO	North Atlantic Treaty Organization
NDAA	National Defense Authorization Act
NGA	National Governors Association
NGAUS	National Guard Association of the United States
NGB	National Guard Bureau

NGREA	National Guard and Reserve Equipment Account
NORTHCOM	United States Northern Command
NPS	National Preparedness System
NRIC	Navy Reserve Intelligence Command
OMB	Office of Management and Budget
OPCON	operational control
OSD	Office of the Secretary of Defense
POM	program objective memorandum
PPBES	Planning, Programming, Budgeting, and Execution System
PSYOPS	psychological operations
QDR	Quadrennial Defense Review
RC	reserve component
RFPB	Reserve Forces Policy Board
RPB	Reserve Policy Board
ROA	Reserve Officers Association
SecDef	Secretary of Defense
SJFHQ	Standing Joint Forces Headquarters
SOCOM	Special Operations Command
TAG	[the] adjutant general
USA	United States Army
USAF	United States Air Force
USAR	United States Army Reserve
USAREC	United States Army Reserve Command
U.S.C.	United States Code
USCG	United States Coast Guard
USCGR	United States Coast Guard Reserve
USD(P&R)	Under Secretary of Defense for Personnel and Readiness
USMC	United States Marine Corps
USMCR	United States Marine Corps Reserve
USN	United States Navy
USNR	United States Navy Reserve
WMD	weapons of mass destruction
WMD-CST	weapons of mass destruction civil support team
WMD/E	weapons of mass destruction/effects